CARIBBEAN MIDDLEBROW

CARIBBEAN MIDDLEBROW

LEISURE CULTURE AND THE MIDDLE CLASS

BELINDA EDMONDSON

CORNELL UNIVERSITY PRESS
Ithaca and London

Copyright © 2009 by Cornell University

All rights reserved. Except for brief quotations in a review, this book, or parts thereof, must not be reproduced in any form without permission in writing from the publisher. For information, address Cornell University Press, Sage House, 512 East State Street, Ithaca, New York 14850.

First published 2009 by Cornell University Press

Printed in the United States of America

Library of Congress Cataloging-in-Publication Data

Edmondson, Belinda.
  Caribbean middlebrow : leisure culture and the middle class / Belinda Edmondson.
    p. cm.
  Includes bibliographical references and index.
  ISBN 978-0-8014-4814-0 (cloth : alk. paper)
 1. Caribbean literature (English)—History and criticism. 2. Popular literature—Caribbean Area—History and criticism. 3. Literature and society—Caribbean Area. 4. Books and reading—Caribbean Area. 5. Popular culture—Caribbean Area. 6. Middle class—Caribbean Area. 7. Blacks—Race identity—Caribbean Area. 8. Social classes in literature. 9. Race in literature. 10. Caribbean Area—Civilization. I. Title.

  PR9205.O5.E357   2009
  810.9'9729—dc22   2009019898

Cornell University Press strives to use environmentally responsible suppliers and materials to the fullest extent possible in the publishing of its books. Such materials include vegetable-based, low-VOC inks and acid-free papers that are recycled, totally chlorine-free, or partly composed of nonwood fibers. For further information, visit our website at www.cornellpress.cornell.edu.

Cloth printing   10 9 8 7 6 5 4 3 2 1

To Gene, Ravi and Dorian, with love

Contents

List of Illustrations   ix
Acknowledgments   xi

Introduction: Making the Case
for Middlebrow Culture 1

1. Early Literary Culture 21
2. Brownness, Social Desire, and the
   Early Novel 50
3. Gentrifying Dialect, or the Taming
   of Miss Lou 86
4. Middlebrow Spectacle and the
   Politics of Beauty 110
5. Organic Imports, or Authenticating
   Global Culture 126
6. Transnational Communities and the
   New Pop Fiction 148

Notes   169
Bibliography   203
Index   217

ILLUSTRATIONS

1. The 1955 paperback edition of Edgar Mittelholzer's
   Children of Kaywana, published by the New English Library   11
2. Louise Bennett, from the cover of *Jamaica Labrish*
   (Kingston: Sangster's Book Stores, 1966). Courtesy
   of Sangster's Bookstores, Jamaica   89
3. Ernest Cupidon and the cast of *Susan Proudleigh,*
   from *The New Cosmopolitan* (February 1931),
   pp. 20 and 21. Courtesy of the National Library of Jamaica   91
4. Mostly women and several children are in the crowd at the
   2004 St. Lucia Jazz Festival. Photo taken by Chris Huxley.
   Permission granted by the St. Lucia Tourist Board   142
5. Cover of *Ti Marie,* by Valerie Belgrave (Kingston:
   Heinemann International, 1988). Courtesy of Valerie Belgrave   165

✤ Acknowledgments

There are many people behind this book. I am grateful to my editor, Peter Potter, for being an early and enthusiastic champion of this project. His careful editing, steady guidance, and pithy advice made this a better book. Sara Ferguson of Cornell University Press patiently answered my almost daily questions. Rutgers' nonpareil administrator Christina Strasburger has been a pillar of strength, bringing her cheerful can-do spirit to bear on computer glitches, copying snafus, and the other day-to-day headaches of manuscript preparation. Thanks also to the writers, filmmakers, publishers, and public relations personnel who shared their insider knowledge with me, especially Nalo Hopkinson, Johnny Temple of Akashic Books, Jaime Levine of Warner Aspect Books, Suzzanne Lee of Jamaica's Novelty Trading Company, Kirby Allain of the St. Lucia Tourist Board, Norman Rae and Esther Figueroa.

A Rutgers Research Council grant enabled me to conduct research in the Caribbean. I also benefited immensely from two fellowships. The first, a faculty fellowship at Rutgers University's Institute for Research on Women, allowed me the intellectual space to do the kind of hard critical thinking needed to jumpstart the writing process. In particular I would like to thank Kim Butler, Josie Saldaña, Carlos Deceña, Sonali Perrera, Marc Matera, and Nicole Fleetwood, whose collective comments helped turn my nugget of an idea into an argument.

A large portion of my gratitude and thanks goes to Cornell University's wonderful Society for the Humanities. My research was greatly facilitated by access to Cornell's excellent Olin and Africana libraries—not to mention the joys of a lovely office with breathtaking views of the beautiful Cornell campus, which should not be underestimated. I could not have asked for a more supportive and congenial group of people with which to work. Big thanks to director Brett de Bary, on whose painstaking notes I relied heavily. Tim Murray, the succeeding director, accommodated my wish for a couple of extra weeks to finish the manuscript when rightfully he should have kicked me out of the building. Administrator Mary Ahl helped with all matters large and small. My fellow Fellows pushed me to be more rigorous, and their contribution here is considerable. In particular I would like to acknowledge the comments of Matthew Hart for helping me to think through issues of class, Seth Suman for pressing me to examine gender issues more closely, Lucinda Ramberg for helpful organizational advice, as well as the comments of Micol Seigal, Phillip Stern, Natalie Melas, Andy Hoberek, Sarah Evans, Steffan Igor Ayora-Diaz, and Gabriela Vargas-Cetina. It was a special pleasure to meet and benefit from the comments of Martin Bernal.

As always, I am indebted to the work of other Caribbeanists who have laid the groundwork for this project. Velma Pollard and Erna Brodber filled in the gaps in my knowledge of Caribbean history. Vera Kutzinski's astute comments provided a roadmap for making revisions to the manuscript. Leah Rosenberg's path-breaking research on early Jamaican magazine culture set the stage for my own work. Leah also generously shared with me the image of H. G. de Lisser's *Twentieth Century Jamaica,* which is reproduced here. Faith Smith read drafts and volleyed ideas back and forth; she is, as always, my best intellectual companion and friend. Donette Francis hunted down articles and kindly provided access to her unpublished 2003 essay, which anticipates some of the ideas of this book. Other Caribbeanists whose work has influenced my own (whether or not they know it) include Michelle Stephens for her work on African American performers in the Caribbean; Rhonda Cobham-Sander, whose excellent dissertation on early Jamaican literature is a must-read for anyone interested in the field; and Harvey Neptune, whose book *Caliban and the Yankees,* on the American occupation of Trinidad, is one of the most enjoyable—and important—books I have read in a long time.

Then there are the organic Caribbeanists, my stalwart friends and family. Thanks are due to my old friend Katrina Scott-George, because if she hadn't invited me after twenty-odd years to that big beach bash I might never have met her husband, Wallace George, who told me all about Guyana's popular radio programs and introduced me to the work of Wordsworth McAndrew. It goes to show that you never know where you might find your material. I learned a lot about the leisure reading habits of the colonial Caribbean from the reminiscences of my mother, Dorothea Edmondson. Family helped in other ways too: my father, Locksley, and Elizabeth Edmondson made our sojourn in Ithaca comfortable with good company and great meals. Magnus and Alisha, if you hadn't babysat the children while I ran off to the Caribbean this would have been a different book, and not for the better. A chorus of thanks to Norma Edmondson, for giving me a home-away-from-home during my research trip to Jamaica; and to Norma Holder, for taking the time to help me find sources on Barbados' Crop Over Festival. Many thanks also to the DeCaires clan: to Denise DeCaires Narain, whose excellent book on Caribbean women's poetry was my constant companion when I wrote chapter 3, as well as to Salvador and Bonu DeCaires, who planted raspberries and roses and took care of my house while I was gone. You gave me peace of mind, thank you. A special shout-out to Salvador, because if you weren't such a fan of Edgar Mittelholzer I could not have gotten my hands on the 1955 cover of *Children of Kaywana* that I've reproduced here.

To the rest of my family, Nona, Chris, Oliver, and Marion, thanks for reminding me that laughter, empathy, and a good dinner are sometimes more important than a deadline. To Gene, Ravi, and Dorian, who have traveled with me from the beginning to the end, this book is for you.

A somewhat different version of chapter 4 was previously published as "Public Spectacles: Caribbean Women and the Politics of Public Performance" in *Small Axe: A Journal of Caribbean Criticism,* no. 13 (March 2003): 1–16. Republished here with the permission of Indiana University Press.

CARIBBEAN MIDDLEBROW

INTRODUCTION

Making the Case for Middlebrow Culture

A milestone of sorts was reached in 2007 when, for the first time ever, a dreadlocked, black Rastafarian woman won a Caribbean beauty pageant. It was no longer news, as it might have been ten years before, that Zahra Redwood, a dark-skinned, black woman, won the coveted Miss Jamaica Universe title. The predilection for light-skinned, long-haired Caribbean women of racially mixed heritage had already begun to fade in the English-speaking Caribbean since the dark-skinned black Trinidadian Wendy Fitzwilliam became the second black woman to win the Miss Universe title in 1998. (The first was the predictably light-skinned Trinidadian contestant Janelle "Penny" Commissiong, in 1977.) "Marcus Garvey must be smiling in his grave," exclaimed one admirer, implying that Garveyesque black nationalism had come full circle.[1] But in a region where Rastafarianism has long been equated with poverty, marginalization, and subversive, millennial black power politics, Zahra Redwood's victory was more than just an ideological triumph of indigenous aesthetics over Western ones. The Rasta beauty queen also heralded the *depoliticization* of black power aesthetics. Rather than the triumph of radical black nationalism, she highlights the cooptation of both Western metropolitan and local working-class culture in the upper echelons of Caribbean society. One interpretation of the Rasta beauty queen is to view her as representative of a globalized indigenous aesthetic, which she is. But even more so, she is the culmination of a long regional history of Caribbean middlebrow culture.

In the beauty contest–obsessed societies of the Caribbean and Latin America, a contestant's chances of winning a national pageant are directly related to the perception that she has a shot at winning an international beauty contest such as Miss World or Miss Universe. By this criterion, critics have long complained, women who look like the majority almost never make it. So it was no surprise when, asked how she intended to improve the nation's chances of winning the international Miss Universe competition, Redwood wrapped herself in the mantle of fellow Rastafarian and reggae superstar Bob Marley, responding that "Bob Marley has long been synonymous with Jamaica and with all the attributes I possess."[2] The beauty queen's university degree and her interests in solidly upper-middle-class pursuits—including "parasailing and horseback riding"—along with her Rastafarian faith, channeled through the global reggae icon, marked her as essentially Caribbean yet—and this is critical—a cosmopolitan black professional.

It is tempting to read the story of the Rastafarian beauty queen as singular to our twenty-first-century moment, a moment when the terms "modernity" and "blackness" are not set in opposition to each other. But what the story illuminates is not so much singularity as continuity. The history of leisure culture in the Anglophone Caribbean for the last 150 years is very much the story of the nascent black middle class and the aspiring black middle class, striving to reconcile their origins in black-identified culture with its aspirations for social ascendance and international recognition. It is this story that I tell here. There are intellectual histories that address the emergence of the black and brown middle class in the Caribbean, but these tell a story of political, not cultural, ascendance. Authentic Caribbean culture is assumed to be the preserve of the working class. This book aims to rectify this perception by sketching a history of middle-class popular culture—or, more precisely, what I term *aspirational* culture—in the English-speaking Caribbean from the mid-nineteenth century to the present moment.

My subject encompasses a broad swath of cultural artifacts, beauty pageants among them. Yet it is framed by an analysis of Caribbean literature—albeit literature broadly conceived, from newspaper features to leisure magazines. Still, even my investigations of other cultural sites, like beauty pageants, inevitably reference literary culture in some way. I begin with a discussion of that most elite, yet most populist, of Caribbean industries: its literature. I do so because it is in the *culture* of literature, in not simply the reading but in the production, dissemination, and symbolic associations of literature, that the rigidly subscribed class distinctions of elite, middle-class, and even working-class Caribbean culture, begin to blur. And therefore it is in the Caribbean's literary culture that we find the origins of middlebrow culture.

The Crisis of Highbrow Culture

In 1970, a book reviewer began his assessment of two anthologies of Caribbean literary criticism with a statement that he considered unassailable: "The two central facts about British West Indian fiction are that it began only twenty years ago... and that most of it has been written in Britain, Africa, and North America."[3] The reviewer had in mind the cohort of now-canonical writers, including V. S. Naipaul, C. L. R. James, and George Lamming, who did indeed pen the Caribbean's most influential narratives in the mid-twentieth century while living in the metropolitan centers of Europe and North America. The newness of Caribbean literature, and its supposed genesis in foreign locations, is framed by the reviewer as a liability. How can one speak of an independent Caribbean literary tradition when the literature owes its existence to a presumably more fertile foreign climate, and the forefathers of that tradition are still young men? While, on the one hand, the independence era required, and did indeed spawn, a singular Caribbean literary culture, on the other hand, the celebration of this newly found foundational literary culture was undermined by the feeling that it wasn't exactly native-born. It was not, in a word, independent. By this estimate, Caribbean literature is a mid-twentieth-century invention of expatriate Caribbean writers who were irreducibly influenced by metropolitan ideas. These "facts" have framed Caribbean discourse for the better part of a century. The Caribbean itself is rarely perceived by critics as a space that fosters a broad literary culture.

If early critics can be forgiven their ahistorical and limited perspective, what about the writers themselves? Barbadian novelist and critic George Lamming opined that his generation in essence created Caribbean fiction because it wrote "without any previous native tradition to draw upon."[4] C. L. R. James, the Trinidadian intellectual, novelist, and founding member of the seminal Beacon group, bemoaned what he saw as the crisis of origins for Caribbean artistic production: "The question around which I am circling is this: is there any medium so native to the Caribbean, so rooted in the tight association which I have made between national surroundings, historical development and artistic tradition, is there any such medium in the Caribbean from which the [literary] artist can draw that strength which makes him a supreme practitioner?"[5]

James's anxieties about the genesis of artistic culture so vividly on display here reflect the wider anxieties not simply of his profession but of his socioeconomic class.[6] The Caribbean literary tradition is perhaps the only tradition in the region thought to be unequivocally middle class, and yet its best practitioners fear that this cultural legacy is not "rooted" in the Caribbean. By contrast, no such anxiety attends scholarly observations on the roots of Caribbean working-class culture. George Lamming's statement that "the West Indian novel... has restored the West Indian peasant to his true and original status of personality" is in effect a concession to the idea that the writer himself has no culture upon which to draw, but rather must channel authentic Caribbean culture via the representation of the peasant. And indeed James's own novel, *Minty Alley*, clearly concedes the cultural territory as it tries to rectify the divide by placing the black, middle-class protagonist in a working-class Trinidadian "yard." The novel mirrors James's view of his own position in Caribbean society: an isolated observer of the "real life" of the working-class multitude.

Fellow Trinidadian V. S. Naipaul had a different view of the divide between working-class and middle-class Caribbean culture of the 1960s. Noting that the Trinidadian middle class loved dialect newspaper and radio stories but not dialect novels, Naipaul opined that the "Trinidadian expects his novels... to have a detergent purpose, and it is largely for this reason that there are complaints about the scarcity of writing about what is called the middle class."[7] In other words, it is not so much that there is no middle-class literary tradition but that *that* tradition is not identifiably different from the tradition of working-class Caribbean culture. Naipaul's remarks find an odd corollary among present-day critics. On the other side of the Caribbean literary continuum, forty years after Naipaul's caustic comment and James's anxious reflection, popular Jamaican author Colin Channer articulates a solution to the crisis of literary authenticity by framing the literary paradigm in terms of working-class Caribbean musical traditions. Or rather, in terms of one particular musical tradition:

> [Bob] Marley is the greatest storyteller that the Caribbean has ever produced. And one of the things I really admire about him is that he didn't "go disco," didn't follow market trends, didn't sell his soul for acceptance by a wider world. As it turns out, global acceptance came over time.... I am currently facing something in literature that he faced in music, a kind of pressure to shoehorn my work into an ill-fitting definition of what "black" is supposed to be. I will resist as he resisted, and if it is the will of Jah, then people will accept me and my work for what we are—Caribbean in origin but global in scope.[8]

Again Bob Marley, now a touchstone of authenticity for everyone from beauty pageant winners to authors. Channer stakes out as his literary forebear not James or other canonical Caribbean authors but rather the reggae superstar. The working-class, black Jamaican singer is an emblem of diasporic black identity, simultaneously embodying the aspirations of the world's poorest people and the glamorous international celebrity of the world's richest. Bob Marley therefore symbolizes a particularly modern idea of Caribbean identity. By canonizing Marley as a storyteller, a romantic nationalist who eschewed "marketing" and yet achieved global appeal, Channer the postcolonial writer answers James's (anti)colonial question, posed almost half a century earlier: authentic Caribbean literature has its roots in that which is at once organic, regionally specific, yet global.

In various ways Channer has attempted to strike a balance between two irresolvable Caribbean positions on race that are inevitably classed: on the one hand, that ethnic hybridity is organic to the Caribbean; on the other, that blackness is the fundamental culture and color of the Caribbean. His medium is the romance novel, and—the taint of "marketing trends" in Marley's case notwithstanding—it is cannily marketed to an international Pan-Caribbean audience. Channer's literary ambitions are larger than the middlebrow nature of his writing suggests; as an older version of his Web site noted, his works have been hailed as a "clear redefinition of the Caribbean novel." Many of his novels are named after Bob Marley songs and feature male protagonists who are intellectuals or artists, with their mixed-race origins given a prominent asterisk in the narrative. Channer's middlebrow genre thus epitomizes, more so than the "serious" (though not necessarily less popular) literature of other contemporary Caribbean authors such as Jamaica Kincaid, the cultural conundrum of the modern Caribbean: the competing desires for authentic culture, middle-class status, and global appeal.

Both James and Channer, in their different ways, speak to the binary that is implicit in Caribbean societies—the binary between authenticity and middle-class status. This binary has persisted despite evidence that the middle class in the English-speaking Caribbean has also been a producer of popular culture from the nineteenth century. My goal is to challenge a dichotomous vision of Caribbean culture by exploring facets of what I call middlebrow literary and popular culture of the modern Anglophone Caribbean. These include, for example, popular novels, beauty pageants, music festivals, and other expressions of culture that are mostly created, maintained, and consumed by the middle or aspiring-middle class. My aim is to both contextualize and historicize contemporary Caribbean middlebrow culture as a phenomenon that reflects more than the obvious connection: a new marketing opportunity for international publishing houses or corporations whose business it is to sell popular literature, beauty pageants, and music festivals to a new demographic of consumers.

Caribbean Middlebrow presents, in a kind of historical chronology, moments in a cultural continuum. It assesses a number of different cultural moments and artifacts, starting with an examination of the commercial literary culture of the late nineteenth-century Caribbean. It interprets newspaper features and magazine short stories taken from the lively print cultures of Jamaica and Trinidad, and often aimed at an emergent black-and-brown middle class. The belief that the Caribbean merely reprinted English stories is given the lie here. Across the Caribbean we find a relatively high ratio of belles lettres from the eighteenth century onward, and in an ironic twist of salesmanship, many original articles and poems first published in local newspapers and pamphlets were *re*published in London and exported back to the Caribbean colonies.[9] Moving from newspaper culture to popular fiction, I argue for the origins of a "brown" aesthetic that provides the foundation for middlebrow culture that is found in early, popular Caribbean novels such as the Trinidadian novels *Emmanuel Appadocca* (1853) and *Rupert Gray* (1907), or in the Jamaican novel *Jane's Career* (1913).

If Caribbean society's consignment of literature and entertainment to separate spheres has produced a schizoid perception of its own culture, then a more conciliatory vision of Caribbean life, one that combines the literary with the performative, is attempted here through an analysis of "dialect," or vernacular, poetry. Popular vernacular poetry links the performative and literary modes of Caribbean middle-class culture. Found on radio and television as well as in the theater and at talent contests, popular dialect poetry has been a staple of middlebrow Caribbean culture for well over a century. It is a familiar presence in almost all of the regional newspapers, and indeed, the earliest published volume of dialect poetry, Barbadian Edward Alexander Cordle's *Overheard* (1903), was culled from his regularly published poetry series in Bridgetown's *Weekly Recorder* newspaper. The themes of *Overheard* still resonate: local issues such as the spread of smallpox, Barbadian relations with neighboring Trinidad, marital relations, and court hearings are treated with the comic tone favored by dialect poets even today.[10] The genre is epitomized by the work of Jamaican Louise Bennett, whose poetry spanned the colonial and postcolonial eras and influenced every part of the cultural spectrum. Yet dialect poets, with the telling exception of the working-class "dub" poets, have been the most understudied authors in the Caribbean literary pantheon. From early on, their local concerns, comic outlook, and status as entertainers guaranteed that they would not be taken seriously as producers of Culture. Nevertheless, in this emphatically local and middle-class genre can be found the origins of everything from the highbrow theater of Derek Walcott to the musical lyrics of Bob Marley.

More recent moments in the middlebrow historical continuum include postindependence beauty pageant culture, the massive commercialization of Caribbean carnivals since the 1970s, the ubiquitous jazz festivals of the last twenty years, and of course the new genres of popular Caribbean fiction found within and without the region. Threading together this diverse history of aspirational culture are three key themes.

The first is the continuing influence of American popular culture from the nineteenth century to the present. Although Caribbean scholarship emphasizes British colonial influence in the nineteenth century and American influence in the late twentieth, this analysis argues for a continuous American cultural influence from the nineteenth century to the present. In *Creole America,* Sean Goudie shows just how interconnected were U.S. and Caribbean commercial and cultural interests in the late eighteenth and early nineteenth centuries, a connectedness that evidently continued to flow both ways into the next century.[11] West Indian businessmen were trying to attract white American tourists as early as the 1890s, and a flourishing commercial trade with the United States is evident in the many newspaper and magazine advertisements for U.S. goods of that period.[12] For over two hundred years American entertainers have been visiting the region, to the point where American culture has become synonymous with entertainment and modern pleasures. African Americans are instrumental in this connection. Harvey Neptune has shown that during the American occupation of Trinidad in the 1940s, for example, the musical tastes and style of African American soldiers fundamentally changed the consumption habits and forms of cultural expressiveness of the society in ways that disturbed the colonial administrators, who felt that African American culture was responsible for the growing discrepancy between West Indians' worldly desires and the provincial designs the administrators had in mind for West Indian economies.[13] Even before this watershed moment, African American society was a constant, if underappreciated, presence in the Caribbean. From the late nineteenth century onward, Caribbean societies followed American racial politics, read African American uplift narratives, and hosted traveling African American theatrical and musical groups. Black America gave the black—and brown—Caribbean a way to be modern and black in the twentieth century.

The second theme articulated here is the affirmation of not a hybrid but a brown cultural identity as a national ideal that has been both celebrated and castigated in the Caribbean. The actual population of mixed race people who inhabit the middle class notwithstanding, brownness is a central category for a discussion of middle-class Caribbean identity because it speaks directly to the middle-class issue of quasi-elite status and humble origins.

The third key theme is the centrality of gender categories in the delineation of middle-class culture. Much of what is identified as middlebrow is also considered genteel culture, or women's domain. If respectability is a category associated with the feminine, then arguably respectable culture is female culture. Gender norms are constantly being negotiated in the interplay between serious and leisure culture that preoccupies the middle class.

It is important to point out what this book is not. It is not an ethnography, or a general history of the middle class, or even a particular history of middle-class reading publics in the Caribbean. A historical, sociological, or ethnographic approach to class inevitably means a materialist reading whereby all narratives become transparent, a means into the society itself. Materialist readings always assume a connection between political events and cultural events: one begets the other.[14] They are synchronic. Yet this relationship is not always the case: for example, the traditional trova music of Mexico's Yucatan peninsula became increasingly "classicalized" even as the government become progressively more leftist.[15] To read the former, therefore, as a reflection of the latter may not ultimately be useful. Thus my analysis asks another kind of question: what do these artifacts of culture tell us that historical, sociological, or ethnographic approaches do not?

Aspirational Popular Culture

In recent years Caribbean cultural studies critics have begun to take note of the shift in Caribbean publishing from what can be called anticolonial literature to a more broad palette of themes and genres, similar to what we see in African American literature, where Walter Mosley's mystery novels and Octavia Butler's science fiction vie for shelf space with Terry McMillan's urban romances. This broadening may reflect nothing so much as the U.S. publishing industry's recognition of the fact that there are all kinds of black people with all kinds of literary tastes, and that they read. Similarly, anticolonial discourse in some ways obscured Caribbean middle-class literary culture as either nationalist or colonialist: between these two polarities it is difficult to judge what middle-class culture reflected, and reflects, "for its own sake." If the antiracist, anticolonial novel is fundamentally linked to a politicized modernism, as has been suggested,[16] then the postmodern moment in the Caribbean has meant a liberation from assiduity; reading, like listening to "smooth jazz," is not laborious but "natural" and pleasurable. Pleasure is key, because without pleasure reading is simply intellectual labor that West Indians do not yet "own." So in this sense I think that postmodern global culture becomes, in the Caribbean, distinctly classed: it is middlebrow culture.

One of the truisms of postmodernism is that it has erased the distinction between highbrow and lowbrow culture, "good" fiction for the few and "bad" fiction for the masses. And, as the Africanist scholar Anthony Appiah famously observed, because the postmodern moment is also in some sense the postcolonial moment, so too has the division between high and low culture been blurred by something akin to middlebrow culture in the infamously elitist postcolonies of Europe. Africanist critics have noted the vibrant popular literature and local film industries of modern Africa, and scholarly attention is now being paid to the phenomenal Indian film industry to examine not just serious Indian films, but also those popular films that speak to a large middle-class audience that is simultaneously cosmopolitan and focused on the local scene. Yet the Caribbean persists in both popular and critical discourse as a region marked by the high/low division, with low the authenticating marker. As Chris Bongie points out, Caribbeanist critics generally reject the idea of a middlebrow postcolonial literature and tend to use the values of colonial modernism to render judgments about contemporary popular fiction.[17] This notion is not to suggest that the necessary corrective is to equate the substance of Colin Channer's novels with that of James or other canonical writers, on the basis of a superficial idea that all cultural exercises are of equal value.

I do mean, though, to highlight the way in which scholars unwittingly reinforce the high/low binary when we ignore the role that popularity and pleasure play in determining the meaning of books or other artifacts of culture. If "popular" has been synonymous with "poor" or "nonserious" in the Caribbean, what does it mean that "serious" Caribbean literature, such as that of Jamaica Kincaid or Edwidge Danticat, appears in such popular American venues as *People* magazine or Oprah's Book Club? Does this sign change the way in which the Caribbean reading audience interprets these books? If the term "middlebrow" is associated with wealthy twentieth-century metropolitan societies with large middle-class populations, is it not misleading to speak of Caribbean middlebrow literature when there is only a relatively small middle-class population in the region? I don't think so. Popular Caribbean fiction was not invented in the present era by U.S. publishing houses and desktop publishing. Several of the literary devices associated with highbrow Caribbean literature, such as the much-commented-on dialectical writing (or responses to European ideas by rewriting European texts), have their origins in popular eighteenth-century parodies of, or rebuttals to, famous poetry, plays, or tracts—parodies that found fertile ground in the popular plays and vernacular poetry of the Caribbean.[18] Thus the dialectical tradition in the Caribbean grew from the bottom up, not from the top down. Popular

Caribbean fiction has been around as long as there have been newspapers, and in the Caribbean almost everyone reads the newspapers. Moreover, the audience for "serious" and "popular" literature has often been the same audience. The difference is in the context.

Take, for example, the Guyanese novelist Edgar Mittelholzer. During the 1940s and 1950s, English publishing houses packaged Mittelholzer's historical novels as both hardcover literature and dime-store paperbacks. These novels tell the story of Guyana through a series of violent historical events, a subject that lends itself to both serious and popular readers. His most famous novel, *Corentyne Thunder,* was published by Heinemann, thus aligning him with the likes of George Lamming and C. L. R. James. His paperback novels, however, were published by commercial publishers and aimed for a whole new audience, the kind of audience that might not have been otherwise interested in stories that illustrate grand national themes. Their covers are instructive: mixed-race Amerindian women with bare breasts; a white creole woman holding a whip over a black, half-naked servant who lies at her feet; two white creole women fighting off threatening black men.[19] Sex and miscegenation were, and are, irresistible topics. Much has been made of the "new" sexuality that pervades so much of today's popular literature,[20] but as the covers of Mittelholzer's books illustrate, there is nothing new about it. It is a question of what is emphasized.

The term "middlebrow" presents its own dilemmas. Lifted from American cultural studies, it suggests a confluence of economic and cultural status, or that consumers of middlebrow culture are, in fact, middle class. This definition may work well for the United States, with its consumer culture and large middle-class population with easy access to middlebrow "goods" like cheap novels. It works less well in the Caribbean, where poverty is endemic, and buying a book, however cheap, may mean not buying something else. Although middlebrow literature is largely read by middle-class readers, I want to emphasize that what people read reflects not just who they are (in terms of socioeconomic status) but who they *wish* to be. This concept is what I call aspirational status. So middlebrow literature reflects the validation of class status, yes, but it also may reflect the desire for higher class status—or the reconciliation of middle-class and working-class status. In short, middlebrow literature reflects the myriad and interlocking facets of the Caribbean class and culture dialectic. However, rather than argue for a globalized circulation of culture, as Paul Gilroy does in *The Black Atlantic,* I am arguing for the circulation of class. There are two axes to what I am terming middlebrow culture: aspirational culture, or a desire for higher social standing; and authenticating culture, or a desire to connect with working-class culture. These aspects are

FIGURE 1. Cover of the 1955 paperback edition of Edgar Mittelholzer's *Children of Kaywana*, published by the New English Library.

sometimes the same thing, though not always. The middle class is, in a sense, an imaginary community, accessed through participatory rituals like reading certain kinds of books, dressing in certain kinds of clothes, and attending certain kinds of public events.

Part of the conceptual problem in establishing a popular middle-class culture is that the Caribbean, unlike Africa or India, has no precolonial culture: the creolized society that we recognize as the modern Caribbean began at the moment of colonization itself. If there are only creoles and no natives, then the idea of a native cultural tradition inevitably begins and ends as a classed notion. As a consequence, much analysis of Caribbean culture starts from the presumption that the society is divided into two discrete and exclusive camps: the derivative "highbrow" cultures of the elites and the authentic cultures of the working classes. Highbrow culture is usually signified by the region's literary tradition, a product of its substantially black and brown middle class. In this region, where the majority of people are poor and comparatively few are what in the United States would be called middle class, the Caribbean middle class is de facto elite. Yet it is still not *the* elite. The middle class does not own the means of production; it owns no factories, media outlets, hotel chains. The real elite of the Caribbean is a haunting presence here, controlling and yet invisible; economically powerful yet culturally marginalized; shaping mass culture through its investments in music, literature, and pageantry, yet not driving it.

The propertied and business classes of the Anglophone Caribbean are, if no longer majority white, certainly disproportionately white—and of course they have always been so. The white elite has long been associated with highbrow culture of the Caribbean. This connection includes early literary culture, which is inevitably viewed as a rarefied by-product of the British education system. In Jamaica, it was an English governor who underwrote early black and brown Caribbean writers like Claude McKay and H. G. de Lisser, and prominent members of white society who built its first theaters and acted in its first plays.[21] Although there were indeed public elementary schools for the black working class that emerged in the post-Emancipation era of the mid- to late nineteenth century, these were not, by and large, avenues to the kind of elite education that was associated with the debating clubs, theater groups, and literary magazines of the era, the kind of education that essentially produced the cosmopolitan intellectuals who defined twentieth-century Caribbean literature.[22] Still, what is left out of these traditional accounts of the privileged nature of Caribbean education is that while elite education was always a raced notion in the Caribbean, it was as often as not raced black or brown. The landowning class was not particularly invested in education. The British writer James Pope-Hennessy, whose grandfather John Pope-Hennessy was the governor of Barbados in the late nineteenth century, noted that it was only those of African origin who would speak to the governor "of subjects about which he was accustomed to talk in his own country: about books, music or religion. English persons on the other hand spoke mainly of tennis-scores, the country-club, whisky or precedence or oil."[23] So: black, educated, propertyless. The more we plumb the narratives of the nineteenth-century Caribbean, the more we find the hallmarks of the emergent black and brown Caribbean middle class. Caribbean intellectuals are, inevitably, descendants of this earlier group. As the intermediaries of metropolitan and local societies, elite Caribbean authors are marked as keepers of Caribbean "high" culture, yet as a group their origins can be found in the local magazines, popular theaters, and debating clubs that characterize early Caribbean literary culture.

The high/low culture distinction that obscures the middlebrow coincides with other traditional scholarly binaries: metropolitan versus indigenous, European versus African, and so forth. Even the innovative recent criticism on cultural hybridity and popular culture has yet to dislodge this enduring presumption of a binary Caribbean cultural framework when it comes to reading actual cultural artifacts. In *The Caribbean Postcolonial,* the most definitive statement on Caribbean hybridity discourses to date, Shalini Puri focuses on the processes of hybridization more so than hybridity itself, with its overdetermined images of cultural harmony. This distinction is an important one because *cultural* hybridization does not, in fact, always correlate with *ethnic* hybridity. "Brown" people who usually identify with the professional class in places like Jamaica and Barbados are associated not with cultural synthesis and the transgression of social boundaries but rather with the consolidation of cultural boundaries. The same might be said of *douglas,* or half-black, half-Indian Trinidadians, who are usually identified as creole, and not Indian, in Trinidadian society.

The ethnically mixed middle class' self-serving nationalist rhetoric that the region's hybrid culture reflects its ethnic harmony, has been significantly punctured by recent scholarship. Puri points out that the "popular" is inevitably linked to the nation-state such that we must not assume that the nation is necessarily repressive or the popular always progressive. Richard Burton astutely notes that despite the revolutionary rhetoric that originates in the Caribbean, Caribbean publics—particularly Anglophone ones—have tended to make pragmatic and cautious political choices rather than revolutionary ones, so that we should view Caribbean societies as a blend of respectability and oppositional cultures, rather than a binary.[24] Yet, for the most part, critics continue to interpret Caribbean culture in mostly oppositional terms: cultural hybridity reflects, if not social harmony, then nothing more than the transformation of culture into state resource; or, popular culture is innately progressive, and thus a threat to a repressive state and to an inequitable social order.[25] And who threatens the social order? Inasmuch as all of the iconic artifacts of Caribbean identity—salsa, carnival, calypso, reggae—are identified with the Caribbean working class, "popular" in Caribbeanist scholarship is synonymous with "poor." And "poor" usually means black or Indian, not mixed race or white. The middle class, itself culturally rootless, is viewed as a consumer of authentic culture, not a producer. As we have seen from James, scholars have presumed that there are no authentic Caribbean middle-class cultural products.

One such scholar, Peter van Koningsbruggen, in his book on Trinidadian carnival, argues that there is an increasing "middle-classization" of Trinidadian society, as the "cultural homelessness" of the middle class makes it dependent on the cultural production of the lower class to the point where the working-class carnival tradition has now been largely appropriated as a middle-class event.[26] What Koningsbruggen and other critics of middle-class appropriation fail to note, however, is that elite appropriation of working-class culture is, far from a Caribbean phenomenon, something that has long and storied roots in Europe, the United States, and around the globe.[27] Elite appropriation of working-class cultural ideas in these other contexts does not inevitably lead to the charge that those middle-class communities or those elites are culturally irrelevant; in fact, often the opposite is true. In other words, why do scholars invert the relationship between political power and cultural power in the Caribbean in ways that we would not consider in other national contexts? There is nothing singular about middle-classization in the Caribbean context. Yet the image of "cultural homelessness" in effect repeats a nineteenth-century claim that the brown and black middle class is an "unnatural" presence in the Caribbean, a claim that persists into the twenty-first century. Nevertheless, Koningsbruggen's formulation of the middle-classization of Trinidad is useful for my counterargument here. As I see it, middle-classization is the reconciliation of two apparently conflicting Caribbean impulses so evident in Caribbean middlebrow culture: the desire for modernity, writ usually as white or First World, and the desire to establish or maintain cultural traditions, or roots—which are usually writ black (or now, in the case of Trinidad in particular, Indian).

A related view is that of anthropologists Deborah Thomas and David Scott, who see the middle class as culturally irrelevant to the working class. Using Jamaica as a case study, they argue that as the power of the state has waned, so has the influence of the state-identified middle class. Now that the black working class no longer sees middle-class status as a conduit to economic power, it is no longer dependent politically or culturally on respectable middle-class institutions such as the church or the school.[28] This point is critical, one with which I fundamentally agree, but only so long as I define middle-class identity solely through its institutions. Or define working-class identity solely through black identity. Although the Jamaica example is reflected in many ways across the Anglophone Caribbean, it should not be taken as the only model of possibility. Race is a critical factor in this argument. A notable contrast would be the working-class populations in Caribbean societies such as Trinidad and Tobago and Guyana, which are heavily Indian-descended, and are forging closer relationships to the state as their political power ascends. My framework for middle-class identity is necessarily more fluid: my point is that middle-classization does not mean solely middle-class appropriation of working-class cultural ideas, nor does it follow the traditional trajectory of the discourses of respectability. It does not mean the socialization of the working class into middle-class institutions so much as into middle-class mores, which have themselves changed. If the poor and working-class constituencies of the Caribbean have no interest in becoming "respectable" along the usual lines, they also have no interest in preserving working-class popular culture in the old formaldehyde of a nationalist "folk" cultural tradition. But if the Caribbean state is no longer a model of emulation, where does the hope for social mobility lie? The emerging working- and middle-class migrant Caribbean communities in the United States and Europe who send barrels as well as cultural ideas back home reflect a different model of possibility. The aspirations of the migrant Caribbean community are those of the working-class communities at home. Those aspirations are mirrored in the discourse of American-style professionalism that now characterizes the region's black and brown Caribbean middle class, a discourse of modernity that has been over a century in the making.

This discourse is informed by a familiarity with American manifestations of middle-class culture, which in the Caribbean take on an added significance, particularly in terms of the act of reading. In the same way that, in earlier generations, the act of reading Shakespeare, or possessing a Shakespeare play, was in itself a signifier of elite, gentlemanly status, so too does the act of middlebrow reading signify cosmopolitan status, the easy marriage between what is modern and what is authentic, or "roots." Unlike so much Caribbean highbrow fiction, middlebrow fiction does not require mastery of any canonical text. There is no status in being able to read a romance or a whodunit. The difficulty and complexity associated with the highbrow—either of form or of theme, is reversed in the middlebrow. It hasn't thematic complexity (although it may imply knowledge of canonical texts); nor has it formal complexity—or if it does, that is not its point. Its accessibility is part of its pleasure. Middlebrow literature's pleasures are heightened by the understanding that the mere mention of particular ideas or social contexts confers, in and of itself, elite or cultural group membership status: say, the heroine's presence at a lecture on behaviorism at the university in the Indo-Trinidadian romance *Hand in Hand,* or allusions to highbrow authors such as John Updike in Jamaican author Colin Channer's *Waiting in Vain.* The work of continuously identifying and defining the Caribbean middle class, its desires and its parameters, is the point of middlebrow literature.

The Domain of Women

Like middlebrow literature, Caribbean middlebrow culture is, broadly speaking, to a large extent women's culture. Much of middle-class popular culture is heavily weighted toward women in that women are more apt to be considered "leisure" (rather than "serious") readers of fiction. Caribbean women's behavior outside of the home is often taken as a barometer of the respectability of the wider community. Much of the popular fiction was and is in the form of the romance, inevitably a female genre. Interestingly, the black Jamaican writer and nationalist Una Marson, whose plays and poems addressed all of the serious themes of the day, was also at one time a writer of short story romances during her stint as the founder and editor of the *Cosmopolitan,* the literary magazine of the Jamaican Stenographers' Association. Romances were indeed the preferred literary mode of the magazine's contributors and, taken together, suggest that the desire to maintain a respectable status as a "pink collar" worker also coincided with larger, "cosmopolitan," desires, all bound up in the pleasurable romance.[29] The *Cosmopolitan* was a site for some of the earliest, American-style professionalism discourse in the Caribbean, where career tips mingled with beauty tips and romances. Another early site of professionalism discourse is the Caribbean beauty pageant, which—even as its appeal fades in its birthplace, the United States—is more popular than ever in the Caribbean and other developing regions of the world. In the Caribbean, as in Africa, Latin America, and Asia, the beauty pageant is the quintessential middlebrow cultural product, a mix of cheesecake, social desire, commercial canniness, and Third World nationalist ambition. Its audience, both the television audience as well as the live audience, is made up overwhelmingly of women. Its winners are overwhelmingly middle class, often university educated and "well spoken," and frequently are used as spokeswomen to promote state initiatives in farming or commerce. The beauty pageant, then, covers roughly the same terrain as the romance novel—social aspiration, nationalism, and pleasure.

This is not to say that there are no male middlebrow cultural artifacts. Calypso and, even more to the point, cricket are both conspicuously absent from my analysis. Calypso and its modern variant, soca, are still mostly masculine, mostly working-class cultural preserves, particularly the "steel pan men" of the carnival bands. But carnival itself, from which calypso and calypso culture originate, is rapidly being purged of its black, working-class male associations, as has been noted by critics and fiction writers alike.[30] Most discussions of popular culture in the Caribbean address calypso and cricket, ever since C. L. R. James was rediscovered by cultural studies critics and his magisterial study of Caribbean cricket, *Beyond the Boundary,* became a cultural studies primer. The conventional reading of Caribbean cricket, as posited by James and others, is that as an upper-class British game it provided a respectable vehicle with which to express an intense anticolonial, nationalist sentiment. (Indeed, cricket is such a signifier of Caribbean identity that Fire, the protagonist of Channer's *Waiting in Vain,* declares that as a "yardie to de bloodclaat core," he prefers cricket to baseball. Here cricket functions mainly as a differentiator between American and Caribbean identities.) So why no analysis of cricket? By way of answer, an example. Cricket's supposed apotheosis—the 2007 World Cup Cricket tournament held for the first time in the Caribbean, to great fanfare—in actuality signaled its descent.

Let us be clear: cricket is still very popular in the Caribbean, particularly in Barbados and Guyana. In Trinidad there is an airplane named after that nation's famous cricketer, Brian Lara. And indeed, Jamaica's populist former prime minister, Portia Simpson, found it expedient to dress up in cricket gear and lace her political speeches with cricket vernacular in order to exhort the party faithful to vote in then upcoming elections. The prime minister hoped to capitalize on the cricket fever that was supposed to be gripping the nation for the 2007 World Cup, with its first-time Caribbean venue. Large crowds were expected, but the stands were half empty for most of the tournament. Ticket prices were exorbitant, and Caribbean-style crowd culture was ruthlessly suppressed: no "wine and jam"[31] music, no food, no drink. "It is like watching cricket at Lord's," complained one English visitor, "It's no bloody different."[32] Cricket clubs like Jamaica's 115-year-old Melbourne Cricket Club now face possible extinction as young men choose sports like soccer and basketball. Which, again, is not to say that cricket is not popular, or indeed genteel—James's formulation still holds true; its popularity crosses class lines—but it no longer offers the same social benefits. What jazz festivals do for Caribbean culture is precisely what cricket doesn't do: establish a link with the U.S.-based black professional class. Cricket is a commonwealth game, after all. It is a game that ties the region to a colonial past and not to the present, where quick, high-scoring American games reflect the new sports consciousness and new possibilities for self-invention.

If cricket is no longer an apt example of male middlebrow culture, what else is there? In terms of literature, detective novels or science fiction are the obvious parallels to the middlebrow romance. Science fiction in particular has always enjoyed the status of being intellectually engaging, if sometimes badly written. The science fiction film genre has always evoked intense interest from scholars that the romance has not, for its perceived ability to promote serious philosophical or scientific issues—witness, for example, the academic industry around *Star Trek* or *The Matrix*—or reflect a particular cultural moment. Science fiction is not a genre associated with the Caribbean in general, however, and there are no male science fiction authors from the region that I know of.[33] So we return to the premise that middlebrow culture in the Caribbean is mostly the domain of women. Much of the marketing efforts for jazz festivals appear to be aimed at families—another code word for women—or at single women. In addition, the influence of African American middlebrow culture on the Caribbean cannot be underestimated. The way Terry McMillan and others literally created their own markets, from selling books out of the backs of cars all the way to making the best-seller lists and signing movie deals, is a lesson in literary social mobility to Caribbean immigrants. Interestingly, the African American women's magazine *Essence* was perhaps the first organizer of a music festival aimed at middle-class African Americans, particularly women: the annual Essence Music Festival in New Orleans. These African American cultural models have been instrumental in combining "real" African American culture with social mobility and modernity, a combination that finds its parallel in Caribbean middlebrow culture, with the emphasis on aspirational, socially mobile, yet pleasurable.

What is "respectable" popular culture? Is there such a thing? Why is this category important? If respectability has been the hallmark of the middle class from the nineteenth century to the present, insofar as respectability has always been tied to what women do or don't do, then respectable culture is, as I've already asserted, the domain of women. Nevertheless, the discussions of "respectability" as a Caribbean category in anthropology discourses are incomplete. The usual academic divide between the "respectable" elites and the not-respectable working class no longer obtains, especially when thoroughly middle-class, often nonblack or light-skinned black women have taken center stage in the "lewd" wining (or gyrating) that now characterizes carnival in Trinidad, Jamaica, and elsewhere. The colonial, female-identified respectability discourse described by anthropologist Peter Wilson in his classic 1973 analysis, *Crab Antics,* no longer applies:—that Caribbean women characterize colonial virtues of domestic or professional respectability, and Caribbean men characterize the opposite in that they aspire to public, "man in the street" models of masculinity. Instead, the divide between public and private, male and female spaces, respectable and not, has shifted. What I call the discourse of professionalism has now superseded respectability as a category, certainly among the upper middle class, which does not see its women "wining" in the streets at carnival as incompatible with the professional discourses of the office and the upwardly mobile home. Indeed, it is arguably a part of the secular Caribbean upper-middle-class experience—even if middle-class black and Indo-Caribbean women are still far more likely to meet with criticism for "bad behavior" at carnival than are brown or white women, middle class or no.

So if middle-class Caribbean women are in the public domain of the "man in the street," resignifying the space in ways that do not merely mean they are viragos, jamettes, streggehs,[34] or any of the various negative Caribbean terms used, this resignification converges with the new professionalism discourse that has replaced the respectability discourses of an earlier generation. And the discourse of professionalism is also, not surprisingly, heavily associated with women. As Carla Freeman observes in her important study of black Barbadian female informatics workers, although these women workers in the multinational computer industry are from working-class backgrounds, and many worked previously as domestics or agricultural laborers for higher pay, they leapt at the opportunity for a job in the informatics industry because of the *atmosphere* of professionalism that pervades the workplace: the air conditioning, the emphasis on "professional" dress (high heels, makeup, business attire), and above all, the "promise represented by the computer." All of these elements combine to make these jobs more desirable and, significantly, more pleasurable to the women.[35]

The investment of women workers in fashion as a symbol of professional status is mirrored by an equal investment of the multinational corporation, which encourages what Freeman calls the "strategic ambiguity" of appearing to be of one class and belonging economically to another.[36] Yet to dismiss the informatics industry as just another example of Western neo-imperialism is to miss two significant changes from the colonial model. In 1990s Barbados, Freeman points out, two of the three informatics companies were owned by black Barbadians, and the third was owned jointly by local whites and an American company; in Jamaica, the owners were all black Jamaicans. In addition, the emphasis on fashion in these corporate spaces is a result of the influence of U.S. popular culture that arrived during the 1980s through the increase in mass tourism, migration, and the sending of "barrels" to relatives overseas. It would be easy to call this willing embrace of corporate culture by the working class an instance of Marxist false consciousness, and perhaps on one level it is. But those of us who have made arguments about the dehumanizing effects of becoming human capital in the multinational workplace must also grapple with the fact that examples such as this one challenge the Marxist concept of the alienation of the worker from her labor. In the same way, I want to challenge the two opposing pillars of globalization theory: on the one hand, that globalization spreads the virtues of democracy through capitalism (it doesn't); and on the other, that globalization is a dehumanizing process that commodifies culture and the global worker (it does, but not always, or not in ways that always mean a repeat of the colonial moment). When the companies are black owned, or when consumer culture is a local phenomenon as much as one that is reinforced by one's relatives abroad—at what point does Commodification simply become Culture? In other words, are globalization and localization the same thing?

In *The Wretched of the Earth,* Frantz Fanon indicts the function of the middle class in Third World societies as both intermediary and imitative, the transmission line between the nation and international capital:

> But this same lucrative role, this cheap-Jack's function, this meanness of outlook and this absence of all ambition symbolize the incapability of the national middle class to fulfill its historic role of bourgeoisie. Here, the dynamic aspect, the characteristics of the inventor and of the discoverer of new worlds which are found in all national bourgeoisies are lamentably absent... this is because the national bourgeoisie identifies itself with the Western bourgeoisie, from whom it has learnt its lessons.[37]

For most critics of Caribbean popular culture, this analysis still rings true today.[38] But while not denying the intermediary role of the Caribbean middle class in international capital, I believe this formulation is complicated by the fact that the international bourgeoisie of today does not necessarily resemble that of 1961. Consumer-driven culture is now as authentic a reflection of the larger society in almost any arena: religious culture is consumer culture;[39] music culture, working class or no, is consumer culture. In other words, even the lodestones of authenticity—carnival, crop-over, dancehall—are being shaped by tourism, multinational profits, and the desire to reach an international audience. Indeed, Bob Marley himself, despite Channer's romantic view, is a triumph of the marketing savvy of Island Records founder Chris Blackwell, whose decision to market Bob Marley and the Wailers as black rock stars (an image more familiar to the white metropolitan audience in the 1970s than the local Caribbean Rastafarian) paid off handsomely.[40]

The presumption has been that the flow of culture is one way: from "the people" to profit. But who is to say that from profit may not also flow culture? If transnational administration is now *necessary* to the flow of local authenticity, we critics must ask ourselves what are our investments in the alignment of Culture against Commodity when the lines between the two are so indistinct. International capital now comes in the form of Caribbean and African American people, middle class and working class, aspiring to and finding meaning in an increasingly converging idea of global black popular culture that is acquisitive, commodifying, but also in some sense truly diasporic, created and consumed right there in the Caribbean.

Chapter 1

Early Literary Culture

On December 23, 1899, on the eve of the twentieth century, Jamaica's oldest and most venerable newspaper, the *Daily Gleaner,* ran one of its many popular competitions. This one was for the best "Nancy story." The entries were to capture, in written form, the stylistic and thematic intricacies of the oral folktales about Anancy the Spider. Anancy is the legendary folk hero brought to the islands by enslaved Africans, whose descendants, the black peasantry, were the supreme practitioners of the genre. Yet, to judge from the competition in the *Gleaner,* Anancy's innate contradictions struck a resonant chord with Jamaicans of all social groups in the late nineteenth century, just as they do in the twenty-first. Both victim and victimizer, Anancy is a wily survivalist and consummate hustler, a fragile member of the animal world who should be among its first victims but often triumphs through deception and trickery. He is profoundly, essentially, Jamaican. Still, the rules of engagement laid out for would-be authors were daunting:

> Competitors may be perfectly sure that they can win no way in such competitions unless they have a good command of English Grammar, and particularly that branch of it that teaches spelling. One misspells of course intentionally in writing dialect, but the English that connects the dialect must be written with correctness.

The next weeding removed those manuscripts whose writers apparently think that because it may be said... that a Nancy Story is a Fairy Tale, therefore it must be true that every Fairy Tale is a Nancy Story. Stories relating to France and England, for instance, are here quite out of it. *What is wanted is one of those semi fabulous, humorous, half-jesting, half-didactic stories, that are set amid local surroundings, and have local atmosphere and colour.*

Competitors however fail, who endeavour to make the story from beginning to end nothing but dialect. It may be clever, but it is quite unreadable to any outside a very narrow circle. All therefore, who look forward to future competitions of the sorts, should take it for granted that there must be breathing spaces of pure and appropriately shaded English, or else, the attempt to plunge through the story is, like getting through a very thick and thorny hedge.[1]

I begin my discussion of early Caribbean middle popular culture with this example of the gentrification of the Anancy story because it reveals so much about the desires and anxieties of the emergent Caribbean middle class in its pursuit of literature and leisure at the turn of the nineteenth century. Although the *Gleaner* was a newspaper for the mostly white Jamaican elite, its readership would have included the literate brown and black middle classes. Further, the competition's detailed instructions on how to balance "a good command of English Grammar" with the "dialect" necessary to the execution of the story tell us that the audience is made up of locals familiar with both. But why such a narrowly telescoped analysis of Caribbean early literary culture? It is true that the nineteenth-century Jamaican middle class is by no means entirely the same thing as, for example, the Trinidadian middle class, which at this period was more fragmented than Jamaica's, as a result of more extensive cultural plurality, immigration, and a much shorter history of English dominance. Nor is it the same as the Barbadian middle class, or the Guyanese middle class, and so on. Nevertheless, by 1899 a definable black and brown middle class had begun to take shape, to a greater or lesser degree, in all of these places. In Trinidad and Jamaica, black and mixed-race (or "brown") men owned newspapers and were active in politics.[2] In Barbados, black and brown men were emerging as merchants and politicians, and the next twenty years would see the formation of black and brown lodges, cricket clubs, and other institutional demarcators of middle-class status on that island.[3] Still, in many ways Jamaica epitomized the consolidation of middle-class consciousness in the region.

By 1899 Jamaica's middle class was fairly large and self-perpetuating; in addition to whites, it was heavily constituted of black and, even more so, brown small landowners, teachers, railway supervisors, ministers, and lawyers who were entering into the civil service, the legislative bodies, and the cultural institutions of the island. This group was distinct and definable: it was increasingly literate and ferociously hungry for literature of all kinds. By the 1890s, black Jamaicans in particular were responsible for the dramatic increase in library reading rooms, newspaper circulation, and book sales on the island over the past five years.[4] As a group, the black and brown middle class were dissociated from many of the "lowbrow" cultural traditions of the black peasantry, but they were also at odds with the politics and attitudes of the white ruling elite. Critics such as Kenneth Ramchand have argued that this dissociation was cultural alienation, borne of the black middle class's isolation and, as he saw it, lack of wealth and privilege. Historian Gordon Lewis went further, painting middle-class culture in the early years as a kind of tragic mulatto problem. Like the region's dependent political status, its culture was "sterile" and "borrowed"; middle-class Caribbean citizens were at best guilty of "militant philistinism" and at worst subject to "the cruel pressures that make life so much of a misery" for this pathetic group.[5]

Yet another picture emerges when we read the black middle class through its members' own newspapers and magazines. In contrast to Ramchand's view, they were, as an economic group, if not altogether prosperous, at least economically stable, having the means to own property, newspapers, and to maintain careers that could be counted on to produce income.[6] In contrast to Lewis's view, the early Caribbean middle class may well have been colonialist and often imitative, but this inclination does not preclude its interest in self-representation. What comes across clearly is its members' profound middle-class desire to see their own cultural reflection, a desire manifested in the stories and other features of Caribbean newspaper and magazine culture from the late nineteenth century through the 1920s and 1930s.

The complexities of this emerging class and its relationship to the peasantry are illustrated with panoramic precision in Jamaican writer Claude McKay's classic Caribbean novel, *Banana Bottom*. McKay himself straddled the Victorian and modern periods of Jamaican history, and his novel reflects his understanding of the extraordinary shifts taking place among the nascent bourgeoisie. On the one hand, some highly educated black and brown characters in his novel go mad or suffer from profound self-hatred because of their alienation from their own society, being neither "fish nor fowl." On the other, we see a stable world of black and brown landowners, teachers, and ministers, people who had their own particular amusements and leisure activities that were tied to neither black working-class amusements nor the English traditions represented by the anachronistic missionaries of the novel. McKay's image is perhaps the only imaginative rendering still in current circulation of this nascent black-and-brown world, so polarizing have been most modern critical attempts either to consign the middle class to comprador status or, at most, to redeem only those figures who articulated anticolonial ideologies.[7]

A more nuanced account of this world, as read through its popular literary culture, is what I attempt here. First, however, we must grasp that the world of Caribbean leisure writing did not appear suddenly in the twentieth or even the nineteenth century. The Anglophone Caribbean already had an entrenched print culture in belles lettres by the nineteenth century, even on the smaller islands. By the end of the eighteenth century, four books of poetry and an English grammar had been published in Antigua alone, and the *Barbados Gazette* had produced a spin-off magazine called *Caribbeana* and dedicated to poetry and other literary writing.[8] Even the Caribbean's famous dialectical tradition, in which Caribbean authors respond to or rewrite (in)famous European texts for a local audience, and which is usually associated with its modern nationalist black and brown communities, is traceable to early print culture.[9] My account here follows a historical chronology, from an analysis of mostly Jamaican newspapers of the late nineteenth century through that of its magazines of the early 1930s. In particular I focus on three central points: the consolidation of brown cultural consciousness; the influence of American popular literature and cultural ideas; and the interpellation of "serious" and leisurely literary cultures in the colonial era of the Anglophone Caribbean.

An Age of Newspapers

Jamaica was an influential island during this period: newspapers from other Anglophone Caribbean countries carried regular news of even mundane events there, and as a comparatively prosperous Caribbean nation with a nationalist-minded elite, it represented a model of possibility for other Caribbean societies. Indeed, Jamaica also had an early engagement with both the printing press and the theater, assuring a long and unbroken association with these two pillars of literary activity.[10] The *Victoria Quarterly,* a magazine devoted entirely to publishing original local creative work, was started in 1889, and the landowning peasantry had organized reading clubs since 1884. At the end of the nineteenth century, Jamaica was home to a bewildering number of newspapers, so much so that the *Jamaica Telegraph,* bemused by its rapidly proliferating competition, noted, "This seems to be an age of newspapers in Jamaica."[11] Many of these newspapers were one-man affairs, run by enterprising black and brown men who were subsidizing or supplementing their regular income as teachers, politicians, or ministers, and who used their newspapers for a variety of purposes: to inform, lecture, bully, or entertain.[12] Whereas the *Gleaner* was unabashedly colonialist in tone, and geared toward a more obviously upper-class audience, smaller newspapers such as the *Daily Telegraph,* the *Jamaica Times,* and the *Jamaica Advocate* were aimed at a wider cross-section of white, black, and brown middle-class and working-class constituencies. Each newspaper carved out a particular socioeconomic and ideological niche: pro-imperialist, white, conservative, and wealthy (the *Gleaner*); moderately nationalist, liberal, and brown and black middle class (the *Jamaica Times*); and anticolonial, radical, and black working class (the *Jamaica Advocate*).

The *Jamaica Advocate* made it clear that it wrote for black people—black, working-class people. It was published by the strident Afro-Bahamian migrant Robert Love, a Pan-Caribbeanist who, after a sojourn in Haiti, settled in Jamaica and eventually became a Jamaican legislator. The *Advocate* was a direct reflection of Love's nationalist, antipapist, unionist beliefs. It had as its motto the title of the famous Robert Burns ode to the working class, "A man's a man for a' dat," a defiant phrase that affirmed both the lower social status of its readers and its advocacy on their behalf. Its editorial page further affirmed its view of its working-class black identity: "We will strive to be the advocate of the rights and interests of the individual as against any abuse of authority.... we will not fail to express our views on all questions which affect the interest of the masses; and which end either to advance or to retard the development of the social and political condition of the common people, of whom we are one."[13] Despite its literary motto, editor Love was not really interested in literature, regarding it as irrelevant. In an editorial titled "Study Your Business," he urges young men to pay attention to their trade and stop straining to "swallow whole volumes of literature and science in a few months." In Booker T. Washington-esque tones he castigates those who "concentrate their efforts upon something quite foreign to their trade. Such men have mistaken their calling, and are wasting their time, so far as self-improvement goes."[14] With the strident political tone of the editorials throughout the paper, Love appears to see literature only in terms of its utility for advancing advance black working interests; the abstractions of the "higher" arts and sciences are not, apparently, self-improving.

This stance was not, however, the attitude of the more famous early black nationalist Marcus Garvey, who later in the 1920s enthusiastically promoted the development of literature among the members of his militant organization, the Universal Negro Improvement Association (UNIA), and ran a series of literary competitions in his magazine, *Negro World*. Garvey himself wrote poetry, often in the Shakespearean mode. Copying the popular format of the day, which combined literature, political analysis, and pictures of female pulchritude, Garvey featured photographs of beautiful black women from around the world, essentially "blackening" the entertainment magazine. The difference between Love's approach and Garvey's is instructive for our understanding of the making of middle-class sensibilities at the turn of the nineteenth century. Whereas for Love cultural products must have strictly material outcomes for the advancement of the black working classes, for Garvey black nationalist culture must also appear as a seamless part of "respectable" culture to be truly transformative. In other words, it must already appear to exist as a part of black people's everyday life. And popular culture, as it appeared in *Negro World,* was distinctly literary: a blend of working-class views and middle-class cultural pursuits. In this way could militancy, literary aspirations, and popular entertainment go hand in hand.[15]

In contrast to the *Advocate,* the *Jamaica Times,* less overtly political and more evidently middle class, gently positioned itself "not so much... a chronicler of passing events... as a magazine for family use."[16] Known locally as "the teacher's newspaper" and widely read among migrant Jamaicans in Panama and Central America,[17] it positioned itself from the beginning as the anti-*Gleaner,* to judge from an endorsement by "Winkler's Choir Leader": "The daily newspapers are too cumbersome in size and too expensive for the ordinary workman to subscribe to, but in the *Jamaica Times,* which is published weekly, we have a little publication that arms the heart... bright, cheery articles, and just a handy size, something that can be bound after a while."[18] Over the years it published a wide array of short stories and serialized novels by local authors and became a forum for the expression of middle-class culture. Even so, the newspaper wished it to be known that it was also for "the folk," as is made evident by the reference to an encomium from one "Charlotte" in the inaugural issue of the newspaper, who said that "De Edita ob de *Jamaica Times* send she a copy ob him fuss numba."[19] This positioning suggests that the editor understood it was important to his more nationalist-minded readership that the paper should at least make the effort to include the black peasantry in its audience, even if that constituency did not contribute to its pages except as fodder for "local flavor." Nevertheless, the *Jamaica Times*'s penchant for rendering quotations from the black peasantry and working class in dialect begins a tradition of popular reportage in the Caribbean up until the present moment, suggesting that the voices—if not necessarily the views—of the working class are considered an essential ingredient to the middle-class medium of newspaper writing.

So it was in the context of these newspaper rivals, with their pages full of stories, amusing anecdotes, political exhortations, and social advice, that the sober *Gleaner* instituted its popular literary competitions. The Anancy story competition illustrates just how invested even the elite of Jamaican elite were in promoting a genre of specifically Jamaican narrative at the close of the nineteenth century. The rise and growing influence of the colored and black middle class suggest that this quest for an identifiably Jamaican narrative form constituted a recognition of what the reading classes across the spectrum wanted: their own story. The Anancy story competition, although not remotely representative of the "folk" culture emphasis of the anticolonial nationalist literary magazines at midcentury, is still evidence of a kind of proto-nationalist cultural consciousness, one that was contained within a pro-imperialist imperative. Significantly, among the *Gleaner*'s many competitions in 1899 was one for a Jamaican national anthem, sixty years before Jamaica actually had one. The paper stipulated that the national anthem should "include the interests of all citizens and not sound like the British National Anthem." The mandate was clear: the anthem must represent the peasantry at some level and not be an imitation of the colonizer. The prerequisites of the Nancy story competition similarly reveal the cultural juggling act that later critics have always subscribed to modern Caribbean literature: the authentic Anancy story cannot be a trumped-up European fairy tale but must have the original features of the oral form ("half-jesting, half didactic"); it must have the authenticating marker of Jamaican Creole speech, yet must be "written with correctness"; most of all, "care should be taken to make details small and large fit into *local surroundings*."[20] The continuous emphasis on "the local" reminds us that the efforts to craft a national literature in the twentieth century were part of a much longer effort from the nineteenth, but what was considered "national" in the nineteenth century did not necessarily spring out of the larger anticolonial movements that characterize the later twentieth century movements. These late nineteenth-century efforts at a national literature were therefore not assigned to the realm of serious literary endeavor: "national" here meant local, comic or sentimental, entertaining, as well as instructive.

The winning entry, "Anancy Wishes to Learn to Read, and the Result," by one Rev. E. D. Tinling, studiously mixes dialect and standard grammar. The didactic storyline features a showdown between Anancy's enlightened desire for social uplift—his desire to read—and his primitive urge—to eat. Obviously the primitive urge wins. The story functions as what was probably seen as a particularly apt metaphor for Jamaica, the war between the desire for "civilization" and the desire to hustle. Many of the humorous stories featured in the *Daily Gleaner* and elsewhere during this period present a clash of cultures between upper and lower classes: the interaction between butlers and mistresses; the conduct of blacks and whites on the same juries; confusion over the colloquial pronunciation of highfalutin words. In a changing world, where black Jamaicans were both butlers and jurists, these comic scenes suggest that comic fiction alleviated the social anxiety about the seismic shift in social classes. The shifting point of view in these newspaper stories, particularly in those of the *Jamaica Times* and the *Telegraph,* is relevant here: stories are written both from both an inside perspective—the Anancy story—and from an outside one—the "scenes of local flavor," with an almost anthropological attention to "local peasant customs" and "the Amusements of the People." The writers, clearly seeing themselves as both "of the people" and "their intellectual and moral superiors," careen constantly between the use of phrases like "our people" and distancing comments about the idiosyncrasies of the populace. In one example, the reporter follows the story of a man who was arrested and charged with practicing obeah (the African-derived popular spiritual practice or "black magic" of Jamaica). The reporter notes that "men of position and intelligence have been to him" and mourned that "our people can be so deluded." Yet, defensively, he also points out "how superstitious Doctor Johnson, and some other great and learned men were." *They* (the peasantry) are superstitious and backward, but so are some of *them* (the Doctor Johnsons and other Europeans). This kind of ideological balancing act is a common feature of these stories. The narrative voices are, by turns, sympathetic, amused, defensive, and haughty toward their peasant subjects.[21]

Nor was it a given that the readers and writers of the Jamaican newspapers believed in the civilizing qualities of the novel, despite the enthusiasm for the many forms of the written word on display in their pages. The genre was still perceived as a purely entertaining form rather than an edifying one, and an acute insecurity was more often than not on display when it came to pondering the meaning of literary output of the island's newspapers. Given that the newspaper was dedicated to the social strivings of the middle and aspiring-middle class, the question of whether one should indulge in nonedifying pursuits such as novel reading was apparently a serious one. In an 1898 editorial titled "Is Novel-Reading Injurious?" the *Jamaica Times* pondered whether modern fiction lacked "brain stuff." Noting that while great strides had been made in literature, the editorial stated that, nevertheless,

> it will not be denied that the high pressure which is the bane of the nineteenth century has invaded the realm of literature, with disastrous results. Speed and excellence of workmanship are only in rare instances found together.

At the same time,

> it is much too late in the day to cry out against the novel. Its place is now secure, and it must be taken account of as a department of literature. If the fact that many people read nothing but novels, be brought as an objection, it must be admitted; but we cannot think that anyone possessed of the real spirit of the student, and a real enthusiasm for literature, will allow fiction—which however valuable, is the least important section of it—to absorb all his attention. The novel is not an unmitigated evil. Rightly used it is much the reverse.[22]

The editorial went on to remind readers of the classic Victorian writers Fielding, Smollett, Eliot, Dickens, and Thackeray, implicitly associating the creative writing in its pages with the indisputably edifying works of English literature in the colonial universe. Dickens et al. not withstanding, the *Jamaica Times* had a prescription for its weekly prize story: "The story must treat of Jamaican subjects or its scenes must be in Jamaica."[23] Thus the beginnings of a popular literary nationalism.

The tension between the *Times*'s democratic intentions and its presumption that "good" writing was essentially painstaking, exclusive, and nonfiction, illustrated the larger tensions of the burgeoning middle class, which was torn between accommodating itself to the goal of egalitarianism—these were, after all, mostly nonwhite people a generation or less away from the laboring class—and the desire for exclusivity, which is the hallmark of social mobility. On the one hand, the *Times* harbored nationalist aims of social uplift, and on the other it was about the business of entertainment. Every week the opening page of the newspaper featured a prominent Jamaican who had worked hard, often pulling himself up by the proverbial bootstraps, to achieve success.[24]

So how did newspaper novels and stories fit into this upward vision? Quite simply, and crudely, they fit by "producing" culture. The aim of this newspaper, and others of its kind, was both to entertain *and* instruct, with the emphasis on "family fare" becoming another way to create a cohesive class, inasmuch as the family itself becomes the foundation for the group. Indeed, the *Times* had a regular beauty column by "A Lady," which also extolled advice for mothers. This pattern of intellectual inquiry followed by beauty and housekeeping advice would be copied and expanded upon by Afro-Jamaican Una Marson's influential *Cosmopolitan* in later years. "Family," however, meant "female," associated with "soft" knowledge as opposed to "hard," easy as opposed to difficult—and novel reading, as conceived in the editorial pages of the *Jamaica Times,* was a feminine pursuit. Novel writing, however, was entirely a different matter. Literature as an act of authorship was still a masculinist affair.²⁵ Between these two poles, leisure and work, soft knowledge and hard, female and male, lay the creation of a distinctly middle-classed literary culture.

Trinidad's Early Newspaper Culture

On the other side of the Caribbean, in Trinidad, a similar if not as dramatic coalescing of the black and brown middle class was also taking place. Since emancipation in 1838, a black and brown middle class made up of free coloreds and descendants of ex-slaves, had been slowly emerging in the region.²⁶ In the late nineteenth century, primarily the result of education, a distinct black and brown middle class emerged, whose members, as in Jamaica, entered the professions and civil service—doctors, lawyers, teachers, printers, journalists. Like Jamaica, Trinidad also experienced a proliferation of newspapers. Five in particular functioned as the mouthpiece of this new class: the *New Era,* begun in 1869 by two brown men, Samuel Carter and Joseph Lewis; the *San Fernando Gazette,* owned by Carter; the *Free Press* in the mid-nineteenth century; the *Trinidadian,* a mid-nineteenth-century anti-government newspaper owned by a brown man, George Numa Dessources; and the *Mirror,* a leftist newspaper started in 1898 by Richard Richardson Mole, an expatriate English journalist.²⁷ These newspapers were vocal about their advocacy for their class in general and pushed ideas important to the black middle class in particular. Topics that came up with regularity were education and the end to exclusivity of schools, an end to Indian immigration from the subcontinent (the burgeoning Indian population was seen as a threat to black and brown power), and the opening up of Crown lands.²⁸ The term "creole" was used frequently, and almost always in a laudatory manner, whereas references to Asians and Portuguese tended to be pejorative or confined to court reports and crime, suggesting the sense of an emerging creole identity that was Anglo, black and brown, and resolutely non-Asian.²⁹ The *New Era* and the *Gazette* were key in promoting two of the earliest books of literary criticism by a black West Indian, the now-iconic *Froudacity* (1889) and the *Theory and Practice of Creole Grammar* (1869) by John Jacob Thomas.³⁰ *Froudacity* was a stinging rebuttal to British historian James Anthony Froude's condemnation of the islands in his travel narrative, *The English in the West Indies* (1888), and *Creole Grammar* was the first attempt to theorize Creole speech in linguistic terms, as a language unto itself. The *Trinidadian* and the *Mirror* also showed a vested interest in local literature. The *Trinidadian* serialized at least one novel, the anonymous romance *Adolphus, A Tale* (1853), the story of two star-crossed brown lovers, which also functioned as a thinly veiled criticism of existing antibrown government policies. In 1907 the *Mirror* heavily advertised what is possibly the first Afro-Trinidadian novel, *Rupert Gray,* which was published by its sister institution, the Mirror Printery.[31]

If there was less of a profusion of literary production in the pages of the Trinidadian newspapers—we do not see, for instance, the literary competitions, comic sketches, and regular serialization of novels that characterize late nineteenth-century Jamaican newspapers—nevertheless, some of the English-speaking Caribbean's earliest novels were published in Trinidad, and in Trinidadian newspapers, in the latter half of the nineteenth century.[32] The heroes and heroines of these early works are inevitably from the brown class, with black characters playing a supporting, often comic role (although this pattern changes dramatically in the first decade of the twentieth century). The representations of mixed-race protagonists are clearly intended to work out local issues about the rights and social status of brown people on the island. In another sense, they symbolize authentic Trinidadianness itself—a hybrid that would appeal to both black and brown reading constituencies.

Trinidadian literature, like its Jamaican counterpart, was completely given over to popular genres of the nineteenth century, so much so that when the now-famous literary Trinidad Beacon group solicited stories for its magazine the *Beacon* in the early 1930s, the submissions were usually harshly evaluated and inevitably rejected because of the group's vision of the "correct" model for a national literature, which was distinctly at odds with popular, genre-driven narrative. In an editorial titled "Local Fiction," the *Beacon* editors wrote, "We regret to write that few good local stories have been received for this competition. The majority of local fiction-writers obviously believe that gross exaggerations contribute to the artistic value of their stories. Several of the stories we have received read like advertisements for the enhancement of our tourist trade; others like anecdotes from the Good Book, and still more, like extracts from *True Story.*"[33]

Perhaps this is why, despite his quick catalogue of early Trinidadian literature—mostly newspaper novels and short stories—critic Reinhard Sander concludes that, until the Trinidad Awakening of the 1930s, the literary scene on the island produced "nothing very remarkable."[34] Yet he also remarks that the entry into fiction of Trinidad's most famous writer, V. S. Naipaul, was essentially effected through the local short stories published in the Trinidadian newspapers of the 1940s, a point that Naipaul himself has made.[35] The influence of the magazine and newspaper culture of Trinidad, as in Jamaica, provided a literary template for a wide range of writers of every ideological, ethnic, and class description. The *Beacon's* editorial collective was a famously nationalist, multiracial group, composed of blacks—among these the scholar

C. L. R. James—whites, Portuguese, and to a lesser extent, Asians. They made a conscious effort to purvey information about Africa and India in order to attract Afro- and Indo-Trinidadian writers.[36] The burgeoning anticolonial sentiment of the country coincided with a coalescing of cross-racial cultural projects, and hence the editors, a highly educated, cosmopolitan group, no doubt influenced by artistic movements like primitivism, indigenism, and negritude, were rightly adamant that Caribbean literature reflect working-class Caribbean realities.

Commerce, Nationalism, and Literature

Another kind of reality is revealed by the "bad" writing dismissed by critics like Sander and Ramchand. In the early twentieth century, Trinidadians, like Jamaicans, were probably reading a lot of travel narratives about the Caribbean, which would be the only kind of "legitimate" writing to feature the region as its subject (hence the "advertisements for the enhancement of our tourist trade"), and lowbrow fare like the popular American romance story magazine, *True Story*. Editor Albert Gomes understood that the serious, proletarian-driven literature he was looking for did not as yet exist, even in the more prolific Jamaica: of that island he wrote that the emerging black and brown middle class followed the lead of the old plantocracy and "showed resistance...to a native literature that was not the English literature that they had been brought up to consider the only literature possible."[37] Ironically, Gomes's critique was confirmed by one of the island's feted symbols of English imperialism, Sydney Olivier, the liberal English governor to Jamaica from 1907 to 1913. Olivier believed that Jamaican authors did not respect local forms of expression, to the detriment of Jamaican writing:

> [They] too often indulge in an unbalanced habit of gushing eulogy...a shallow, pictorial, ignorant and often vulgar and frivolous fashion of writing about the men and women who form the mass of the population and their reputed psychology, habits and superstitions, and in a recurrent unintelligent serving up of old dull legends and antiquarianisms...which ceased long ago to have any little of significance in the consciousness of the island community. I do not know of any really completely truthful and unaffected book about Jamaica, either as a country or as a society.[38]

Although Gomes is essentially correct, the problem is that what he—and Caribbeanist critics such as Ramchand and Sander—defines as "literature" is limited to a version of the modernist or proletarian novel. Both genres, like the reviled "pictorial" writing or popular romances, originated in Europe and the United States. Yet for Gomes and other members of the intellectual class, authentic literature should only be a "serious" effort that, in reflecting life as it "really is" in the Caribbean, would contribute to the anticolonial politics of its own class. The consequence of this view is that the folk novel is essentially an intellectual invention, *about* the folk but not *of* them. As a class within a class, early Caribbean intellectuals did not write novels about themselves. By contrast, the broader Caribbean middle class was indeed producing and consuming its own literature in the late nineteenth and early twentieth centuries, but it produced and consumed it with a range of motivations contending together. The literature was often ephemeral, such as the serialized novels and the poetry that appeared in the newspapers of the era, most of which were themselves ephemeral, or the literature produced by the early literary debating societies in Jamaica, Trinidad, and Barbados.[39] Their writing was sometimes nationalistic, or pedantic, but always intended to entertain a broad audience; the aims of commerce were never far from what I am terming early Caribbean middlebrow literature.[40] The view that this literature should entertain or have a calculable economic benefit—entertainment and commerce being intimately aligned—was paramount. Thus could a 1951 editorial in the venerable Jamaican magazine *Spotlight,* geared toward the black and brown middle classes, opine without irony, "Maybe the Board ought to interest the West Indies University into giving a fellowship or something to some writer who will delve into the legends and folklore of Jamaica and make not only written history of them, but provide ear-tingling and hair-raising stuff to sell to tourists. The other Caribbean countries—who also have good food, good rum, good scenery and good hotel beds—are doing it. Why can't we?"[41] The respected black Jamaican poet Evon Blake was founder and editor of the magazine, and what this editorial suggests is that the black and brown middle class did not necessarily see nationalism and commercial interests as incompatible.

The content of the late nineteenth- and early twentieth-century serialized newspaper novels provides some links with what we find in later, more explicitly nationalist and black-and-brown-identified magazines of the 1930s, 1940s, and 1950s, such as *Spotlight,* the *Beacon,* and Jamaica's the *Cosmopolitan.* Because the newspapers were often the only, or the cheapest, forum for producing literature, many serious practitioners, such as Jamaican writers Claude McKay and Thomas MacDermot (known popularly as Tom Redcam), and later Una Marson, published regularly in local newspapers and magazines, and later published their serialized fiction as full novels, as did popular writer H. G. de Lisser (who later became editor of the conservative *Gleaner*). Claude McKay, in particular, enjoyed early popularity in Jamaica with his newspaper-published dialect poetry. He was then known as Jamaica's Robert Burns, and people memorized his poetry avidly, including the young Louise Bennett, Jamaica's most popular dialect poet of any generation. (The poetry of the anticolonial, dialect-writing Irishman Burns was hugely popular during this period, and Jamaicans were given to memorizing the poems whole.) McKay's early poem "Agnes o' de Village Lane" (1911) was published in the *Daily Gleaner*, which reported that it was the "general favourite of McKay's poems."[42] Although contemporary critics situate McKay's work by contrasting dialect poetry to the colonialist mimicry encouraged by the Jamaican literary establishment, McKay's origins as a popular Jamaican newspaper contributor who was well regarded by this same establishment cannot be overlooked; the conservative *Gleaner* welcomed and published his poems, and he crafted his model for his later 1912 volumes, *Songs of Jamaica* and *Constab Ballads,* on these earlier newspaper entries.[43]

The popular and the highbrow were hardly distinguishable during this period. The exclusionary "white" Jamaican author H. G. de Lisser,[44] famous for his editorship of the *Gleaner* and the snob magazine *Planter's Punch* of the 1920s, as well as for his gothic potboiler romances and adventure stories such as the *White Witch of Rose Hall* (still a best seller in Jamaica today), nominated the black dialect poet Claude McKay for the Musgrave Medal in 1912. McKay asserted that he was often invited by the literary clubs, usually devoted to English authors, to give a reading.[45] These examples suggest a creative flowering that crossed ethnic, class, and high/low culture boundaries. McKay wrote popular poetry; de Lisser's popular novel *Jane's Career* (1913) is an important work that had as its heroine a black, working-class Jamaican maid and was, as even his critics acknowledge, an early precursor to the proletarian, anticolonial, barracks-yard novel.[46] In the first decade of the twentieth century, "white" Jamaican Thomas MacDermot created the short-lived but influential All Jamaica Library publishing house, dedicated to the "literary embodiment of Jamaican subjects" "at a price so small as to make each publication generally purchasable" and specifically "written by Jamaicans."[47] His sensationally titled novel *Becka's Buckra Baby* (1904), published by All Jamaica Library, was an earnest morality tale about the harm caused by racial self-hatred. In the novel, Becka is a black girl who is given a white ("buckra") doll by her English teacher. The doll comes to symbolize all of the virtues and high ideals associated with whiteness to which Becka is encouraged to aspire. Accordingly she becomes devoted to the doll. Her devotion is compared to her aunt's pride in *her* illegitimate "buckra" baby, the offspring of an affair with a white man; despite the stigma of illegitimacy, the aunt sees the child as giving her prestige. Becka's devotion ends with her tragic death. The high sentimental mode of the writing no doubt contributed to its best-seller status: *Becka's Buckra Baby* quickly sold out, and a second edition of a thousand copies also nearly sold out.[48]

American Influences

The whiff of illicit sex no doubt contributed to the fascination with MacDermot's sober story, and most likely he understood this. The murder mystery, the romance, and the adventure story—often a combination of two or more of these—is an inevitable staple of the newspaper fiction of this period, and many of the Jamaican newspaper stories feature a combination of Christian piety and lurid sex-murder-and-intrigue. The influence of American popular writers should not be underestimated here.

American influence on early Caribbean popular culture can be traced as far back as the late eighteenth century, when America's patriotic Continental Congress banished comedies from American stages, deeming them a "fatal" distraction from the serious purposes of the Revolutionary War. The result was that the American Company of Comedians came to Jamaica for two sojourns, the last during the 1774–84 revolutionary period, creating an "unprecedented" level of activity on the Jamaican theater scene.[49] Racist American popular culture also left its mark on the mid-nineteenth-century Jamaican comic plays that featured American-style burnt-cork blackface minstrelsy adopted by native black Jamaican comedians.[50] American influences on colonial Jamaican popular culture from the mid-eighteenth century onward are thus consistent with a historical equation of American culture with comedy and pleasure culture, not—ironically, given America's anti-British origins—with the overtly political or the serious.

In the Anglophone Caribbean, American dime-store novels were as popular as they were denigrated: serious writing was European; fun reading was American. In *A House for Mr. Biswas,* V. S. Naipaul's classic story of the second-rate writer/journalist Mohun Biswas, we are treated to a catalogue of Biswas's leisure reading, which has a thoroughly American flavor. Many of the stories serialized in Jamaica, and perhaps even more so in other countries that featured less local talent, were taken from American newspaper services.[51] One such story, "Libertas C, or Died for Cuba," about the Cuban war of independence by "one of the rising young novelists of New England," was prefaced by this revealing editorial note: "'Libertas C' is a thrilling story, but devoid of all the features which make the dime novel objectionable. It is pure in tone and instills lessons of patriotism calculated to benefit young readers."[52] Clearly, the editorial board felt the need to defend its selection of the "dime novel" by playing up its moral benefits, such as instilling patriotism—albeit an abstract patriotism that could not be confused with the more pertinent forms of anti-British nationalism that would soon emerge in Jamaican public discourse. Such a space-clearing gesture also suggests that the readers themselves need to be reassured that they are not merely engaging in purely entertaining fare, lacking in "brain stuff." In addition to thrills, the popular literary culture of the time also required instruction. The "thrills plus instruction" model is a consistent feature among the widest range of literature produced at this time.

The focus on racial ambiguity and illicit sexuality in many of these stories further underscores the issue central to the emergent middle class in the consolidation of its own respectable antecedents, that of the question of racial origin. The status of the African American community, so similar to and yet so different from that of the black and brown Caribbean communities, provoked a range of ambivalent responses in the Caribbean. On the one hand, the parallel existence of a relatively large African American middle-class community, its members subject to vicious Jim Crow laws, clearly drew the interest of Caribbean black and brown readers, themselves struggling to define their shifting status in the still antiblack, colonial Caribbean. The *Jamaica Times* carried regular stories about African American life in its pages, and in 1898 it published an item from the *New York Evening Post* about an "Afro-American Conference," held in Rochester, that raised the alarm against the prohibition of intermarriage of the races, and the concomitant promotion of "immorality" in black-white relations. The prominence given to this excerpt suggests that nonwhite Jamaicans were concerned about the respectability of a black and brown identity beyond the Caribbean. Like their Caribbean counterparts, middle-class African Americans had their own debating societies, produced their own newspapers, and wrote novels about black life during this period. Much of this writing focused on questions of class, social obligation or "uplift," and the intraracial color line.[53] Brownness, whether racial or cultural, was emblematic of the newly emergent middle class of the Caribbean (and to some extent, of the African American community), and the acceptance of its legitimacy, both locally and internationally, was perceived as an important development. Therefore stories of the educated African American class, and its triumphs, found an audience in the pages of black-and-brown-oriented Caribbean newspapers. Booker T. Washington's rags-to-riches memoir *Up from Slavery* was a familiar text in many Caribbean societies, including the world of a young V. S. Naipaul.[54]

In this sense African American ideas and struggles were taken seriously by the emergent black and brown Caribbean middle class.

On the other hand, an 1899 letter to the editor of the *Gleaner,* titled "A Negro's Christmas Message to His Race in Jamaica," illustrates this concern with American views from a decidedly hostile point of view. After emancipation there was serious discussion among white elites in Jamaica to import African Americans to the island. Jamaican governors supported this initiative, one going so far as to describe African Americans as "of industrious habits, and superior as a class to the present country of the West Indian islands" by whose example "the existing population would be improved and stimulated."[55] As if in response to such proposals, the letter writer urges his fellow black Jamaicans to oppose an immigration "scheme" that, "if attained," would bring "the scum of America...to this spot." The "scum," apparently African Americans, would "intermingle with our people and make them worse than they are":

> I ask you to remember that our condition is far in advance of the American Negro. We have the rights of citizenship, we have the rights of the franchise. Already a member of our race has found a seat in the Legislative Council Chamber. We have the advantages of a modern education in the same school as the white man's children....*We see the intermarriage of the black and white, and they have shown themselves to be good husbands.* There is not one single instance in which it can be proven that a black who has taken a white woman to be his companion has not only treated her with the same love and respect as any white man would. Indeed, the ladies of Jamaica feel perfectly safe in our presence....We love our white friends, and time will come, when by the rapid growth of education, we shall make them like us.[56]

Intermarriage between black Caribbean men and white Caribbean women is viewed here as one more sign of the progress being made by black people on the island, in contrast to the lack of "progress" among African Americans, who could not marry whites and suffered from segregation and disenfranchisement. Education is viewed as the black population's primary leveraging tool. The fact that the letter received such a prominent place in the elite *Gleaner* suggests that its sentiments were likely to have found a grudgingly positive response in the heavily white and elite readership as well, even if they did not return the "love" shown by the black populace toward them, according to the author's depiction of black-white relations. At the very least, the writer suggests that brownness, as the racial designation of the new middle class, was either an acceptable category or understood to be an inevitable one, and thus may have been preferable to a black cultural identity by many in both the black and white populations.

Creolizing Asianness and Brownness

The Jamaican newspaper novels during this period stand out for what they reveal about class and color in late nineteenth-century, middle-class Jamaica. In particular they reveal a fascination with the contact points between social and ethnic classes, and much of the action in these stories revolves around blacks and browns, and occasionally Asians, in love affairs with whites. Many of the stories also involve foreign countries that Jamaicans would have reason to be curious about—Haiti, for example, with its bloody history of black and brown revolt, and China, given the influx of Chinese onto the island. The stories mix descriptive elements about the societies with a common formula of adventure and romance. One of these stories, "The Mandarin's Daughter: A Romance of Chinese Life," is one of the earliest examples I found of Asian-authored fiction in the Caribbean. The editorial preface notes that the author, Wong Chin Foo, "is an educated Chinaman and has already won for himself a name as a bright and entertaining writer.... It is both entertaining and instructive, and will give you a keener insight into the character of a people about whom so little is known than can be obtained by reading volumes of history."[57] The story has the distinct themes of the modern English historical romance: a young Chinese woman, who has taken "a collegiate course" and has "better command of math, sciences and classics than most young men," decides to run away from home after her parents try to marry her off. Seeking knowledge, she dresses as a man and goes to the wharf, where she is kidnapped by sailors who have stolen treasure. The handsome captain of the stolen treasure ship is taken with the "young boy." Although the story teaches little about the Chinese "character," it suggests that for educated Asians of the Caribbean, stories of this kind, featuring liberated young women who would have been the antithesis of how Asian women were regarded by Caribbean people, may have been a way of "creolizing," or becoming a respectable member of Caribbean society.

More common, however, were the interclass, interracial love affairs such as that depicted in "Carvalho," published in the *Jamaica Times* in 1899. This romance featured a rivalry between a white man and a white-looking brown man for the affections of a white creole woman. The white man, jealous of his brown rival, reveals the brown man's parentage, to the horror of the young woman, who admits, "I was West Indian enough in my feelings to have a certain innate horror of colored blood." The woman's mother inveighs against the brown man's parents; his mother kept a school for brown girls and had the gall to marry a Jew in the church: "Just like those brown people. Their grandmothers never married." The heroine considers: "Poor mamma always made it a subject of reproach against respectable brown folk that they tried to live more decently and properly than their ancestors used to do in slavery times." The young woman marries the brown man after all, and "when I took [his mother's] hand in mine ... and kissed her, and called her mother for the first time, I felt that I had left the guilt and shame of slavery for ever behind me, and that I would strive ever after to live worthily of [his] love."[58]

Although "Carvalho" has a white female narrator, the triumph of brown male respectability, and in particular the elevation of the brown man to the status of romantic hero, suggests that the author is most likely himself brown. The strategy of using a white creole woman to legitimize brown people by her marriage to one is telling: the narrative seeks to persuade the planter class to see that it is guilty of the "shame of slavery"—indicting a class of people for the marital status of their grandmothers, a guilt that can only be erased by social acceptance of the new brown class.

The newspaper competitions seem to have spawned their own coterie of popular writers, some of whom went on to republish their stories as books. One such prizewinner was a relatively prolific local man, Alexander MacGregor James, who authored a series of prizewinning stories, including "Soul's Sacrifice" and "The Mysterious Murder," a story involving "planter-princes" and a "coloured detective" hero.[59] He later reprinted "Soul's Sacrifice" in *Four Stories and a Drama of Old Jamaica,* as well as a novel titled *The Cacique's Treasure.* In his introduction to the anthology, he grumbles that he is forced to be his own publisher and bookseller, and he scolds the government for only rewarding education and not "literary or artistic attainment." Apparently this statement is intended to explain the advertising that covers the book's back and inside covers: innumerable advertisements for sugar, cigarettes, malted milk, a steamship to Cuba, and the like, giving us some clue as to the means of his audience. Advertisers were, then as now, a notoriously conservative group that represented the commercial interests of the country. The racial sentiments of the stories must not have conflicted with those of merchant interests to get such clear financial backing, and yet at least one tale features a brown hero. The alignment of commerce with popular genres of literature such as the detective story, as well as the fact that many of these stories feature a "brown" subjectivity, altogether suggest an emerging, popular literary culture for a brown middle class weaned on American popular culture, and a class that wished to see itself as the subject of its own leisure reading.

The Age of Women: The Growth of Magazine Culture

In most studies of the growth of West Indian literature, the period between the two world wars is left severely alone. This interwar period is usually noted only for the formation of the Beacon group in Trinidad, the only serious, nationalist-minded literary forum of the time. The explosion of Caribbean fiction that characterizes the post–World War II period is largely due to the local creative magazines like Barbados's *Bim* (1942), edited by the legendary Barbadian poet Frank Collymore, Guyana's *Kyk-Over-Al,* also run by a poet, and Jamaica's *Focus.* Further, the editors, especially Collymore, had regular contact with Henry Swanzy of the BBC, who created the now-classic radio program *Caribbean Voices,* which helped to launch Derek Walcott, V. S. Naipaul, and other canonical Caribbean writers. These magazines were consciously engaged in creating a literary tradition of the Caribbean that reflected the "real" society, the peasantry, the urban poor, the Creole speakers. The period before World War II is not notable for its literary output, and critics tend to point to only a few meritorious volumes, which anticipate the folk themes that characterize most published Caribbean writing at midcentury.

These magazines are not my focus here, however. Rather, I look at more broadly conceived leisure magazines of the 1920s, such as Jamaica's *Cosmopolitan* and *Planter's Punch*. Although both supposedly catered to different audiences—the *Cosmopolitan* to mostly middle-class and aspiring-middle-class, employed, brown and black women, and *Planter's Punch* to the white upper and upper-middle classes—nevertheless together they paint a portrait of a variegated middle class of the early twentieth century, rife with color and strata distinctions, and with a thriving entertainment culture. The *Cosmopolitan* was the official publication of the Jamaican Stenographers' Association and billed itself as intended for the "business youth," which was another way of saying that it was an entertainment magazine for the upwardly mobile, young working woman, usually brown or black. One of its editors was Una Marson, the black, nationalist-minded Jamaican playwright and poet who later became well known for her work with *Caribbean Voices* in London, but who in the 1920s was herself a stenographer. *Planter's Punch,* run by H. G. de Lisser, also seemed geared to women, but white "society" types, and its tone, like its title, suggested that it was purely "fun." The editor never used the word "editor"; rather, the caption under the *Planter's Punch* masthead reads, "mixed by H. G. de Lisser." Unlike the *Cosmopolitan, Planter's Punch* invited a readership of those who had "already arrived," a creole aristocracy. But this audience is mostly fictional. The planter in the title connected the readers to the plantocracy of an earlier century, a group more or less vanished from the Jamaica of the 1920s. The white Jamaican elite of the early twentieth century were mostly from the mercantile class, heavily Jewish,[60] and, like the brown and black middle class, also aspiring to cultural dominance. Taken together, these two magazines reveal a middle-class culture torn between competing poles of modernity. On the one hand, modernity was writ as the resuscitation of a vanished, English-identified planter class; on the other, it had an emerging nationalist, race-conscious, American-identified sensibility.

The post–World War I period saw a surge of leisure products on the island. This growth reflects the consolidation of the black and brown middle class, whose members, with more leisure time, were forming innumerable social clubs and organizations, and many of these focused on women. Whereas white women had typically controlled charitable and social welfare organizations, middle-class black and brown women now became major players, to the point where, according to Una Marson, white women complained that they were being usurped in their "special privilege of doing charitable work for coloured people."[61] Veronica Gregg has provocatively suggested that H. G. de Lisser was actually instrumental in securing the vote for white Jamaican women during this period in order to retain the cultural authority of the fading white elite in the face of rising black and brown power.[62]

Novelty Trading Company, which still operates a thriving business selling popular local, regional, and American fiction in Kingston today, began during this period. Its creator, a "mixed race black man" who worked as a superintendent of the railroad, in response to clamoring from his family and friends, began to procure American fashion, family, and news magazines such as *Family Circle* and *Radio News,* and later, popular American novels from Random House.[63] In this newly expanding cultural universe, *Planter's Punch* and the *Cosmopolitan* began their quests to create a cultural space for what they saw, respectively, as the cultural center of the country: the former to preserve—or more accurately, to create—the cultural dominance of the elite, the latter to assert the cultural presence of the middle class. Both magazines combined the same mix of news commentary, social photographs, and short fiction, often romances. Both were also geared for a female readership. *Planter's Punch* featured a photo of a society lady once a month and was intent on showcasing the charms of white Jamaican women. But its anxiety over their representation illustrates the facade of its own upper-crust conceit. The inaugural issue of the magazine carried an article titled "The Fair Daughters of Jamaica: Characteristics." The editor describes the magazine's mission as, in part, to right the wrong that has been done to Jamaica's elite white women:

> The people of Jamaica have often been represented as peasants merely, the woman shown pictorially have mostly been women of the working classes. Sturdy dames trudging it down to a market town...giggling servant girls saying eternally that "the heatment is great"—these have been shown again and again, and the outsider who has never been to

Jamaica may well be excused for believing that the country has no other women to show, can boast of no daughters to compare with those of Northern countries. The pictorial representation of Jamaican life in the past has been largely in the direction of the burlesque. The other side of the picture has hardly ever been seen.[64]

Although de Lisser concedes that "in former days the Jamaican girl spoke with a decided drawl, her accent was broad, flat, unpleasant," he then emphasizes that "amongst the better educated classes it is not so today." The rest of the article goes on to delineate the characteristics that make the "best people," who, the reader is informed, are not necessarily the richest; they could be the daughters of rich men, or men "with incomes computed by 100s," "but by their manners and appearance you shall know them."

This strategy, of emphasizing "manners" over any material differences, seems geared to allay the middle-class anxiety of the magazine's readership, a strategy underscoring the possibility that the actual readership for *Planter's Punch* was not necessarily the stated readership that its language implies. Further, Rhonda Cobham observes that the release of *Planter's Punch* always coincided with Christmas, "when the average middle-class Jamaican who probably read little apart from the newspapers, could be more easily persuaded to fritter away one shilling on a magazine." Despite its high-class pretensions, the magazine offered a wealth of articles about all aspects of Jamaican life and culture. Cobham states that "there were historical articles on famous buildings, documentaries on small local groups such as the Chinese business community, and intriguing vignettes on such subjects as Jamaican dancing girls over the years and the history of Jamaican theatre. In this way *Planter's Punch* gained a readership among the new middle class for which the *Jamaica Times* had formerly catered, and for whom the dazzling portraits of society belles added a touch of fantasy to a lively and diverse source of information."[65] As such, *Planter's Punch* was really a middle-class venue. The magazine's serialized fiction was mostly de Lisser's, which he later went on to publish in book form. A few other pieces that were published reflect de Lisser's vision of what entertaining fare for a Jamaican upper-class woman should look like: several adventure stories of revolutionary Haiti, one in particular in which a French creole virgin, bartered to a colored man ("vile" although "educated"), becomes "a helpless pawn in the intrigue of the black empire"; sentimental stories of the Jamaican "nobility"; and some notable sidebars involving criticism of Marcus Garvey and his lack of democratic principles.[66] Despite its reactionary politics and elitist aims, *Planter's Punch* managed to pull in a brown and black middle-class readership whose political views were antithetical to its own, a feat of popular culture engineering that would not be rivaled by a Caribbean literary magazine until the politically radical Trinidad *Beacon* became popular with a great swath of Trinidadians, across ideological lines, in the 1930s.[67]

The *Cosmopolitan* was far more contradictory in its social views than was the solidly colonialist *Punch*.[68] Jamaica had been grappling with the issue of "respectable" women in the workplace from the late nineteenth century, and two decades into the twentieth century these women were at the vanguard of a new cultural class: working, mostly (but not always) middle class, often single, socially ambitious, and willing to spend money on leisure entertainments.[69] The cover of the 1928 inaugural issue shows the members of the Stenographers' Association, the majority of them brown women, with a few whites and a few men. The name suggested the magazine's desire to see itself, and its readership, as representative of a new, modern, urban aesthetic. While *Planter's Punch* was establishing the cultural credentials of the white and near-white Jamaican elite, the *Cosmopolitan* was extending a much broader reach to capture not simply those readers who were middle class but also those who aspired to middle-class status. Its editorials raised serious issues facing working women, in addition to the "light" fare. As might be expected, the articles reflect a lot of social patrolling to create this new urban class. Articles on the "health and efficiency of stenographers" ("ten minutes of exercise at 7 a.m., brisk walk...in bed by 10 p.m."), how to dress for business success, and "The Importance of the Comma" vie for space with "Hints for Housekeepers," "Kiddie's Corner," and "The Hygiene of the Child." The readers, young, brown and black, working women, were in some sense representative of the society itself, poised between colonial submission and personal autonomy, English cultural heritage and American cultural influence, and a growing sense of Caribbean identity that synthesized all of these traits. As the middle class grew, so too did the number of young, brown and black women trained to be typists, nurses, teachers, and nurses. These women needed jobs to fit their new educational attainments, as well as cultural pursuits that reflected their newfound social status. As one contributor put it:

> Thirty or more years ago the business woman was almost an unknown factor in the Commercial life of Kingston. There were, of course, thrifty hard working women who eked out a precarious living by making and selling luncheon delicacies...bright faced negro girls clad in clean print frocks, wearing bright coloured bandana kerchiefs which were then the popular head dress of their class...the young women of Kingston have advanced far in that time which to us, who can look

back, appears so very short. Still, though the young women of Kingston have discovered and exploited many outlets for their activities still more must be found.⁷⁰

The *Cosmopolitan,* and later entertainment magazines for the black and brown middle class such as *Spotlight* in the 1940s and 1950s, consciously set out to provide just such an outlet by creating a reading community where social information was traded, and class mores instilled and codified. The magazine had a special sympathy for single women and championed causes that were important to this constituency: it had remarkably progressive views on birth control (although not on what it termed "companionate," or common-law, marriages), and advocated for an unemployment bureau, a minimum wage, and sick days. One editorial lambasted men who "set themselves up as judges of our dresses" and manners, and another decried the lack of sports facilities for women.⁷¹ Time and again, the magazine's writers compare the condition of women in Jamaica to that of women in the United States, always with the view that Jamaican working women should aspire to the independent status of American women.

Its social politics veered between the almost radical and the moderate, and its paradoxical views on culture challenge academic charges of middle-class cultural philistinism or insularity. One of the more intriguing articles on literature is titled "Sappho—The Lesbian Poetess,"⁷² in which the Greek poet is lauded as the president of the first woman's literary club, "a kind of sacred sorority" in which "the members were bound to each other by sacred ties and regulations." The article suggests that Sappho's "club" be the model for a kind of Caribbean literary sorority. The Caribbean interest in American race issues is continually underscored with a constant flow of articles on Jim Crow and commentary on racist slights to respectable African American figures such as the editor of the *Chicago Defender.* A review of a visiting African American theatrical troupe at the Ward Theatre in Kingston reminds us again of the pervasiveness of African American culture and views in Jamaica. The reviewer extols "The Coloured Follies" and compares the negative reviews it received in the *Gleaner* with the enthusiastic reception accorded a similar white musical review in the same newspaper:

> We cannot help but wonder if there is not some deep-rooted psychological reason for their objections. Is there a more disastrous effect on sex morality in looking at brown nudity than at white?... If our Councillors are concerned merely with nudity or semi-nudity why differentiate between [either show]?... Why let the extraordinary displays of fair bodies go unchallenged—indeed they were greatly applauded—and

ostracize that of bronze ones? We do not pretend quite to understand the objections.[73]

The magazine also followed the case of seditious libel against Marcus Garvey, who was sentenced to six months' imprisonment for remarks made as editor in chief of the *Blackman*. The editors of the *Cosmopolitan* weighed in with this ambiguous remark: "The responsibility of an Editor-in-Chief... cannot be admitted to be negligible. The influence of the press on the public mind is great and any attempt to abuse in any way its liberty cannot be overlooked. So often is not what is said that makes trouble, it is how a thing is said and wisdom, restraint and discretion, with a due regard and deference to others in our expressions is always the wisest policy."[74] In other words, what Garvey was guilty of, in the view of the magazine, was not what he said regarding race in Jamaica, but how he said it. This middle ground, poised between what we might now call racially progressive politics and conservative public discourse, characterizes much of the early middle-class, black-identified magazines such as the *Cosmopolitan,* and later, *Spotlight*.

What distinguishes the *Cosmopolitan* from other extant magazines, however, was its vision to create a popular literary culture that would reflect this new, aspiring female class. Like the old *Jamaica Times,* the *Cosmopolitan* also aimed to "develop literary and other artistic talents" in combination with a "regard for financial results," and modeled itself on what it saw as the American "thirst for knowledge." Hailing the decade as "the age of women," the editors particularly sought to develop and promote women writers and artists, and featured a prominent woman artist every month.[75] Local literature was published in every issue, and in 1929, like the *Times* and the *Gleaner* before it, the magazine sponsored a short story contest. As Leah Rosenberg points out, however, the editor's directions to contestants "lacked all the traits we have come to associate with Caribbean nationalism: the use of Creole language, the focus on the Afro-Caribbean peasantry or working class, and attention to the land. In fact, the stories were not required to represent Jamaicans or Jamaica." In stark contrast to the *Gleaner*'s Anancy story competition of 1899, dialect stories were also rejected, unless "exceptionally good." Editor Una Marson asked contestants to conform to American spelling conventions because she planned to sell the winning story to American magazines and give the writers a percentage of the fee. As Rosenberg asks, "How could stories tailored for a U.S. market constitute the foundation of Jamaica's national literature?"[76]

For the early twentieth-century Caribbean, the United States, then as now, represented modernity. And Jamaicans wanted to be modern. In particular, African Americans represented, especially for Afro-Caribbean people, a way to be black in modernity. W. E. B. DuBois's famed anguish over African American "double consciousness" ("An American, A Negro; two strivings in one dark body whose dogged strength alone keeps it from being split asunder") played out quite differently in the Caribbean. If, on the one hand, African Americans were the victims of a relentless racism, on the other they had their own colleges and universities, and even more to the point, their own celebrated culture: jazz music was the apex of modern music for the Western world, and black jazz musicians were especially feted by Europeans. From the late nineteenth century onward, Caribbean people closely followed the doings of African Americans, particularly those in Harlem, where so many West Indians had emigrated during the great migration of the early twentieth century.[77]

More generally, even during the heyday of the British empire at the end of the nineteenth century, American popular magazines were to be found in every English-speaking Caribbean country. American popular stories were serialized regularly in all of the Caribbean papers, even in that most Anglophilic of Caribbean countries, Barbados. The marked American cultural presence has gone virtually unremarked by critics and scholars. British literature was taught; American literature was consumed.[78] Edification versus consumption; modernity is intimately tied not simply to what we learn but to what we imbibe—what we eat, what we watch, how we play. Consumption does not reflect what we think we should be but what we desire to be, which is not always the same thing. Jamaicans of the 1920s understood that they were supposed to be made in the image of Britain; that image, however, did not reflect the quotidian desires of the middle class, surrounded as it was by American films, American music, American popular literature. By that measure, the relationship of the early twentieth-century Caribbean to American popular culture, and Caribbean understandings of what constitutes the modern, are inescapably tied to American identity.

The work of Una Marson encapsulates the dialectic between British and American literary influences in the early twentieth-century Caribbean. Marson's plays and poems sought a different audience than the one she pursued for the *Cosmopolitan*. The theme of her plays and poems was a critique of the colonial relationship, and as such they are seen as part of the birth of national literature in the Caribbean. Even if serious writers like Marson only engaged the colonial relationship to Britain when they were writing "serious" work, those same writers could also be part of another kind of literary culture, one tied to profit, entertainment, ephemerality, newness, individualism—in a word, to Americanness. As Rosenberg points out, the stories published in the *Cosmopolitan* were inevitably romances in which were combined black or brown ethnic pride, social ambition, and a relentless purveying of Jamaica as a modern nation.[79] The editorials served to underscore the magazine's literary emphasis on American-style modernity. The literature column of the magazine often advocated American books or the American view of books. ("When a novel fails to excite discussion the Americans apply to it one of their telling phrases, 'It lacks the forward look.'") Declaring the city's modernity yet chafing at its lack, the magazine's editorials charged Kingston with a host of ills, all in one way or another related to not being "modern" enough. In one editorial, the ubiquity of goats is decried as primitive: "Is there any other city with our claims and aspirations to Western civilization which would unmoved see its thoroughfares turned into runs for goats?... Visitors think that better is hardly to be expected from a people whose ancestry is at least partially from the Dark Continent."[80] Despite the fact that Kingston had plenty of theaters, concerts, and film houses, another writer was mortified that Americans had remarked that Kingston had no night life, and opined that

> this is a disgrace to Kingston at this stage of her civilization.... When we speak of night life, we specially think of the middle class people who have no motor cars to go out for a drive, no radios to listen in, and who cannot always afford to go to a picture show.... Then again, our youth are fond of dancing. Why not have a large airy dance hall, with good music in attendance... and run it in such a way that respectable people could pass an evening there without any embarrassment.[81]

Yet in the *Cosmopolitan*'s literary renderings of Kingston, there are motorcars and radios aplenty, and the black and brown characters are self-assured, educated, and "modern." In other words, modernity does not necessarily look like Kingston's actual modernity but like an American ideal. "Sojourn," Marson's own contribution to the magazine, is typical of the *Cosmopolitan* stories.[82] The romantic hero, an Englishman named Sydney, comes to Jamaica expecting to find tropical squalor and improbably finds "no insects of any description." The inhabitants are smartly dressed, and he is glad he decided to bring his tweed suit. Kingston is the real focus of the story, in many ways: through the validating persona of the Englishman, the city itself is "romanced." Sydney discovers that the city is clean, the people are multiracial (not all black, as he feared), and there are plenty of "large buildings, motor-cars, [and] buses," suggesting a "prosperous business centre." In phrases strikingly reminiscent of 1980s tourism ads, Sydney discovers that Jamaica is "not a beach but a country," and its countryside is described to him in terms lifted from tourist guidebooks. The market women in bright bandanas, the bane of the *Planter's Punch* set, are relegated to "picturesque figures who illustrate that Jamaica is a modern country populated by middle-class citizens who have control over a hardworking peasantry and working class," in Rosenberg's apt phrasing.[83]

Sydney is astonished to find that the "coloured girls" are pretty and have fine figures. Eventually he falls for his black host's sister Helen, an elegant woman with "a complexion not unlike an East Indian's" and "abundant hair."[84] Although "Sojourn" is a romance, it is one that is tellingly devoid of erotic detail—Sydney asks permission before he kisses Helen, and when he does so it is "reverently and devoutly as though she were a goddess." In the end, the romance is never consummated: Sydney goes back to England and his English fiancée, although not before he considers that "the lure of the tropics was catching him in its spell."[85]

The heroine Helen reflects the tentativeness of the new black middle class, caught between Victorian deportment and modern black pride. The validation of Europe, read here as male, is the essence of the story. Although the modern ideal may be American, it is the British who must accept and approve this new black/brown modernity, and accordingly we see Jamaica, and Helen, only through Sydney's eyes. In the end, Sydney's respect—his "reverence"—is more important than his love. The story's emphasis on Kingston as "a prosperous business centre" rather than as aesthetically pleasing sets the stage for a paradox that is to be repeated throughout Caribbean popular fiction: the clash between competing representations of desire. On the one hand, the reader is presented with commerce, modernity, nationalism; on the other, the stereotypes of black/brown eroticism and the lush beauty of the region, fused to connote the primitive. How to manage the erotic in a nationalist romance is a problem that haunts not just these stories of the 1920s but the romances of both an earlier and a later age as well. In Helen's representation we find many of the problems of how to represent the modern black woman, one who is educated yet erotic, beautiful yet businesslike. The image of the black romantic heroine as more Indian in feature than African is one that is repeated throughout the history of Caribbean popular literature, from de Lisser's historical romance *Psyche*, to contemporary Trinidadian author Valerie Belgrave's historical romance *Ti Marie*. Even if the goal of the romance is to assimilate blackness into modernity by making it the object of white romantic desire, it seems that "pure" Africanity, in the form of distinctly West African physical features, is not quite assimilable. Apparently not even black female readers wish to see themselves portrayed as purely black. Hence the compromise of using a heroine with a "brown" physiognomy that stems from Asian, not white, blood. The accepted beauty of brownness is divorced from its class connotations and thus acceptable for a nationalist romance.

In fleshing out the contours of Jamaica's early literary culture, I have rewritten the view that the Caribbean's middle class had none. I hope I have also corrected the view that the lively literary magazines of the 1940s and 1950s, which spawned most of the Caribbean's seriously regarded writers, owed nothing to the middle-class societies from which their practitioners came. The development of a creole culture is generally recognized to be the driving force behind a truly Caribbean national literature. Creolization is the development of a society that is a blend of ethnicities and influences, but how those ethnicities and influences gel is still a debated issue in Caribbean studies. Cultural critic Rex Nettleford has described the process of creolization in the Caribbean as a battle for cultural space, a view to which I have long subscribed, and still do.[86] Orlando Patterson distinguishes between what he calls "segmentary creolization," or the development of parallel local cultures by each ethnic group, and "synthethic creolization," or the forging of a local culture from all available cultural resources.[87] My picture of Jamaica's—and to a lesser extent Trinidad's—early literary culture conveys that all of these processes may contend at the same time. For example, if Jamaica's white elite was reinventing itself in *Planter's Punch* in a kind of segmentary creolization, it was also participating in the construction of a synthetic creole society through the *Gleaner*'s stories and contests. The visions of Caribbean society to be garnered from these many sources of middle-class cultural production, black, brown, and white, altogether suggest that the struggle to establish a cultural space by all constituencies created the conditions for the nationalism that was to mark the literature of the society in the decades to come.

CHAPTER 2

Brownness, Social Desire, and the Early Novel

> Caribbean literature, whether it be, in its early stages, European literature on the Caribbean theme or, later, a Caribbean literature set on native grounds, has never been able to afford the posture of art for art's sake. In both of its manifestations, it has been the child of a philistine, brutalized society, literally struggling for survival.
>
> —Gordon Lewis, *Main Currents in Caribbean Thought,* 1983
>
> [The imperial period] can never form the basis for an indigenous culture.
>
> —Bill Ashcroft, Gareth Griffiths, and Helen Tiffin, *The Empire Writes Back: Theory and Practice in Post-Colonial Literatures,* 1989

In Trinidad, in the years 1853 and 1854, long before the famed Trinidad Awakening of the 1930s, two novels about brown people, both by brown authors, found their way into circulation. *Emmanuel Appadocca,* by the well-known Trinidadian lawyer, editor, and orator Michel Maxwell Philip, was a gothic adventure of Caribbean pirates on the high seas. Published in London in 1854, the novel went on to become a Trinidadian best seller of sorts: the royalties were enough to support Philip's expensive legal studies.[1] The other, *Adolphus,* was a romance penned by an anonymous author and serialized in 1853 in the "radical" newspaper the *Trinidadian* (radical for its pro-black-and-brown, antigovernment views). Critics speculate that the author was more likely than not George Numa Dessources, the brown proprietor and editor of the *Trinidadian,* who wrote many of the paper's features himself.[2] These two novels constitute the earliest literature by nonwhite Anglophone Caribbean authors. Ignored or belittled by contemporary critics for their "bad" writing and compromised views of black people, they reveal to us the society for which they were written: an emergent brown middle class whose members were familiar with the devices of the gothic adventure story and the American sentimental novel, and who were chafing at their lack of representation in politics and seeking their own reflection in the stories they chose to tell about themselves and their society.

What I seek to do here is tease out the social desires of an emergent class by looking at representations of "brownness" in a variety of early novels. The colored class has been the most ambiguous class in Caribbean social history. Black Caribbean people were always presumed to have a culture of sorts, even if it was viewed as debased and primitive by early European travel writers and white creoles, and even if it was reviled and rejected for exactly those reasons by the black middle class. Historically, however, brown people have always suggested a problem of cultural representation, a cultural "otherness": were these "colored" white people, or were they black people with a desirable color? "You brown man hab no country, only de neger and de buckra [white man] hab country," declare the Jamaican slaves of the 1828 novel *Marly*,[3] a sentiment that neatly summarizes the view of the mulatto as a nationless—and therefore ethnicity-less—aberration. But brown people early on declared themselves to be native Caribbean citizens, if for no other reason than that, as one early spokesman put it, "we have nowhere [else] to go."[4] Later Caribbean authors, most notably Derek Walcott, used mulatto identity as a metaphor for a creolized aesthetic, an originary view of brownness that celebrates European and African (and more recently, Asian) heritage as a cultural, not racial, ideal.[5] In other words, cultural brownness is what makes the Caribbean the Caribbean, an idea that has seized the popular imagination. This view of brown identity, however, has never produced any literature that was so seamlessly associated with its corresponding ethnic group: the brown class is associated in the minds of most scholars not with creolization but with the cultural decreolization of the Caribbean.[6] So thoroughly have members of this class been associated with cultural sterility and a profound indifference to art and creativity that as late as 1970, critic Kenneth Ramchand could declare with confidence that "the Coloureds did not read or write fiction in the eighteenth or nineteenth centuries."[7] The residue of that moment is still with us: Walcott's short-lived experiment notwithstanding, it is ideologically suspect to speak of a "brown aesthetic," in much the same way that it would be to speak of a white one, so completely aligned are whiteness and brownness with a neo-imperialist ideology. Thus could Michael Manley, the charismatic "white" (or brown) Jamaican prime minister, in the heady nationalist flush of the 1970s, align himself with Afro-Jamaican, Rastafarian culture, an association with no social consequences whatsoever but with huge political ones.[8]

Accordingly, in the literary world there are nationalist texts—and imperialist ones. There is an Afro-Caribbean aesthetic, an Indo-Caribbean aesthetic, a creolized or hybrid aesthetic, but no brown aesthetic.[9] Regardless, both popular and critical celebrations of a creolized cultural sensibility rest on the struggles of an earlier age to define the contours of a cultural brownness, a brownness that nevertheless was connected in some material way to actual, physiognomical brownness. In this analysis I contend that these early Caribbean novels aimed to provide just such a definition of a creolized society, and that their emphasis on popular genres bespoke their authors' desire to create a middle class that was naturalized. In other words, it was not so much an endlessly proliferating hybridity that was the goal—the celebrated "out of many, one people" model—but rather brownness as a homogenous, consistently reproducible type. Brownness as an ideological category is itself fluid: the authors of the following "brown" novels are, variously, a black Pan-Africanist, a "white" imperialist, and brown Anglophile nationalists. Despite these apparent ideological contradictions, brownness figured as a physical representation of a cultural norm for all of these constituencies. I interpret brown desires for political power by investigating novels about brown people by brown people, as well as interpret black desires for social mobility through the vehicle of intermarriage: what I call a kind of social "browning" of black people. I therefore look at *Emmanuel Appadocca* and *Adolphus* alongside three later texts: *One Brown Girl And*—(1909) by brown (or "white") Jamaican Thomas MacDermot, *Rupert Gray* (1907) by black Trinidadian Stephen Cobham, and *Jane's Career* (1913) by "white" (or brown) Jamaican H. G. de Lisser.[10]

Recuperating the Philistines

In trying to reconstruct the West Indian literary tradition, contemporary critics are divided as to where these novels belong. The more traditional view is to consign them to the ideological dustbin. From this perspective, these stories constitute the irrelevant flotsam and jetsam of the culturally "philistine" middle class: they are efforts to copy British literature, and poor efforts at that. In this vein, the respected Trinidadian historian Bridget Brereton wrote of *Emmanuel Appadocca* that "the novel is an extremely bad one, the plot absurd, the characters incredible, the prose turgid; the whole production is a fourth-rate 'Gothick' romance by a very young man with high-flown literary pretensions.... The novel has no real literary merit."[11] More recently, Trinidadian scholar Selwyn Cudjoe, who has done much to resuscitate interest in the Trinidadian books by reprinting them, justifies so doing by declaring that *Emmanuel Appadocca* and *Rupert Gray* constitute the earliest articulations of literary Pan-Africanism and African diasporic sensibility, to be read alongside such early black nationalists as Liberian Edward Blyden and

Trinidadian Pan-Africanist Sylvester Williams. Emphasizing the nationalist credentials of their authors, these books collectively demonstrate for Cudjoe "that Afro-Trinbagonians were part of a larger diasporic discourse about race and identity"; the novels therefore are the "foundational" texts of Caribbean national literature.[12]

To drive home the African connection, Cudjoe, in his Calaloux Publications edition of *Rupert Gray,* features familiar images of African women wearing elaborate head wraps and posing as workers, mothers, and elegant ladies.[13] The viewers are cued to read these African women as Afro-Caribbean women, and the arc of women—from worker to mother to prosperous lady—implies both a kind of three-tiered progression of the female state and an embodiment of all three within the modern Afro-Caribbean woman. This image implies that the book we are about to read is a story that reflects the heritage of these Afro-Caribbean women. It is they who are the inheritors of its nationalist trajectory, and it is for them that this black nationalist romance is conceived and written. Given that *Rupert Gray* is about a black accountant who falls in love with a white creole heiress, this reading is a fairly tall order. Cudjoe's recuperative strategy seems thus poised between two tantalizing gender discourses: one a masculinist, Pan-Africanist discourse and the other a nationalist discourse that equates modernity with the social progress of black women. After all, who do we expect wants to read a romance that involves a black male hero but black women? Then as now?

The introduction to *Emmanuel Appadocca* by American scholar William E. Cain similarly situates that novel in another dimension of African diaspora discourse, that of the American antislavery discourses of *Uncle Tom's Cabin* and the abolitionist movement. Making no mention of the text's racial specificity—*Emmanuel Appadocca* is interested in the rights of brown, and only brown, people—Cain, in his analysis, performs the same function as Cudjoe does in his contextualizing afterword for *Emmanuel Appadocca* and introduction to *Rupert Gray*. By redirecting our attention from the novels' narrative "badness" to their animating critiques of race and inequality, these interpretations are meant to mask the residue of these novels' unmistakable racism, classism, and genre-driven sensibilities, the clichés of the pirate adventure, and the sentimental romance of the star-crossed lovers. In this new vision, we must read both *Emmanuel Appadocca* and *Rupert Gray* as only about colonialism and racism.

Precursors to Cudjoe and his strategy to recuperate these early novels were Kenneth Ramchand and Mervyn Morris in their attempts to recover *Jane's Career*. That novel, unlike *Emmanuel Appadocca* and *Rupert Gray,* even de Lisser's critics admit is an engaging and well-written work. Nevertheless, *Jane's*

Career has been sidelined from the nationalist oeuvre because of the well-known racist and colonialist views of its author and has fallen into neglect.[14] Ironically, it is de Lisser's distinctly racist gothic murder-mystery romance, *The White Witch of Rose Hall* (1929), that is Jamaica's all-time best seller, outselling contemporary American popular novels even today.[15] De Lisser's current status is that of a popular author still serialized from time to time in his old newspaper, the *Gleaner*, but he is not a canonical author catechized in the school curriculum like his contemporary Claude McKay is. McKay, however, is a black author with unimpeachable Pan-Africanist credentials; resting on the solid rock of McKay's love for black people, his novel can be recast into popular literature with no harm done to his canonical status. No such recuperation in the other direction is likely when the author is an unapologetic, sometimes racist, colonialist. The racial residue of *Jane's Career* is impervious to all cleansing efforts; it remains at the level of a curio—once popular, interesting in passing, but ultimately, not "good."

It was not always thus. As Ramchand and other critics have noted, for a short period during his years with the *Gleaner* (including 1913, the same year that *Jane's Career* was published), de Lisser was sympathetic to the aims of Fabian socialism and a critic of colonial rule. As de Lisser moved from proofreader to editor, his political views became more establishment and reactionary, culminating in his *Gleaner* editorial of 1938 opposing universal suffrage and self-government on the island: "From complete self-Government for Jamaica, Good Lord deliver us. Not even Full Representative Government can be considered at a time when...the tail is wagging the dog, and tub-thumping is practically the order of the day."[16] De Lisser died in 1944, a few months before the proclamation of universal suffrage in Jamaica. In death, his legacy was inescapably linked to the demise of the old planter class.

In 1971, however, almost a decade after Jamaica had achieved independence from British rule, black Jamaican prime minister Hugh Shearer attempted to resuscitate de Lisser's reputation by proclaiming *The White Witch of Rose Hall*, de Lisser's gothic best seller, "a treasure in our history."[17] The novel relates the apocryphal story of the white creole owner of Rose Hall, Annie Palmer, a bloodthirsty woman who, according to legend, practiced voodoo, had sex with her black slaves, and killed her white husbands. Critic Laura Lomas writes that Shearer's praise occurred as part of a speech given at the opening of the refurbished Rose Hall plantation, a tourist draw, which was simultaneously advertised as a "national historic trust" that belonged to all Jamaicans.[18] At a time when Jamaica needed to reinvent its own nationalist version of history and create its own pantheon of national heroes, the unlikely de Lisser was presented in the guise of a "successful" (profit-producing) author who was inscribing "Jamaican history." The prime minister's speech went on to encourage Jamaican artists to use national themes in their art: Jamaicans, he observed, "were reluctant to identify themselves with their legends, folklore and customs." By invoking the Annie Palmer legend as a piece of Jamaican "history," to be read alongside the story of the black and brown leaders of the Morant Bay rebellion of the 1860s, Shearer attempted to reinvent de Lisser as a "blackened" nationalist. The effort failed. But the fact that Shearer made the attempt at all is instructive for what it reveals about state interests in recuperating even the most intransigent of colonial authors in the postindependence phase of Jamaican history. Although ideologically de Lisser's opposite, Jamaican author Thomas Henry MacDermot ("Tom Redcam"), de Lisser's contemporary, created work that is significantly tied to that of de Lisser, Philip, and (in all probability) Dessources. Although MacDermot referred to himself as a white man, apparently he was "high brown."[19] MacDermot does indeed differ from the other authors investigated here in that his name is still recognizable in the public sphere as synonymous with early Caribbean nationalism, and he instituted the short-lived All Jamaica Library publishing house, out of which came *Becka's Buckra Baby* and *One Brown Girl And—*. Although MacDermot's name survives, however—principally through Kingston's Tom Redcam National Library—his novels have not. The only critical appraisal of the latter that I have found is Kenneth Ramchand's assessment in his groundbreaking book, *The West Indian Novel and Its Background* (1970), and even Ramchand terms this and other MacDermot works as "not of a high order" and "disappointing," especially given their "comic" and romantic emphasis.[20] MacDermot, however, was important for more than the nationalist literary effort; as Ramchand observes, MacDermot's push to publish books locally became the blueprint for de Lisser's far more successful effort with *Jane's Career* a few years later, and MacDermot saw more clearly than most the importance of having popular, not institutional, appeal. In the preface to *One Brown Girl And—*, he defends his decision to charge a shilling for the novel:

> I desire to get from this novel a reasonable return in money.... Now I would make it very clear that I ask no one, on the sentimental grounds of patronizing a local writer or supporting local literature to pay a shilling for what he or she does not want.... All the fine talk in the world, and all the nice expressions of enthusiasm and regard will avail little if the enthusiasts do not buy the local publication that they declare so well deserves support.[21]

Thus, unlike later nationalist efforts such as C. L. R. James's *Minty Alley* (1936), I categorize MacDermot's work with that of those writers I term the brown popular nationalists. His literature sold well, emphasized a local audience, and aimed to appeal to women in particular, especially brown ones. As such, MacDermot belongs on the list of early Caribbean authors who defined brownness as a uniquely Caribbean attribute.

Finally, we have Stephen Cobham, the Afro-Trinidadian schoolteacher and aspiring lawyer who wrote *Rupert Gray*. Cobham was indeed a Pan-Africanist, as Cudjoe emphasizes, having founded a local branch of the Pan-African Association in Port of Spain in the early 1900s. An opponent of Crown colony government, Cobham was a member of the growing community of black and brown intellectuals who were beginning the push for more autonomy that would eventually become the anticolonial struggle. He belonged to a literary circle in Port of Spain and wrote poetry, which was published in the local newspaper the *Mirror*, a reformist publication whose sister printery, the Mirror Printing Works, published *Rupert Gray*. The novel is filled with the distinctive features of the black intellectual class—for example, there is an approving mention of John Jacob Thomas's 1886 attack on English stereotypes of the Caribbean, *Froudacity*—and because of these and the author's solid Pan-Africanist credentials, contemporary scholars such as Cudjoe as well as Bridget Brereton, Rhonda Cobham, and Lise Winer (some of the commentators writing in the recent edition of the novel) read *Rupert Gray* as a form of protest literature. Addressing the incongruity of a Pan-Africanist protest novel that features a melodramatic love affair between a black man and a white woman, Brereton et al. persuasively argue that the model for the black hero is clearly the Trinidadian Pan-Africanist Sylvester Williams, whom Stephen Cobham knew and who was married to an Englishwoman despite her family's hostility. Further, they note that "throughout the region there were well-known cases of professional men of African descent whose marriages to white women, though at first the subject of scandal, eventually helped establish their social credentials," and they point to some of the most prominent political families in the region—the Manleys in Jamaica and the Adamses in Barbados, both founded by brown men who married white women.[22]

This reading of the black-white interracial romance as not simply a local concern but a regional one is critical to the way I conceptualize the notion of "brownness" here. Indeed, one of the early newspaper reviews of *Rupert Gray* declares that it lays bare "the greatest social problem in the West Indies" and as such is "a true pen picture of certain conditions to be found in every British West Indian colony."[23] Doubtless the reviewer was describing the problem of color prejudice, but his delicacy in treading the issue ("certain conditions") revolved around its problematic sexual aspect. The advertising for the novel first read "A New Local Novel. Read *Rupert Gray* The Lover of the Hour, by Stephen Cobham" but was subsequently changed to "The Book of the Hour," apparently to minimize the novel's sexual implications. The racism unmasked by the novel has nothing to do with the hero's blackness in and of itself—he is celebrated and promoted by his white employer and colleagues—but rather with their objections to his relationship with a white woman (his employer's daughter). If the marriage of a black Pan-Africanist to a white Englishwoman provides the template for the novel, then it is also the template for what may be seen as a desirable kind of Afro-Caribbean nationalism: one that "marries" black nationalism to white culture; one that, in effect, produces a sociopolitical "brownness." And literal brownness too: for who are the products of interracial marriages but brown people; and what are the results of the unions of black political figures with white women but the famous brown and "white" political families of the English-speaking Caribbean? What the protest novel argument for *Rupert Gray* misses is precisely its point: an argument for Caribbean identity that fuses the disparate creole identities and ideologies into one singular "browned" black body, one single "brown" belief.

Brown Nationalism and the Problem of Sex

In mid-nineteenth-century Trinidad, the brown population was already well established. As early as 1825, the free colored population outnumbered the whites and "constituted over one-third of the total population, making the island unique in the British Caribbean."[24] The brown population of the Caribbean has often been described as a buffer class, filling, "without truly bridging, the social gap between the upper and lower class," as if created for this purpose.[25] Mulattoes, however, were a thorn in the side of the ruling elite, particularly in places like Trinidad, where as property owners, and even slaveholders, their growing influence was feared more by authorities and local whites than were rebellious slaves.[26] The specter of brown power had been growing across the Pan-Caribbean since the eighteenth century, and different forms of containment were deployed to stave off the colored political threat. In 1733 the Jamaican legislature, under pressure to counteract the threat of a black majority, literally invented more white people overnight by giving full rights and privileges of whiteness to any colored person who was at least three generations removed from black ancestry (the so-called octoroons).[27] Going in the opposite direction, the French colonies attempted to stave off the growing brown population by instituting the infamous Code Noir, which stripped mulattos of rights and forbade white men to sleep with black and brown women, albeit to no effect. By the end of the eighteenth century, mulattos owned one-third of all slaves in Saint-Domingue,[28] and across the Caribbean mulattos continued to amass property and education. It was not uncommon for white men to leave property to their illegitimate mulatto children, and doubtless this financial and social security must have been an incentive for black and brown women who consented to sexual relationships with white men. Early accounts of brown women in particular remark on their independence, arrogance, and conspicuous consumption as shopkeepers, owners of boarding houses, and mistresses of white men.[29] An early novel, *Creoleana* (1842), by white Barbadian J. (or I.) W. Orderson, has as a subplot the story of real-life mulatto woman Rachael Pringle, who survives rape and hardship by becoming the mistress of successively wealthier white men until she arrives at semirespectable status as the legendary owner of the Royal Navy Hotel. Pringle hosts the British prince regent and his entourage at the hotel, then shakes him down for large amounts of cash after he trashes the place. Her story encapsulates the source of brown angst and white fear: brown peoples' disreputable origins and sexual history are also the source of their economic and social mobility.

Although he was apparently the child of an enslaved mother, the author of *Emmanuel Appadocca,* Michel Maxwell Philip, came from an old free colored family;[30] his cousin was Jean-Baptiste Philippe, the brown author of the famous 1824 treatise *Free Mulatto,* republished in 1882. (Ironically, Jean-Baptiste was himself a slaveholder.)[31] The grievances of *Free Mulatto* bear noting here, because they form the template for the plots of *Emmanuel Appadocca* and *Adolphus.* Complaining about the truncated rights of the brown population of Trinidad to the secretary of state for the colonies, the treatise goes into particular detail about the public humiliations of colored men and the sexual degradation of brown women at the mercy of white men. Inveighing against the common practice of white men seducing brown women, Philippe in *Free Mulatto,* argues for brown men's political rights by protesting their inability to protect their women:

> Suppose, then, a girl of colour to be flattered by the amatory professions of a white man; she listens to his vows, and returns his affection; overcome, at length, by the tenderness and frailty of her sex, she yields to the warmth of her lover's solicitations, leaves her home, and sacrifices every moral and social duty to her fondness. In such a case, what *legal* redress is there for a parent,—what satisfaction for a brother? Can he challenge the vile seducer, and wipe out the stain of dishonour *with his blood*? Alas! the *customs* of the country forbid it! In Europe, my Lord,

what epithet does the man deserve who tamely suffers his mother to be insulted,—his sister to be prostituted? is it to be supposed, that we alone are unconscious of such tender ties, or ignorant of the duties of sons and of brothers?... Custom, equal to law, unhappily protects the luxurious villain, who only dares offend because the hand which should avenge is manacled by the galling chain of despotism. Is it to be borne, I ask, that one particular set... should enjoy the privilege of triumphing with impunity over the honours of the mothers, wives, daughters, and sisters of another class; should enjoy the right of robbing an aged father of his only child, and bowing down his hoary hairs with sorrow to the grave? (186–88)

The plot of *Adolphus*—of a beautiful young brown woman and only child, who is kidnapped from her parents' home by a wealthy white creole with political connections—is a literal rendering of precisely the scenario that Philippe outlines in *Free Mulatto*.[32] The honor of brown women is clearly the pretext for establishing the legal rights of brown men, and to make the point stick Philippe must wrestle with the apparent willingness or even enthusiasm of otherwise respectable brown women to enter into illicit liaisons with white men, a theme to which Frantz Fanon, over one hundred years later, would return when delineating the contours of colonized psychology.[33] Philippe continues:

It has been said, too, by their traducers, that the coloured women, independently of affection, generally prefer living with white men, to marrying individuals of their own class. This, as applied generally, is the basest of libels. That many cases could be cited to warrant the accusation, I must own to my sorrow; but it has only occurred amongst the emancipated and illiterate, and has arisen more from poverty than inclination. Unfortunately, education had not formerly diffused any liberality of sentiment among them: few could scarcely read and write....I dare challenge the testimony of persons acquainted with [Trinidad's] rising generation of coloured females, to say, whether they are not... characterized for their religious principles, and the suavity of their manners? and whether there is not an equal share of virtuous pride diffused amongst them, as is possessed by any other class of women in the colony? (190–91)

For brown men to be full-fledged citizens of Trinidad, armed with full political rights as well as the force of "custom," much hinged on the perceived sexual status of brown women. How could men rise to positions of authority and influence who could not control the sexual lives of their women?

The historical images of mulatto women in the Americas as promiscuous and lascivious have been much remarked on elsewhere, and I do not belabor the point here.[34] The historical image is relevant, however, in that Philippe finds it necessary to discount, as "the basest of libels," brown women's apparent proclivities to be mistresses of white men rather than wives of brown ones. No respectable woman would choose concubinage over marriage; accordingly, he emphasizes brown women's "religious principles," "suavity of manners," and "virtuous pride," even going so far as to dare the hated governor of Trinidad, Ralph Woodford, to "vouch for the individual correctness of his select circle" (191, asterisked footnote), implying that he cannot. The contradiction is stark; on the one hand, brown women are, after all, women, and it is up to their husbands, fathers, and brothers to protect them from their own womanliness, the "tenderness and frailty of their sex." This docile version of brown women, the very antithesis of the arrogant, sensual, and showy mistresses depicted in both local white and European accounts, brings them into line with the familiar traits of Victorian womanhood—weakness, emotion, vulnerability. By this reasoning, brown women are sympathetic victims in need of protection: arm their men with rights to shelter them! The other version of brown women presented by Philippe is less easily subsumed into Victorian views of the sex: brown women who do enter into illicit sexual relations with white men do so because they are poor and illiterate, and therefore "without the liberality of sentiment" that education provides.

Brown women's sexuality is pivotal to the understanding of these early romances because brown men's social status hinged on the status of their women, and their women were compromised subjects. Caught in a nexus of contradictory visions of black and white women by black, brown, and white men, brown women's subjectivity was a hall of mirrors, reflecting and refracting the gaze of whatever constituency was watching. Next to white women, they were promiscuous. Next to black women, they were respectable. Next to black women, they were romantic subjects rather than erotic objects; next to white women, they were erotic objects rather than romantic subjects. Brown women's ambiguous sexual status can be read as a metaphor for the unstable, ever-shifting possibilities of an emerging black and brown middle class, whose bid for legitimacy depended so heavily on the status of its women. Brown women were, simultaneously, an asset and a liability: they were privileged and victimized; respectable and wanton; eroticized and desexualized. For brown men to become the heroes of their own stories, their masculinity must be legitimized by their relationship to their women—their mothers and their wives. In this sense, both

Emmanuel Appadocca and *Adolphus* are written as protests against brown second-class status, and as models for brown (male and female) virtue. There are no brown—or black—women of loose morals in either novel, or brown women whose compromised marital status cannot be explained by a critique of existing custom. MacDermot's *One Brown Girl And*— later extends this focus on brownness as a model for a creolized identity by concentrating specifically on brown women and their complex sexual status in early twentieth-century Jamaica. The critical point here is that brown people, both men and women, are constructed as romantic heroes of the archetypal quest-romance genre. As one that both mystifies and codifies subjectivity as a given, the romance genre essentializes the traits of brownness from an unstable "mulattoness"—an unsteady blend of black and white, embodying neither—into something natural, the characteristics of a people with their own habits, their own society, their own traditions.

The Template: The American Antislavery Novel

The American antislavery novel provided the perfect synthesis of themes for the early brown novels: a passionate invocation for political rights wrapped in the gauze of the sentimental romance and the adventure story. Both *Emmanuel Appadocca* and *Adolphus* feature heroes who are the children of enslaved mothers, and so these postslavery texts begin with a critique of slavery, although this topic is not their main one. In their prefaces both authors contextualize the slavery theme. Philip writes in *Emmanuel Appadocca* that

> This work has been written at a moment when the feelings of the Author are roused up to a high pitch of indignant excitement, by a statement of the cruel manner in which *the slave holders of America* deal with their slave-children.... [The author] has ventured to sketch out the line of conduct, which a high-spirited and sensitive person would probably follow, if he found himself picking cotton under the spurring encouragement of "Jimboes" or "Quimboes" on his own father's plantation. (6, emphasis added)

Who are the Jimboes and Quimboes to whom Philip alludes but other black men who may be plantation foremen and as such stand "over" a mulatto? What Cudjoe and Cain do not remark on is that this statement suggests not just a critique of slavery's evils but a critique of the way in which it puts naturally superior characters—the "high-spirited and sensitive" brown individuals—under apparently inferior (black) ones. The anonymous author of *Adolphus* is less combative and seeks to neutralize any "disagreeable feelings" that may be aroused by examining such an ugly period in Trinidadian history. Its author declares that his

> principal object is to shew the contrast between the present position of the coloured people and that in which they stood formerly, that they may see the better the great step that colonial society has made in advance... that it may prove amusing and interesting to all, and offensive to none, are the only rewards hoped for by The Writer. (5)

The official disclaimer is, at best, disingenuous, since the novel is as critical as *Emmanuel Appadocca* is on the slights to brown male authority, and even more so on the evils visited on black women by white slaveholders. The "advance[ment]" of brown society is not the issue here but rather the obstacles in the way of that advancement. *Adolphus,* unlike *Emmanuel Appadocca,* was serialized in a newspaper with a strictly local audience, and it was important to the author not to annoy the local authorities, whereas Michel Maxwell Philip, publishing in London, could afford more license.

The eponymous hero of *Emmanuel Appadocca* is the son of a white creole planter and his black mistress, or slave; the text is deliberately hazy about the status of the hero's mother. Slavery is mentioned only once, and that almost halfway through the book, yet slavery and its relation to the degraded status of the hero's black mother form the crux of the book, as both Cain and Cudjoe note. For Cain, the centrality of slave status means that the novel is essentially a Caribbean replay of *Uncle Tom's Cabin,* that is, a sentimental antislavery novel meant to appeal to American and British readers' abolitionist sympathies. *Emmanuel Appadocca,* however, was written after slavery had been over for more than a decade in most of the Caribbean. Further, the text's political concerns are focused on the status of free brown people, not on enslaved blacks, so this reading seems off target. These early Caribbean novels appear to be aimed squarely at Caribbean and English readers.

Although the influence of *Uncle Tom's Cabin* is self-evident in this and other early Caribbean novels,[35] we must ask what, beyond its obvious dramatic and sentimental power, is this American novel's appeal for a free colored population in the Caribbean where slavery has been over for a generation? The mulatto hero and heroines of *Uncle Tom's Cabin* are the draw. To gain perspective on the centrality of mulatto characters in the antislavery story, we can more fruitfully group *Uncle Tom's Cabin* with other popular mid-nineteenth-century African American slave testimonials, such as Frederick Douglass's 1845 autobiography, or William and Ellen Craft's 1860 story of their daring escape. White audiences could view mulatto characters as both heroic and victimized in ways that apparently they could not extend to purely black characters. If white audiences showed a predilection for light-skinned protagonists, so too did African Americans, who had a color hierarchy not as entrenched but certainly as pervasive as that in the nineteenth-century Caribbean. Early African American authors used mulatto heroes and heroines almost exclusively until well into the twentieth century. These popular American stories, with their emphases on mulatto heroes and heroines with "white" characteristics, gave Caribbean authors a way to talk about brown people as victims that made them into heroic, desiring and desirable, subjects.

The first known novel by an African American, *Clotel; or, the President's Daughter* by mulatto ex-slave William Wells Brown, was published in London in 1853, the same year and in the same place as *Emmanuel Appadocca* was published. *Clotel*'s main themes parallel those of *Emmanuel Appadocca* and *Adolphus* to an uncanny degree: the difficult lives of mulattoes in the United States, and the immorality of sexual relations between wealthy white men and victimized brown women. London in the 1850s was a hotbed of abolitionist ferment, a safe harbor for refugee African Americans such as Douglass, the Crafts (who published their story there), and Wells Brown. London provides the missing link between early African American and Caribbean literature, since London is where educated black and brown men like Michel Maxwell Philip completed their studies to become lawyers, doctors, or members of other professions. It was London where several literary traditions connected: the English tradition, American antislavery writing, and the Caribbean newspaper stories that were repackaged as novels and sent back to the Caribbean. So it was London where educated nonwhite West Indians could familiarize themselves with an American genre so enthusiastically favored by the English reading public. The warm reception in England of biracial African American authors such as Wells Brown and Frederick Douglass could not have been lost on the brown West Indians longing to tell a story of brown identity that would be validated by a cosmopolitan reading public.

For Michel Maxwell Philip and his contemporaries, therefore, the stories of African American slavery symbolized by *Clotel* and *Uncle Tom's Cabin* were foundational, but not because of the books' representations of black, illiterate Uncle Toms. Rather, for Philip and his contemporaries, the beautiful and intelligent mulattos Eliza and George are the main point of *Uncle Tom's Cabin* and other antislavery narratives. The American antislavery narrative provided a template for the brown hero, not the black one. And indeed the story of Emmanuel Appadocca, the hero-pirate, is a cautionary tale to white people of what happens when brown men go wrong.

Emmanuel Appadocca is set on the Caribbean high seas, a location with far more romantic possibilities for heroic subjectivity than the slave plantation, as

Faith Smith notes.[36] Appadocca's father refuses to acknowledge him or support him, and his black mother dies in despair and destitution. In response, the young brown man, after a promising start as a brilliant university student in Europe, embarks on a life of crime as a pirate on the Caribbean Sea, robbing vessels carrying the cargo of the wealthy planter class. These exploits are not robbery, for, as Appadocca tells his old English friend, "If I take away from the merchant whose property very likely consists of the accumulation of exorbitant and excessive profits, the sugar which by the vice of mortgages he wrings at a nominal price from the debt-ridden planter, who, in his turn, robs the unfortunate slave of his labour, I take what is ethically not his property, therefore, I commit no robbery" (115). Thus is piracy's criminality neutralized as a relative point in a thieving, immoral society. The handsome young pirate gathers about him a handsome young brown lieutenant, of good family, and a band of educated pirates, whom, we are told, "had been of a superior class in society, before they exiled themselves from it" (121). Together they capture a ship from Trinidad carrying a beautiful brown woman, Lorenzo's love interest, as well as Appadocca's hated white father, James Wilmington. Appadocca's pursuit and subsequent treatment of his father form the basis of the novel.

The lieutenant, Lorenzo, performs a kind of doppelganger function in the narrative as the good pirate who in the end goes straight, marrying his lady love Agnes and living happily as master of his father-in-law's plantation. His actions make up for the "blighted life" of the hero, who despite the redeeming love of a Venezuelan señorita and that of the English admiral's son, is devoured by his hatred of Wilmington. Appadocca accuses Wilmington of the inhumane crime of abandoning his progeny, before, in turn, abandoning his father to die on the high seas. After Wilmington dies, Emmanuel Appadocca commits suicide. There is no heroism, apparently, in killing the white father, bad as he is, and going on to health and good fortune.

English Nobility, African Bravery: The Brown Heroic Ideal

The descriptions of the brown characters reveal much about how brown people desired to see themselves. There is pronounced emphasis on their "Spanish" characteristics, and it is not coincidental that both Appadocca and Lorenzo take on Spanish names; Appadocca acquires the name Admiral Appadocca, after the Spanish general who set fire to the Spanish ships when the English seized control of the island. Spanishness is everywhere, as if to provide a way to be both brown and white at the same time.[37] Independent South America, and in particular Venezuela, so close to Trinidad, represented a kind of postcolonial space for brown West Indians of the English-speaking Caribbean; in Venezuela, the brown, or *pardo,* population most likely constituted a majority of the population, and free nonwhites had more rights than did brown people in Trinidad and the other Anglophone countries.[38] Despite the irony that slavery still existed in 1854 Venezuela, both brown authors of *Emmanuel Appadocca* and *Adolphus* idealize that country as a kind of utopian brown space, where brown men have rights. Thus Hispanic identity becomes an alternative to a colonial, white creole identity. The lingering descriptions of their physiognomies, so central to the romance genre, here dwell on their brownness. When the reader is first introduced to Appadocca, whose genealogy is still unknown, we are told that he is "light olive," showing a "mixture of blood" that "proclaimed that the man was connected with some dark race, and in the infinity of grades in the population of Spanish America, he may have been said to be of that which is commonly designated Quadroon." The description continues:

> But the features of this femininely formed man were in deep contrast with his make; they were handsome to the extreme; but there was something in his large tropical eyes that seemed to possess the power of the basilisk.... His high aquiline nose, compressed lips, and set jaws, pointed clearly to a disposition that would undertake the most arduous and hazardous things, and execute them with firmness in spite of the perils... there was a power in that mind which was reflected on his face... men must, unknowingly to themselves, obey him, and act as he acted.... The shape of his head was what the most fastidious could but admire; his forehead rose in the fullness of beautiful proportions, while, at the same time, those skilled in reading others' skulls would have declared that, with his high intellectual development, he did not lack those necessary moral accompaniments. (24)

This description of Appadocca is a tense balancing act of antithetical racialist views of humanity. He is clearly meant to be seen as brown, but what kind of brown? The kind with an "aquiline nose" and "tropical eyes," the kind that was undeniably of some African extraction but nevertheless aesthetically pleasing to European eyes. The passage reminds us that brownness traditionally has had its own hierarchy, where "bad" mixes—that is, where black features dominate white—are undesirable.[39] Further, the capacity to "read' skulls reminds us of the racialist beliefs of the period, wherein moral character and intelligence could be literally mapped onto the body.[40] So despite his African ancestry and criminality, Appadocca is cast in the body of a beautiful intellectual, a pirate who reads Aristotelian philosophy and essays by Francis

Bacon (24). The tension among his physical desirability, his intellect, and his illegitimate legal status as both bastard and pirate begs the question of what kind of society could make this "natural" hero into Satan?

The noble masculine ideal posed by Appadocca requires, almost by definition, a contrast, and Philip provides it in the character of Jack Jimmy, the black Trinidadian fisherman whom Appadocca's crew captures, and who comes to adore the pirate captain, remaining his loyal servant until Appadocca dies. The character of Jack Jimmy seems so thoroughly a racist, plantation stereotype that it comes as some surprise when Selwyn Cudjoe declares that he represents the novel's distinct "Afro-Trinidadian voice," a character who joins the pirate not out of admiration but rather to rebuke the plantation system: "Reading between the lines or beneath the surface of the text—in spite of Philip, as it were—one sees a very human figure in Jimmy, someone who is fed up with the system...a black man who is willing to give his life to a cause.... He too is committed to the eventual overthrow of the colonial system."[41] Jimmy Jack's consistent Trinidadian dialect is meant as comic relief, however, and his physiognomy bears out his status as comic sidekick to the brown hero: when he crouches in fear, he is "difficult to distinguish... from the ideal of a rolled up ouranoutan [orangutan]" (29); his movements "were as brisk and as rapid as those of a monkey," and he lacks courage, "his large white eyes... stretched open to their utmost width" (50). If this novel establishes the brown man's credentials as a heroic figure by imbuing him with the characteristics that make him a desirable husband and leader, he must lead someone, and Jack Jimmy is born to follow, in spite of Cudjoe's recuperative efforts. Appadocca's courage and intellect are contrasted with those of his "natural" father, who prevaricates when his son confronts him, shrieks for mercy when captured, and disgusts the fair-minded British officers to whom he flees upon escape from the pirate ship.

It is instructive that all of the respectable men who admire Appadocca are English naval officers. A consistent thread in all of the novels of this period is that English characters, in contrast to white creole ones, are never guilty of racism or narrow thinking and are always voices of reason and fellowship. It is with Englishmen that Appadocca has all of his most philosophical and erudite discussions, and one may suppose that part of the book's trajectory is to persuade the English, not white creoles, to accept the brown class as their equals. But the sympathetic views of the English permeate all of these novels, from *One Brown Girl* to *Rupert Gray* to *Jane's Career*. The good English characters are almost always contrasted with bad white creoles, as if the authors' message to white creoles is "we all agree that, as Englishness is the white ideal, and your views are at odds with the English, you are therefore not sufficiently white"—a charge, incidentally, that had been leveled at the white creoles by the English themselves.[42]

From this perspective, it makes sense that, although Philip's portraits of Afro-Caribbean men are relentlessly racist, his view of African heritage is not. Given that brownness is essentially linked to an African ancestry, if not to an Afro-Caribbean present, Philip's brown aesthetic requires that the European stereotype of Africa as the "child of civilization," and African culture as essentially primitive, violent and immoral, must be, if not entirely revised, at least partially salvaged. In the following scene Appadocca chastises Charles Hamilton, the Englishman who is his former university friend, for his conflation of commerce with advanced civilization:

> It is not in the busy mart, not at the tinkling of gold, that [the human mind] grows and becomes strong; nor is it on the shaft of the steam-engine which propels your huge fabrics to rich though savage shores that it increases.... The mind can thrive only in the silence that courts contemplation. *It was in such silence that among a race, which is now despised and oppressed, speculation took wing, and the mind burst forth,* and, scorning things of earth, scaled the heavens, read the stars, and elaborated systems of philosophy, religion, and government: while the other parts of the world were either enveloped in darkness, or following in eager and uncontemplative haste the luring genii of riches. Commerce makes steam engines and money—it assists not the philosophical progress of the mind. (116, emphasis added)

Remarkably, Appadocca is tackling one of the central foundations for the argument that Western civilization is superior to all others: its technology, its wealth, and its trade. In so doing Philip anticipates modern Afrocentric arguments that Egypt was advancing "while other parts of the world [Britain, perhaps?] were enveloped in darkness," and that Egypt's knowledge systems constitute the foundation of Western knowledge. Like modern Afrocentrists, Philip (through Appadocca) conflates Egypt with Africa and thus with "the despised and oppressed race" of black Africans who became an enslaved people in the Americas.

Emmanuel Appadocca is a book about brown masculinity and brown political desire, but its thesis is dependent on the largely absent women who inhabit its fringes. As I've said, Appadocca's illegitimate status is tied to his black mother's sexual relationship with his white father, and although we never see the mother—she dies before the novel's action takes place—we are meant to understand that all of Appadocca's "crimes" are intended to revenge her memory: "How to wreak retribution now engrossed his whole intellect—retribution on the man whom that mother had once too fondly loved, and whose placid nature had, no doubt, long long forgiven" (226). The only time the pirate becomes emotional is when his Venezuelan sweetheart suggests that his pursuit of Wilmington may offend his dead mother (228). The black mother's absence is critical to the fulfillment of the brown romantic ideal. Whereas black male characters like Jack Jimmy help to construct the brown hero as a Caribbean leader and the intellectual equal of the English by their contrasting positions as loyal and stupid servants of brown men, black women's representation poses something of a problem for the brown masculinist romance. The black woman is the Mother, figuratively and often literally (as in Philip's case), of the brown population. She cannot be so easily reduced to plantation caricature in the way that black men could, because her threat lies elsewhere. Whereas black men are an omnipresent model of "other" masculinity from which brown men must distance themselves, the status of black women, as forebears, must be explained. The description of Appadocca's mother as someone who "had once too fondly loved, and whose placid nature had, no doubt, long long forgiven" her white exploiter, shifts the emphasis away from her legal status—was she a slave, or wasn't she?—to her "fond" and "placid" nature. These ideal maternal characteristics bring the black mother into line with the Victorian female ideal and away from the more disturbing nineteenth-century images of black women as promiscuous, loud, and independent.[43] Although white male exploitation is a major theme here, we are told that the black mother "loved" her exploiter, so Wilmington's crime is not rape but rather lack of love in the larger sense. Slavery is thus stigmatized not as a sign of black or brown inferiority but as a sign of white creole debasement, even as it is never mentioned—the one direct reference is in the quotation given earlier. The illegitimate brown hero is legitimized not simply by his innately superior intellect and physical capabilities, but by his love for his black mother, whose absence is nevertheless necessary for brown heroism to exist.

The other absent woman in the novel is Agnes, the brown quasi-heroine who marries Lorenzo. The rapturous and detailed description of the character at the beginning of the novel suggests that she will be his love interest:

> She was exceedingly beautiful; such a species of beauty that we meet only in the tropics,—*a beauty which we can compare to no known standard: something that belongs entirely to the warm clime by which it is produced;* something that is more of the fanciful than of the real. She was...slender, and of a perfect figure; her features were delicately and nicely chiseled; her complexion was of the clearest white, tinged with

the slightest olive; her dark brown hair hung over a high and nicely moulded forehead, while her dark gazelle-like eyes imparted to her face a character of tenderness and softness. (51, emphasis added)

Agnes's description bears more than a passing resemblance to that of Appadocca himself—the olive complexion that somehow is still "of the clearest white," the emphasis on the forehead (a marker of European heritage), the "tropical" beauty. Yet even as her white credentials are emphasized, Philip makes a point of saying that her beauty is an original product of the Caribbean ("the tropics") and as such it cannot be compared to any "known standard." Assuming that the "known standard" is the European standard of feminine pulchritude, it appears that Philip is clearing a space for brown beauty, recognizing that the success of the brown romance requires a brown heroine who complements the brown hero. Agnes has other appealing characteristics of the Victorian ideal—she is religious, delicate, and faints often—but perhaps her most important quality is that she forms a template for the brown heroine.

Philip has little to say about his brown heroine other than to emphasize her beauty and religiosity. There are no other brown women in the story. The paucity of characterization suggests that while brown women are necessary, in the story of brown mobility they are also a liability; any characterization more complex than giving one brown woman beauty, virtue, and a handsome plantation would be to undermine the image of a fully formed brown society awaiting recognition. Similarly, in *Adolphus* there is a paucity of brown female characters. Antonia, the brown heroine, despite her more central role, is sketched in roughly the same contours. The reader is told that her "colour was of that light Italian *brunette* which commands admiration throughout the world" (9), and that she loves reading learned tomes and is profoundly religious. The story hinges on her love for the brown hero, Adolphus. Their trials begin when she is kidnapped by a local, wealthy white creole, DeGuerinon, who tries to rape her. She is rescued by Adolphus and his plucky brown friend Ernest, who must escape to Venezuela to avoid prosecution for striking a white man and other, false, charges. Antonia's aged parents expire from the ordeal.

Like *Emmanuel Appadocca,* the real story of *Adolphus* is that of the brown hero and his brown friend. Their heroism is largely dependent on exculpating the virtue of black and brown women. Adolphus's sorrow is the status and demise of his mulatto mother, herself the product of a rape, who was in turn raped by her white owner. The forcible sexual degradation of black and brown women is given both explicit and implicit explanation here: explicit in the case of black slave women, implicit in the case of brown women who cohabit with white men (a scene, incidentally, that we are never shown). Adolphus's mother dies giving birth to Adolphus, and he is subsequently raised and educated by a priest. The description of Adolphus bears striking similarities to that of Appadocca, most notably to the emphasis on an aristocratic bearing that belies his illegitimate origins: "on his brow he bore the impress of nature's nobility" (18). Adolphus's heritage is both maroon and creole; as an infant he is handed over to the priest by his granduncle Jimbo, the leader of the runaway slaves. Jimbo has hated whites since he saw his sister's husband sold and his sister, and then his niece, raped by "Christian" white men, and he vows to "study revenge." (He and his men respect the Spanish priest, however, again signaling the novel's interest in preserving an idealized view of Hispanic race relations.) Although the other black men in the novel are portrayed almost exactly like Jack Jimmy in *Emmanuel Appadocca*— that is, as buffoonish dialect-speakers—in this instance, this black man—an African—carries all of the traits of heroic masculinity: Jimbo is strong, brave, a protector of women and children, and, most notably, he speaks in standard grammar. Unlike the other black male characters, Jimbo is an African who was captured by a slaver. Similar to the positive characterizations of persons of African heritage in *Emmanuel Appadocca*, the positive characterization of Jimbo suggests that the author of *Adolphus* has a similar investment in retaining a positive image of African heritage, if not of creole blackness.[44] Thus is the heroic image of the black maroon subsumed into the brown heroic model.

Perhaps the most interesting description of physiognomy in the novel lies in the term "white mulatto," the phrase used to describe the white creole DeGuerinon. A lecherous but wealthy local white who is repeatedly described as "dull" despite his residence at the best European universities, DeGuerinon and his white friends first enter the story when they invade a respectable brown man's home, where a party is being held, in order to dance with the women and make sexual advances toward them. Although the brown women "shudder with indignation" at their overtures, the white men persist, and the young brown men must stifle their urge to strike them because of laws forbidding black or brown men to assault whites for any reason. The author struggles to keep the masculine dignity of his brown male characters while showing them to be victims:

> The four *gentlemen* neither knocked at the door nor asked for admission, but *sans gene* walked coolly into the apartment where dancing was going on.... The host, old Navetto, a fine looking old man, who, with the exception of his dark complexion, was a perfect portrait of the "real

old English gentleman," came, and making a bow, such as those of his class usually made to the potent whites, asked, "will you, gentleman, be pleased to tell your humble servant what is your desire?" (25)

The contrast between the rude white gentlemen who are anything but and the real gentleman, who, except for his brown skin, typifies the "real old English gentleman," instantly communicates the story's thesis, to wit: Local whites are not true whites because they do not measure up to the English gentleman ideal. This view returns in a more overtly political guise later on. Brown people, by contrast, are the true inheritors of the English ideal and, as natural gentlemen (in spirit if not in fact), should not have to kowtow to inferior whites. This ideological race reversal is further problematized when we find out that DeGuerinon is not really white but rather a brown man like Adolphus himself. DeGuerinon's mother is also, shockingly, "to him unknown" (29); later she is found out to be his old black slave, whom he sells in an effort to pay his debts. Covering his curly hair with a glossy wig, DeGuerinon passes as white more easily in that the local whites "saw not the dark tinge of his complexion, because it was overspread by a white veil of dollars" (30).

An elaborate distinction is made between physiognomic Caribbean whiteness—inevitably connected with moral degeneracy and cultural philistinism—and an idealized Englishness, which is rendered in love of books and good manners, and which is apparently accessible to all. The stereotypes that Europeans held about the degeneracy of whites in the tropics were stereotypes that brown people held as well;[45] or, one might argue, brown people simply tarred and feathered whites with the same stereotypes as those held by whites of brown people. At any rate, in contrast to the conventional scholarly view that the early brown middle class simply wished to be white,[46] *Adolphus* makes a point of showing that its brown characters are proud of their brownness and have no desire to be otherwise. Early on, DeGuerinon finds out from a black servant that Antonia's family is held in high regard by black people because "dem give charity to poor niggers, but me no tink dem like white folks" (30). This pointed rebuttal of a supposed brown inferiority complex is further emphasized when Ernest asks DeGuerinon's black slave Cudjoe to sit down at the table with him and his brown friends. The black man, shocked and grateful, offers that "country buckras [whites]" such as Ernest are truly good, not like the urban whites, who would never eat with a black man at their table. Ernest replies coldly, "I am not a buckra, my friend, that you can see yourself, therefore think not to flatter me with so blind a compliment—if I may term it a compliment" (48). As in *Emmanuel*

Appadocca, the validation of brown men's heroism and rectitude by poor black people is necessary to the legitimization of brown subjectivity.

The distinction between good and bad brown men in *Adolphus* hinges on the treatment of yet another marginalized character, the black mother. Adolphus honors his mother's legacy by embodying the fighting maroon spirit and refusing to bow to white authority. By contrast, DeGuerinon sells his own enslaved mother, literally, to pay off his debts. The black mother symbolizes the African heritage of the brown class; the refusal of "good" brown people to disinherit her is a form of specifically brown nationalism that is simultaneously characterized by a dismissal or belittling of black identity. Brown female chastity is also an important underpinning for brown masculine subjectivity. The novel trades on the idea—the fantasy—that respectable, desirable brown women would never choose white men, even wealthy white ones like DeGuerinon and friends, as sexual partners over marriage with brown men of their own class. This fantasy stands in sharp contrast to the reality of what appears to have been the widespread practice of brown women cohabiting with white men. Brown nationalism in these novels thus combines elements of black nationalism, gender fantasies, and a concomitant idealization of Englishness.

Even as the narrative idealizes Englishness, however, the English themselves are critiqued. Simón Bolívar, the father of Latin American nationalism and "that model of patriots" (73), enters the story in deux ex machina mode to rescue Adolphus. When he hears the story of Adolphus's heroism and unjust persecution on false charges, Bolívar exclaims, "Ought England not to blush! She that pretends to be the greatest and most magnanimous of Nations, to tolerate such things in any part of her dominions?" (74). Bolívar's presence serves to underscore the Hispanic alternative—if over here in the Caribbean we are second-class citizens, over there in the birthplace of Latin American nationalism we are equals; brown citizenship is simply a question of geography and not of nature.

The Caribbean Uplift Novel

The idealization of Englishness is also apparent in more overtly nationalist, early twentieth-century "brown" texts, such as Stephen Cobham's *Rupert Gray* (1907) and MacDermot's *One Brown Girl And—*(1909), in which English characters are presented as sympathetic, racially progressive, and open-minded. This portrayal is particularly so in *Rupert Gray*, whose eponymous black middle-class hero falls in love with a wealthy white creole woman in Port of Spain. When the hero arrives in Britain, he is as jubilant as if he had made it to the promised land: "At last, at last! The dream of boyhood realized—an ambition capped—hope crowned. Every black man in the West Indies expects to see England some day" (98).[47] England and Englishness function throughout as an ideal world in which the black hero is seen as an equal among men. When Rupert Gray and other black guests are snubbed at a party by whites, the heroine opines that "in England that could never happen" (35). As in the earlier texts, it is white creole men who are the most demonstrably racist and the most reluctant to embrace social change, which is signaled through interracial marriage. The English characters, by contrast, are confidants of the interracial couple. One is an English female doctor whose "modern woman" persona underscores that interracial love affairs are no big deal among modern, cosmopolitan people; the other is an English countess and amateur botanist who is impressed by Rupert Gray's extensive knowledge of botany. In the end it is the countess's money, as well as that of other English nobility, which comes to the rescue of the outcast black hero and funds a proposed Booker T. Washington-esque Negro-Industrial Institute of the West Indies (123). Thus the interracial romance ends with American-style black racial uplift, funded by English money.

If it is unsurprising that the discourse of loyalty to England can coexist so easily with a Pan-Africanist sensibility here, it is noteworthy that that Pan-Africanist sensibility finds its ultimate expression in an African American solution. In the later nineteenth century white planters toyed with the idea of annexation to the United States, and in this context loyalty to the Crown constituted a bulwark against American-style racial inequality.[48] Yet it is the African American experience, in the form of the Tuskegee Institute, that provides the resolution for the impasse created by Pan Africanism and Crown loyalty. *Rupert Gray* is a peculiarly Caribbean version of the African American uplift novel, a story founded on the concept of black self-determination and respectability that reconciles black nationalism with a desire for brown status and English approval.

The story follows the travails of the love affair between Rupert Gray, a black Trinidadian accountant, and his white creole employer's daughter, Gwendoline Serle. Although she is a native Trinidadian, the text emphasizes that Gwendoline's extensive travels and foreign education render her "almost a foreigner" in her native land, in her father's words (9). The author implies that Gwendoline's more cosmopolitan worldview allows her to see Rupert Gray as a leading man, not just a good worker, as does her father Mr. Serle. When we first meet him he is described from her point of view: he is, significantly, a "full-blooded negro" (not brown, in other words, so none of his good qualities can be imputed to any European heritage); his "rich baritone" is "masculine, musical," full of "vigour"; "there is character in that face of his"; "his manner bespoke refinement and habitual self-respect"; and "he stood tall and athletic" (8–9). Their relationship grows as Rupert teaches Gwendoline shorthand and typewriting, and we understand that Gwendoline's attraction to Rupert is as much about his superior knowledge as it is about his physical qualities.

It is tempting to read *Rupert Gray* as simply a political fable of black self-determination in a romance genre guise, as Cudjoe and the authors of the introduction to the University of the West Indies Press edition do. But the narrative does not allow us that expedient interpretation. Gwendoline's villainous white father is also, as it happens, a great admirer of black political leaders: in one revealing dinner table conversation, he enthusiastically lists the great black men of Caribbean and Trinidadian history, from "the genius of Toussaint L'Ouverture" to Michel Maxwell Philip, "the demosthenic lawyer" (59). Therefore the problem with Serle, and whites like him, is not that they lack respect for black talent or leadership ability, since, as Serle declares, "We are ready to receive the black man with open arms into the professions, the service of the Crown, and in commerce" (59). Rather, it is that such political acceptance does not come with social acceptance. As Serle concludes, "but when it comes to mixing up in the company of our wives, and wanting to marry our daughters—I say, 'No, sir.'...'Thus far and no farther'" (59). Given Serle's eager promotion of Rupert Gray, we are meant to take his words at face value. The common interpretation of white hostility to interracial romance has always been that it is an essentially political struggle played out through the control of nonwhite men's sexuality, an argument that has made particular sense in the American context, where African American voting rights were eviscerated by the Reconstruction-era image of black men kissing white women, a nightmare that would soon come to pass, white Southerners warned, if black men got the vote.[49] But here, in the early twentieth-century Caribbean, in a society whose white minority has far more reason to fear political eclipse by the black majority, the Pan-Africanist author consciously de-links the objection to interracial marriage from the political argument. Why is the threat of black masculinity represented as essentially, almost exclusively, sexual?

"I do not deny the equality of man," says Serle, "but I do think that the West Indian negro barely stands within the threshold of *culture*" (58, emphasis added). Serle's distinction between political ability and cultural deficiency is what lies behind Cobham's contradictory portrait of him. Cobham's concern with black uplift had as much to do with white acceptance of black manhood as it had to do with black social mobility. Among other things, interracial marriage, and the institutionalization of black/brown society as a respectable norm, threatened the cultural primacy of whiteness. As Serle puts it, "I believe that our coloured people are enlightened enough to form an aristocracy of their own" (58). In other words, Cobham is implying that white fear of interracial marriage stems not from an antinationalist viewpoint, but rather from a fear of social extinction. A parallel black aristocracy would—in theory, anyway—pose no threat to the white one, but a "browned" black aristocracy, a synthesis of black and white, would obliterate it.

If Cobham envisioned such social reengineering as part of the new Trinidad, he obviously believed that black people would also have a problem with the new dispensation. In the novel, the people who object most to the interracial romance, other than Gwendoline's father and other white creoles, are black people themselves. The black characters who object to the interracial romance are cast as inferior to Rupert Gray in every regard: intellectually, socially, economically. They represent what Frantz Fanon calls a "colonized mind," blacks who have so much self-hatred that they cannot stand to see a black man get above his station. This attitude is shown to be pervasive in the working world of Afro-Trinidadians in Port of Spain. When the interracial couple eat at a hotel, the black waiter grumbles that the "Nigga too black, set down close bakra gul, tink heself big guvanah [Nigger's too black, yet he sits down next to the white girl and thinks himself a big governor]" (10). When Rupert Gray helps a down-at-luck friend get a good position, the friend, jealous, repays him by scheming to ruin him and end his love affair with Gwendoline. Nevertheless, throughout all of these trials Rupert Gray is solidly problack, exclaiming, "We must forward the race. We must do good, and if we cannot, we must do no harm to other negroes.... Race-uplifting should be our reward" (48).

Rupert Gray ends, predictably, with the marriage of Rupert and Gwendoline, the "patter [of] tiny feet," and—unpredictably—with an incongruous speech on miscegenation by a black bishop. The speech is given to a lofty gathering of aristocrats and "all the blacks in England," gathered for the purpose of devising ways of erecting the proposed Negro-Industrial Institute of the West Indies. Opines the bishop, "Miscegenation would soon obliterate the strongest traits of race. West Indian negroes, be proud to perpetuate your seed unmixed. Fraternize and hold your heads up. Variety is a law of nature. You represent one of the four ruling colours in mankind.... Why vex your souls when called negro? Which white man, or yellow man, or red man does that?" (123–24). In a note, the editors of the University of the West Indies Press edition find the speech "puzzling because in it the bishop seems to oppose the miscegenation that the novel has just resoundingly approved in the marriage of Rupert and Gwendoline. The speech may reflect black pride...or it may have been tailored to its audience, with an eye to pleasing [conservative English leaders], assuring them that Rupert and Gwendoline's case is exceptional, not the beginning of a trend towards mixed marriages" (168).

The bishop's speech is contradictory only if we persist in reading the story as exclusively about Pan-Africanism and racism. The conclusion in fact emphasizes the interracial marriage theme as a template for future blackness, not as its aberration. Cobham needs to reassure his black audience, not his white one, that the marriage of a proud black man to a member of the ruling elite does not signify the self-hatred the novel has gone out of its way to depict. The black bishop's speech emphasizes that interracial marriage "would obliterate the strongest traits of race," meaning the unwieldy extremes of blackness and whiteness. He then urges black men to be "proud to perpetuate your seed unmixed," which seems less a call to racial purity than to qualify his first statement—in other words, don't feel that you are inferior if you do not have a white partner, because after all, "variety is a law of nature." In naming the "four ruling colours of mankind"—white (or European), red (or Indian), yellow (or Chinese), and black (African)—the bishop is assuring black men that the fruit of the black-white alliance—those brown pattering feet—will come under the rubric of black identity. Brownness, in other words, will be a stronger form of blackness—without the rough edges.

Just as *Emmanuel Appadocca* and *Adolphus* subsume the desirable traits of Africaneity into a model of brown masculine subjectivity, so too does *Rupert Gray* subsume brownness, both physical and cultural, into a politically black identity. The final sentence of the novel describes Rupert Gray as "liv[ing] for the good of his people, entering *without fear of contamination* into their every phase of social life...a brilliant jurist...whose deep wise counsel is almost indispensable in the Senate...the rising hope of Trinidad and the West Indies...Rupert Gray" (124, emphasis added). Rupert Gray's rising political star suggests that he is, indeed, the foundation for a new political class of black leaders, one who in his upward social trajectory still does not wish to de-link himself from the black majority, with its inescapable associations of cultural backwardness and poverty. The making of this new breed of black political hero, one who does not fear social contamination by the black masses below him, is equally predicated on his social alliance with whiteness. In other words, brown identity, ideological and physiological, can be remade in the black image. This recombinated form of black nationalism is distinctly culled from an African American template, where problematic mulattoness was subsumed into blackness, and a tradition of black leadership could be produced by institutions such as Tuskegee, or the "Negro-Industrial Institute of the West Indies."

Reclaiming Black Chastity for Brown Women

The 1909 Jamaican novel *One Brown Girl And*— also focuses on black respectability, but unlike *Rupert Gray,* the emphasis is on that of females rather than males. MacDermot attempts to write the story of modern Jamaican society by investigating the domestic lives of brown and black women. The brown heroine of the title is Liberta, a mulatto whose white creole father had bought a mother and daughter out of slavery in the United States and brought them back with him to Jamaica, where he married the daughter. MacDermot provided this slave genealogy for Liberta so that the character's brownness is more emphatically associated with a conscious pride in the relative freedom for blacks of the modern Caribbean, in contrast to the racism meted out to black people in the United States. The genealogy also makes Liberta's brownness more clearly a blend of Africa and Europe, in contrast to that of the centuries-old brown class whose members characterized early twentieth-century Kingston. Liberta's status as a first-generation mulatto allows the novel to dwell on the dilemmas of brown identity in a way that an established brown cultural identity would not. The focus is on more than one brown girl, however, as the title implies. The other two main characters are Ada, a light brown servant, and Fidelia Stanton, a "pure" black one, a "Coromantee girl who did not have a drop of white blood" (42). The novel traces the dilemmas of sexual temptation and romantic love for the three women. Ada, who is led into sexual temptation by her white creole seducer, the Mephisto-like Meffala, is rescued from moral disgrace by two predictably upright English characters, an angelic Sunday school teacher and a Salvation Army major.

With the exception of Liberta's father, the white creoles are portrayed as immoral, money minded, and violent. Although wealthy in her own right, Liberta lives with her father's sister Henrietta, who hates Liberta because she is brown and yet richer than Henrietta herself. Henrietta enjoys abusing the servants (a subject raised in *Jane's Career* as well) and boxes Ada. But "striking of servants in any part of their corporal being is decidedly a dangerous pastime in the West Indies of today [because] the sufferer is as likely as not to return the gift with interest" (16); indeed, Ada boxes back and leaves the household. The question of how young, urban, working women can make a living and remain respectable is investigated in great detail in this novel, and even more so in de Lisser's *Jane's Career.* Young black and brown Jamaican women were migrating from the country and joining the urban work force in unprecedented numbers at the beginning of the twentieth century, and what to make of the modern working woman was a subject of intense interest. Like de Lisser, MacDermot was fascinated by the urban middle-class home, which was both the contact point between the races and classes of Jamaica and a microcosm of the emerging creole nation. Accordingly, in *One Brown Girl And—*, the servant Ada is presented as a more complex figure than even the putative heroine Liberta. Ada is brown and relatively well educated, but she has few choices because, unlike Liberta, she has no money and must support herself. Ada considers it her social right to live a middle-class life and therefore sees no alternative but to marry a respectable brown man or become a mistress of a dissolute white one.

The story's lone brown man, Harold, is rendered not in heroic terms but as an ordinary man with ordinary morals. Harold finds Ada sexually attractive but does not wish to marry her, and she goes off with Meffala. Unlike Philip and the author of *Adolphus,* MacDermot does not attempt to avoid or erase the stereotype of brown female promiscuity through his portrayal of brown women; rather, his earnest depiction of Ada's dilemma shows her as, yes, of permeable morals, but as also having serious economic incentives to choose the wrong path. Even the chaste Liberta suspects that own her respectability and desirability hinge on her money, or lack thereof. She worries that her English suitor, a naval captain, wants her only for her wealth; she is anxious that she looks too black—the "plague mark"—and that if she marries him her children will show their African ancestry. Even with this fear of blackness, Liberta exhibits indignant racial pride; she believes that her English suitor is reluctant, having to "persuad[e] himself first, and his people in England afterwards, that I am an exception to other Jamaican brown girls" (18). She imagines that they ask if her hair is "very woolly" and that he replies, "Only a little wavy.... She is not black ... and I can tell you she is as well educated as you are and indeed a great deal better for she started with some natural advantage of having some brain" (18).

The third main character in *One Brown Girl And—*, the black Meffala servant Fidelia Stanton, represents black female beauty and respectability. Similar to the descriptions of the brown heroines of *Emmanuel Appadocca* and *Adolphus,* MacDermot's description of her is animated by the racialist view of European physiognomical superiority, even as Fidelia's looks are meant to contradict it. Her beautiful face "contradicted the opinion that every black face has the same broad features, the flattened nose, the low forehead, the thick lips" (42). Again, we read of a high forehead, not low; thin lips, not thick; narrow features, not broad. Before Fidelia utters a word, her intelligence is linked to her beauty, and her beauty is African, yet not black.[50]

MacDermot uses Fidelia to upend the idea that black people are immoral savages; like his nineteenth-century brown forebears, he too is invested in revising European stereotypes about African heritage. Fidelia's virginal rectitude is the result of her African heritage, we are told:

> To this day tribes of the Upper Creek River, where the backwash of European advance has not corrupted the simple but vital virtues, take rigid precautions to preserve their girls' chastity. In some cases so rigid is the tribal conception of this virtue that a girl is held to be unchaste if a man, other than her nearest blood relations, has even touched her person. Neat, clean, grave-looking Fidelia Stanton, with blood in her veins [was] drawn from a source such as we have indicated. (42)

When the dissolute John Meffala attempts to sexually assault her, she hits him. Fidelia's natural chastity and pride are contrasted with the viciousness and greed of her employer, Mrs. Meffala (who, when her son dies, worries about the loss of the five hundred pounds of insurance money). Mrs. Meffala accuses Fidelia of "laying traps" for her son, to which Fidelia replies, "I am a woman.... I am not different to you or your daughter. If a man had spoken so to your own daughter or to you, My God, would you not strike him?" (47).

If *One Brown Girl And—* is a novel about brown identity as *the* Caribbean identity, as I assert here, why then should MacDermot be so assiduous in making the case for African female chastity? Again, the answer lies in the Africaneity of blackness, not in the blackness of blackness. Although these novels posit Englishness as a citizenship ideal, African *heritage*—if not actually visible African cultural manifestations, such as language or religion, for example—is also posited as contributing essential ingredients to the moral character of the brown hero or heroine. MacDermot's novel is not really about the one brown heroine, after all; rather it is a rebuttal of the idea that brown women, the backbone of middle-class society, have innate inclinations toward unchaste behavior. He uses a black female character to prove that the brown heroine's rectitude is the result of her African heritage, not in spite of it. Any promiscuity on the part of a brown female, such as Ada, is the result of circumstance: it is economics and white creole prejudice that create sexual immorality, not African heritage. As we have seen in the earlier texts, the exoneration of black sexuality is a necessary component in the consolidation of brownness as the organizing cultural principle of middle-class Caribbean identity.

The First Black Heroine: *Jane's Career*

The most intriguing of all of these early novels is de Lisser's *Jane's Career*.[51] It is ironic that this Caribbean novel, written by a "white" defender of imperialism, was the first to use a black (not brown) working-class woman as the central heroine. As I have indicated, de Lisser was a complex figure, one who at different times inhabited two different social classes and two different races, and who flirted with two widely divergent political ideologies. His novels, almost all of them first serialized for a local audience, focus almost exclusively on black or brown women's lives. His first—and best—novel, *Jane's Career*, tells the story of a poor black woman, whereas his later stories concentrate on brown people, from the poor but attractive brown heroine of the eponymous *Susan Proudleigh* (1915), who marries up, to the financially secure brown man who marries a poor but ambitious Englishwoman in *Under the Sun: A Jamaica Comedy* (1937), to the rebellious brown heroine of the adventure story *Morgan's Daughter* (1953). Nevertheless it is the black woman's story in *Jane's Career* that best reflects an aesthetic "brownness." Its brilliance is that it consciously refuses easy co-optation by any constituency.

The story follows the format of the classic bildungsroman. The heroine Jane is an ambitious but poor, virtuous, black peasant girl. Seeking a better life, she leaves her rural Jamaican home to work as a live-in maid in the home of a brown family in the city of Kingston. She learns about life the hard way. Domestic service is rendered as a form of slavery: Jane's brown employer, Mrs. Mason, is pretentious, racist, physically abusive, and pathologically cheap; and Mrs. Mason's stupid but predatory nephew sexually exploits her. Seeking more freedom and more money, Jane moves in with a friend and goes to work in a factory. But "independence" is no picnic either. Factory work is tedious and pays little; Jane's black supervisor sexually harasses her; and Jane's jealous roommate kicks her out of their bungalow. Jane's dilemma is presented as a conflict between virtue and pragmatism. The moral virtues instilled in Jane from her rural upbringing seem anachronistic and useless in the face of the different social fabric and new economic landscape of the city. Despite her excellent work ethic and good character, Jane is never far from destitution, and she fears that like all of the other black working girls she meets, she too will have to take on a male "friend" to support herself. In Jane's case, she must choose destitution or the black supervisor who will fire her if she doesn't become his mistress.

What has any of this to do with brownness, ideological or physiognomical? The author appears to be most interested in black womanhood, not brown. Indeed, brown characters are the most villainous, to the point where, as one black servant declares, "I know that God meck two colour, black an' white, but it must be de devil meck brown people, for dem is neider black nor white!" (56). De Lisser goes out of his way to illustrate the pretentiousness of brown privilege next to "real" white privilege:

> Jane still admitted that Mrs. Mason was a lady, but Jane felt that Mrs. Mason was only a lady of sorts. She lived in a street where all the houses were small and shabby, and if she did have the merit of possessing a brown complexion, if at least one-half of her physical composition was white, there were thousands of others lighter in colour than she could claim to be. More, there were a few thousand white people in Kingston, and of these Jane had seen not a few. What was Mrs. Mason compared with these?...Kingston contained about a million people, and...vast numbers of these were white. What was Mrs. Mason among so many?...Who, after all, was Mrs. Mason? (69)

It seems as if de Lisser has an investment similar to that of later Caribbean nationalists in denuding brownness of its social power by identifying only two "real" categories for Caribbean identity—black identity, originating in a rural heritage and with its own language; and white identity, a center of "real" economic privilege and "real" society. Mrs. Mason puts on social airs although it is clear her origins are far from wealthy: she speaks "broken" English, much like her servants do, a characteristic meant to show her crassness, lack of education, and stupidity.

By contrast, de Lisser's portrait of his black heroine is admiring; when she, or the other black characters, speak in Creole dialect, it is not meant to be taken as a sign of lack of intelligence, as it is with Mrs. Mason. Jane is unpretentious and honest, and decidedly not brown. Although she appears to have "some white ancestor," Jane is described as "darker, strongly built and robust." Her beauty does not conform to the standards of middle-class society, but that is of little import, since "any one accustomed to the Jamaican peasant's appearance would have pronounced her good-looking, an opinion with which she would have entirely agreed" (12). Jane represents a new breed—the independent black working woman, confident and cognizant of her own value—whose members are flocking to the city looking for a new life. De Lisser sees these young women as the foundation of a modern, urban black sensibility. He consciously de-links them from the bygone passive plantation-era stereotype represented by Jane's mother, a well-meaning but subservient woman who urges Jane to be a "good girl" and obey the abusive Mrs. Mason; Jane becomes estranged from her mother, and her upbringing, when she understands that subservience is antithetical to independence. In this perception she follows her compatriots, who dislike domestic work and see themselves as the equal of their brown employer. When Mrs. Mason tries to cheat the other female servants of their pay, they call the police; when she curses them, they curse her back—with interest. The author says of this new breed, "They were rebels; they had no humility in them; in their own way they had aspirations; they wanted to be free" (102).

Jane's "career" is her movement from poor peasant girl to married, middle-class matron; her journey is that of the new black middle class. Similar to Jane's journey is that of Bita Plant in Claude McKay's *Banana Bottom*. McKay's educated heroine returns to the country, rejects respectable brown suitors, has a baby out of wedlock, and then marries her lover, a humble black laborer—albeit with her own home and inheritance. McKay's primitivist romance makes it necessary for the middle-class Bita to consciously choose rural heritage and custom—with its disregard for the legalities of wedlock and "legitimate" children—in order to validate his thesis about the equality of black peasant society and "civilized" society. De Lisser's story is far more realistic, and accordingly, Jane's trajectory moves in the other direction. She rejects the country for the city, becomes the common-law wife of an enterprising brown (not black) printer, and ascends to middle-class status. They live in a suburb where "to be a resident there is to bear the hall-mark of respectability, and a house [there] is eagerly sought after by those persons of the lower middle class who are blessed with social aspirations" (192). De Lisser tells us, with some irony, that this new personality "is Jane perfectly contented at last, and dreaming of no higher fortune. It is Jane, who now herself employs a schoolgirl, who submissively calls her Miss Jane, and obeys her slightest command" (196). Like Bita, Jane, after having a baby, decides with her common-law husband to make their union legal. They have a grand marriage, with all of the garish accoutrements of the newly arrived. Mrs. Mason's fashionable nieces make a point of attending the wedding because, now that Jane is respectable, she is their social equal. The novel concludes with the image of Mrs. Mason's nieces stretching out their hands to Jane, whose "cup of joy was full."

Critic Kenneth Ramchand argues that de Lisser turns on his black heroine at the conclusion, driving her into an "imitative dead-end"; in this way, according to Ramchand, the novel is similar to V. S. Naipaul's critique of Caribbean mimicry of European identity in his 1969 novel *The Mimic Men*. Further, Ramchand believes that the authorial about-face at the end mirrors de Lisser's "real-life attitudes" toward black people and his gradual loss of sympathy for them.[52] I don't think what we are reading indicates a "loss of sympathy" for black people, just a final stab at brown people.

The novel's concluding embrace of brown people and middle-class status reveals the working-class origins of brown middle-class identity; by showing Jane's ascension, de Lisser strikes at what he considers the pretensions to high society by the brown middle class. The joke is not on Jane—she got her just reward, and we're happy for her; the joke is on her erstwhile employer, Mrs. Mason. The seismic shift taking place in Jamaica's color-coded society is the novel's central theme, and brownness is a central trope in that new alignment. Brownness starts out villainous and ends up triumphant, but with its lowly pedigree exposed. Jane is assaulted by one brown man and marries another; she is abused by the brown matron but welcomed by the brown nieces. If indeed Jane is imitating the brown social class that once derided her, her mimicry is represented as the inevitable result of those "social aspirations" with which the ambitious are "blessed." And if brown peoples' sins are imitation and rank hypocrisy, for de Lisser those drawbacks are still, apparently, preferable to black political power, the ominous specter haunting the fringes of the story.

One of the most intriguing incidents in the novel concerns Jane's husband, Vincent Broglie, who is a leader of the impending printers' strike. The description of the strike is rooted in a historical event: in 1908–9, the printers of Jamaica formed a trade union and struck for higher wages. One of the leaders of that strike was Marcus Garvey, who would go on to become one of the most famous Pan-Africanists of the twentieth century. The novel focuses on the strike to an unsettling degree, given that it appears to have little relationship to Jane's "career." An indignant de Lisser dwells on the image of middle-class black and brown men demanding more money and benefits. The novel also makes several references to the American union agitators who are stirring up trouble on the island. Vincent's employer, a benevolent white man, urges Vincent not to join the strikers who have led him astray, a view with which Jane concurs. She is worried that the would-be strikers will betray Vincent and that he will lose his comfortable position. De Lisser informs us that Jane's antiunion views are in sync with those of the working classes, whose distrust of the strikers' motives illustrates their pragmatism and good sense (175). At one point de Lisser pointedly aligns Vincent's predicament with Jane's: when Jane tells Vincent that she has decided to become her supervisor's mistress because she has no other economic option, she echoes her own advice to him on the strike, "Can't do better, an' it's no use forming [acting] independent when y'u know that y'u can't afford it" (187).

Vincent wisely chooses not to strike and reaps the reward in the form of a job promotion and a happy marriage to Jane. The new lower-middle-class community in which he and Jane live is resolutely apolitical: "it cares little about politics; it simply loves to think of itself as poor but respectable" (192). In marking this characteristic, de Lisser is delineating the difference between this kind of desirable black middle class and that of the discontented strikers, who are not content to wait for progress in their economic and social life to be decided on by the ruling class (170). Jane and Vincent, despite their hard work and independent characters, cannot, ultimately, "form independent" on their own. So Jane finds herself a respectable brown man, and Vincent stays with his respectable white man; the social order is preserved, and the new black middle class, minus its independent political ambitions, is welcomed into the ranks of respectable Jamaican life. The novel is a colonialist appropriation of rising black social power. For de Lisser, so admiring of black women yet so fearful of black men, a black middle class is fine as long as it doesn't "form independent." So, too, a brown middle class is fine if it has no pretensions to whiteness. De Lisser clearly had an investment in preserving the old colonial order. If we consider that de Lisser was a brown man until he was "whitened" by his enhanced social pedigree, his searing indictment of brown middle-class pretensions may be read as an erasure of his own past. Jane's "career" from poor black peasant to "browned" middle-class matron reveals the blackness latent in brown middle-class respectability; by contrast, de Lisser made no such examination of the white elite society to which he claimed allegiance. The mystification and reinvention of ethnic and class origins are, after all, a brown story.

The trajectory of the "brown" novel covers a wide ideological sweep, from Philip's antislavery agenda through de Lisser's imperialist nostalgia, from Cobham's peculiar brand of Anglophilic Pan-Africanism through MacDermot's equally peculiar brand of Afrocentric Anglophilia. What connects these disparate novels is their one constant: a commitment to a social agenda that views a "brown"-identified Caribbean middle class as the foundation of modern Caribbean society. Maxwell Philip and the author of *Adolphus* wrote fiction that naturalizes brownness by valorizing its African antecedents while erasing its black creole connections; by contrast, black Cobham and "white" de Lisser were committed to exposing the black creole roots of brownness. In all of these racial maneuvers, women's sexuality is the most slippery category. Chaste black and brown women are necessary for the claims of black and brown nationalism, yet these stories provide tantalizing glimpses into a treacherous sexual universe that suggests a more complex portrait than that of harlot or victim.

These early novels also illustrate the constantly shifting terrain of blackness in the Caribbean. Blackness here, as in later texts, is read as an international identity as much as a local one. The striking printers in *Jane's Career* are incited by a Garveyesque figure who has imported radical ideas of equality from the United States. In *Rupert Gray* prominent black men from around the world meet, in Pan-Africanist fashion, in London to envision a Tuskegee-like school for black people in the Caribbean. The narrator of *Emmanuel Appadocca* reminds us of the African American experience in making his case for brown equality. Both *Adolphus* and *One Brown Girl And*— utilize a heroic African past. These early novels were written for a local audience, and their "brown" concerns are ultimately local. Yet they persistently invoke, for good or ill, the wider black world. They challenge current views that it was only the "serious" literature of later generations that engaged the ideas of global blackness. If we recognize this shift, then the distinctions made between the popular and the serious, the local and the international—distinctions on which Caribbean literary criticism is founded—begin to blur. The omnivorous ideological brownness found here, so out of critical favor, flying as it has under the canonical radar, is nevertheless a constitutive element of popular Caribbean nationalism. It has threaded through much of the cultural expressions of succeeding eras all the way to the stories of the present postcolonial moment.

CHAPTER 3

Gentrifying Dialect, or the Taming of Miss Lou

> From the beginning nobody ever recognized me as a writer.
>
> —Louise Bennett, interview in *Caribbean Quarterly*, 1968

On August 9, 2006, Jamaicans were riveted to the funeral of the Honorable Louise Bennett Coverley, member of the British Empire and Order of Jamaica. The wildly popular Jamaican folklorist, actress, and poet had died at the age of eighty-seven. Miss Lou, as she was called informally, had been almost single-handedly responsible for legitimizing the use of Jamaican Creole, or "dialect,"[1] in the island's schools and in the arts. Miss Lou's career had spanned an incredible seventy years. An icon of true Jamaicanness, she wrote dialect poems that are standard fare in Jamaican national elocution contests, and recordings of her recitations occupy Air Jamaica's entire on-flight folk channel.[2] Miss Lou's importance to modern Jamaica was underscored by her state funeral, attended by prime ministers past and present. The tributes were effusive. As one politician put it, "She more than any other brought recognition and value to our indigenous culture, our folklore, our dialect... the things that indelibly make us who and what we are—Jamaican."[3] Miss Lou, her casket draped with a large Jamaican flag, was laid to rest in Jamaica's National Heroes Park, as befitted her status of Jamaican national icon.

It was not always thus.

Forty-odd years ago, V. S. Naipaul, no champion of Caribbean working-class culture, wryly commented on popular resistance to the use of Creole speech in Caribbean writing:

GENTRIFYING DIALECT, OR THE TAMING OF MISS LOU 87

> The lively and inventive Trinidad dialect, which has won West Indian writing many friends and as many enemies abroad, is disliked by some West Indians. *They do not object to its use locally;* the most popular column in Trinidad is a dialect column in the *Evening News* by the talented and witty person known as Macaw. But they object to its use in books which are read abroad. "They must be does talk so by you," one woman said to me. "They don't talk so by me." The Trinidadian expects his novels... to have a detergent purpose, and it is largely for this reason that there are complaints about the scarcity of writing about what is called the middle class.[4]

Naipaul's observation—that it is the people (specifically, the middle class) who police their own literature as much as any literary critic—is a challenge to the view that it is postcolonial critics who are responsible for the two-tiered system of literature that prevails.[5] So too is the career of Louise Bennett, which reveals the politics of the evolving Caribbean middle class as does that of perhaps no other writer.

The career of Miss Lou is both representative and singular: representative in that it embodies the terminal trajectory of the local dialect writer, as does Naipaul's long-lost "Macaw"; singular for its length and its not insignificant part in the reification of Creole into a global signifier of Caribbean originality. Her Jamaica-centric (or more accurately, Kingston-centric) focus notwithstanding, in international circles Miss Lou is the best known of a welter of obscure Caribbean dialect poets-cum folklorists—writers and actors who came to local prominence in the 1950s and later. Aside from Miss Lou, these authors, such as Guyana's Wordsworth McAndrew and Ken Corsbie, and perhaps the most famous regionally, Trinidad's Paul Keens-Douglas,[6] are a by-product of the quest to legitimize "authentic" Caribbean culture as heralded by a clutch of influential Caribbean arts magazines of the mid-twentieth century, such as Barbados's *Bim,* Jamaica's *Focus,* and Guyana's *Kyk-Over-Al.* (As comic "folklorists," however, none of these writers would have appeared in their pages; Miss Lou once complained that "I was never thought good enough to be represented in that anthology *Focus.*")[7] Critics have already linked these magazines to the surge in literary activity in the Anglophone Caribbean during the latter half of the twentieth century. Less investigated is the effect that surging nationalism had on local, popular middle-class artists whose audiences were themselves heavily middle class. Usually comic radio personalities or newspaper columnists, these writers were—and are—beloved quotidian presences in the lives of the Caribbean middle classes, but emphatically and distinctly their work is not meant for international consumption.

Miss Lou's case is unusual in that her career began in the 1930s, more than a decade before the popular clamoring for independence in the Anglophone Caribbean.

Miss Lou and the other writers did not, of course, invent the first dialect fiction or poetry. Nor was Miss Lou, or even Claude McKay, the first published author of a book of dialect poetry. (That honor goes to Barbados's Edward Alexander Cordle, who in 1903 published *Overheard,* a book of dialect poems, in Bridgetown.) Nor did they popularize it: there was a taste for dialect poetry even in the Caribbean of the late nineteenth century, as we have seen. The significance of these popular performers lies in the way their renditions of Creole speech and their visions of Caribbean life have been so seamlessly integrated with state interests in the postcolonial Caribbean. Wearing an anachronistic Madras "head tie" and peasant dress, the iconic image of Miss Lou reflects a vision of "authentic" Jamaica that, curiously, disturbs neither the black-identified Jamaican government's vision of an independent creole nation, nor nostalgic tourist visions of a land of pleasant peasants, nor the old plantocracy's version of a colonial state.

Dialect performers, as opposed to today's working-class-identified Spoken Word poets such as Jamaican Rastafarian Bongo Jerry or former convict Oku Onoura, were hardly antiestablishment types. They inevitably hailed from the middle class themselves. The conventional middle class may well have frowned on the use of Creole speech in public, but it had no problem accepting it from its own members on radio, stage, or other popular venues. Indeed, evidence suggests that the genesis of today's popular, working-class-associated dub poetry and Spoken Word performances in the Caribbean lies in the stage and radio performances of artists from this earlier, more genteel, generation.

Lest we assume this phenomenon was mostly Jamaican, it is critical to emphasize that some of the earliest examples of the connection between popular performance and Caribbean literature can be found elsewhere. For example, in colonial Guyana (then British Guiana) the advent of film generated the original indigenous theater movement. Local performers seized the opportunity to present their "dialect playlets" before cinema audiences. In 1916, one of these performers, Portuguese Guyanese comedian Sidney Martin, published a collection of his sketches and witticisms. In the 1920s, Afro-Guyanese actor Sam Chase performed his dialect plays before both urban and rural audiences and even toured other Caribbean islands such as Trinidad, spreading dialect performance as a genre. A contemporary of Miss Lou and a performer whose career spanned forty-four years, Chase created plays based on contemporary events, and he invited audiences to decide the outcomes.[8]

FIGURE 2. Louise Bennett, from the cover of *Jamaica Labrish* (1966 ed., published by Sangster's Book Stores, Kingston). Courtesy of Sangster's Bookstores, Jamaica.

Meanwhile, in Jamaica as early as 1931, popular Afro-Jamaican actor and comedian Ernest M. Cupidon was part of a multiethnic cast who performed the theatrical version of de Lisser's novel *Susan Proudleigh,* and he was singled out for enthusiastic praise by reviewers for his portrayal of "everyday people" who spoke in patois. Cupidon is a central, if little studied, actor in the history of Caribbean dialect performance in that he was the first actor to bring dialect into the widely influential but "serious" Jamaican theater.[9] In one review, the critic enthuses that the "burlesque of Jamaica peasant life" played four performances before packed houses at Kingston's respectable Ward Theatre and asserts that

> "Cupid" had discovered that a Jamaican audience is happiest laughing at itself or rather, at caricatures of people whom it meets any day of the week. At first the idea must have sounded audacious even to the originator [de Lisser] and we may be sure that when the box-plan first opened, all those who were in any way responsible for "Susan Proudleigh" must have had some anxious moments. The tremendous success... is concrete proof that Jamaica is not only giving birth to an art essentially native, but is capable of appreciating that art.[10]

The passage reveals what the reviewer thinks is essential for a "native art form": the representation of "ordinary," peasant or working-class, people; and a theater-going audience that recognizes portrayals of these people as a form of art. The importance of local artists such as Cupidon lies in their paving of the way for legitimation of Creole speech and Creole culture by representing them as worthy of art. They gave Caribbean societies a way to see themselves.

The problem, of course, is the laughter.

The middle-class audience appears to be laughing *at* the black, patois-speaking characters of *Susan Proudleigh*. In the interstices of the reviewer's amended comment that the Jamaican audience most enjoys "laughing at itself *or rather,* at caricatures of people whom it meets any day of the week" is a world of ambiguity. The audience recognizes itself in the dialect-speaking characters because local dialect is a signifier of Jamaicanness. But the middle-class audience would have been horrified if anyone had suggested that those comic characters represented the members of the audience themselves. Recognition brings laughter, but also fear. Does laughter reflect kinship or alienation? The problem for the brown and black middle classes of the Caribbean is not their distance from the Creole-speaking working class, but precisely their proximity to it.[11] In the English-speaking Caribbean, certainly in the mid-twentieth century, the middle class was not so well

GENTRIFYING DIALECT, OR THE TAMING OF MISS LOU 91

FIGURE 3. Ernest Cupidon and the cast of *Susan Proudleigh,* from *The New Cosmopolitan* (February 1931), pp. 20 and 21. Courtesy of the National Library of Jamaica.

established that it could acknowledge its own black, or Asian, working-class or rural roots without fear of social backsliding. Creole is not something that resides only in lowest economic registers of Caribbean society; it is also the lingua franca of the middle classes, who have always used what Gordon Rohlehr calls a linguistic spectrum, from standard grammar to Creole, for personal and public uses, moving easily among the various social registers of Caribbean society.[12] Yet whether as "broken" or "bad" English, or as anticolonial, African-identified "nation-language" (to use Kamau Brathwaite's phrase), Creole has been so firmly established as the antithesis of English that to an emergent middle class, for whom the acquisition of "proper" grammar was an essential characteristic of class identity and an article of faith in the armament of social identity, to identify with Creole speech beyond the realm of the apparently superficial or nonserious entertainments of the comic play would have been unthinkable.

It is this push-pull factor—the simultaneous recognition and rejection—that accounts both for the popularity of dialect poetry and performance in the Caribbean and for the traditional academic difficulty encountered in attempting to move these art forms beyond the ephemeral level of popular performance to the printed page. Print means "for the record," and the record is, inevitably, aimed at the international audience—it means analysis, and analysis is "real." Performance is fleeting and local. It cannot be pinned down, it is inevitably tied to entertainment. In other words, it is popular culture. For the logocentric professional classes, the oral and the written have inevitably occupied two separate spheres of existence. Traditionally, even when the dialect poem or play was committed to print, from a middle-class perspective it retained the categorical features of the oral performance: local production, comic packaging.

Yet the surge of nationalist sentiment that accompanied independence from Britain in the 1960s for most of the English-speaking Caribbean meant that these respectable dialect performers could now be celebrated for the very quality that rendered them unserious—their local appeal. In the rush to identify what is truly West Indian, dialect performance filled a niche. It was indigenous. It was popular. Its reliance on old folk stories and proverbs accorded with the state's imperative to elevate folk culture to reflect a more autonomous version of Caribbean history. Shortly put, it was now respectable and therefore ripe for the state seal of approval. Indeed, the identification of this earlier generation of dialect performers with (newly minted) tradition is so inevitable that one well-known Jamaican writer sees Miss Lou as his literary antithesis. When asked how he saw himself as a writer in relation to Miss Lou, the author responded testily that he saw her as a sort of "Cro-Magnon" or "Aunt Jemima" figure who spoke only in a "comedic and countrified" voice ("countrified" despite the fact that Miss Lou was a product of the city and reproduced the language of its inhabitants), not the gritty, sensual urban voice he wished to emulate. "I could not have become who I am with Miss Lou," he concluded.[13] Echoing these sentiments, Colin Channer recalls that his discovery of the working-class dub poet Mutabaruka evoked an epiphany: that "the time had come to skank away from the wheel-and-tun of her [Miss Lou's] *mento-minded minstrelsy,* for a poetry grounded in the esthetics of reggae, and its compelling argument...that Caribbean art would achieve its highest height when it broke out of the space that it was deeded by a White man system preserved by its brown inheritors."[14]

It seems that for a younger, particularly middle-class, generation of male writers, Miss Lou is merely a colonial-style nostalgia act, someone whose cheerful evocation of city life is akin to a "countrifying" of the city, a denial of the violence and complexity of urban reality. In the same vein, young Jamaican writer Marlon James links his own use of dialect to American writers and rejects the "patronizing" use of dialect by earlier Jamaican novelists such as Roger Mais, who, he writes, held the "belief that anything in patois must be a Louise Bennett minstrel show."[15] Their emphasis on Aunt Jemima and minstrelsy suggests an American vantage point, not a Caribbean one: few Jamaicans or other Caribbean nationals would have much knowledge of these African American stereotypes. By contrast, the comparatively young, middle-class Jamaican female poet Joan Andrea Hutchinson casts herself as an heir to Louise Bennett. She embraces Bennett's visual persona of the large, garrulous black woman and performs similar dialect poetry for radio, stage, and downloading; Hutchinson's dialect poetry books are ubiquitous in Jamaica. Her work is now lauded by the very academy that shunned Miss Lou decades earlier.[16] So although the working-class view of Miss Lou appears to be universal admiration, middle-class views are refracted by gender politics and a self-conscious view of what "foreigners" may see when they look at a fat black woman in peasant costume. It cannot have helped that Louise Bennett—like so many first-rate Caribbean performers who have had bit parts in American comedies set in the Caribbean—was relegated to playing an ethnically stereotyped character in the 1986 film *Club Paradise*. Certainly from an American perspective, her role as the large, and loud, turbaned black cook in a tourist hotel appears distinctly Aunt Jemima–like. Miss Lou's crime is her "minstrel," "comedic" voice and her ability to make people laugh. At what, precisely, are they laughing?

Even Mervyn Morris, the first Jamaican literary critic to recognize the value of Louise Bennett's poetry, acknowledged in 1963 that middle-class audiences and readers may have, with their laughter, distorted the purpose of the poetry and distanced themselves from the stigma of the illiterate Creole speaker who could speak only Creole and nothing more.[17] In this critique, the young critics of Louise Bennett sound similar to the African American critics of the 1930s who denounced Zora Neale Hurston, the Harlem Renaissance author, for caricaturing black people and invoking racist stereotypes through the use of exclusively dialect-speaking characters. Ironically, black nationalist working-class icon Mutabaruka, their acknowledged role model, was also a favorite of Miss Lou, and he credits her with being the creator of two undeniably working-class, male-associated artistic forms, dub poetry (the Jamaican ancestor of Spoken Word, which melds "dub" rhythms to poetry) and deejaying.[18] After her death Mutabaruka lamented, "When we hear Miss Lou we neva tek har serious... [yet] Miss Lou wasn't just a comic. Miss Lou was a social commentator."[19]

What to make of such distinctly opposed views of the cultural legacy of Louise Bennett? What are the stakes in acknowledging or rejecting her influence? By way of answer, I sketch the trajectory by which Miss Lou and the first generation of modern dialect performers became the establishment, and yet not.

"Not Even Lickle Language Bwoy?" Alienation and Dialect

Part of the humor in Naipaul's comment on the rejection of Creole by the middle-class is Naipaul's acerbity in noting that one of the objectors to Creole literature herself spoke in Creole, even as she makes a class distinction between who she is and who those Creole speakers are. The funny anecdote underscores the very unfunny problem, for Caribbean writers bent on writing "serious" literature in 1962, of using Creole speech. Naipaul's early Caribbean novels, steeped in dialect-inflected grammar, were highly influential in illustrating for other canonical writers, such as Derek Walcott, how to capture the complexity and energy of Creole on the page. But inflecting standard English with regional Creole speech patterns is not the same thing as writing entirely in Creole. Times have changed since the 1930s, when C. L. R. James and other members of the Beacon group complained about the lack of Creole speech in Caribbean literature. Now the use of Creole speech is de rigueur in Caribbean fiction.

What has not changed, however, is Creole's status in "serious" fiction. Excepting the poetry of Barbadian critic and poet Kamau Brathwaite, whose international reputation arguably rests as much on his work as a historian and literary critic as it does on his poetry, there is no important, internationally disseminated work of literature in the Caribbean that is written entirely in Creole. This problem transcends the Caribbean. In 1982, when Kenyan writer and critic Ngũgĩ wa Thiong'o declared that from then on he would write fiction only in his native language of Gikuyu, his declaration was hailed as radical, but it was so only because Ngũgĩ wa Thiong'o is an internationally recognized author. Moreover, his reputation is such that he can get his work translated into other languages (although he continues to write his more influential criticism in English). For writers like Miss Lou who always wrote in dialect, there can be no after-the-fact ascription of radical literary politics to their preferred narrative mode.

Claude McKay is, like Miss Lou, recognized in the Caribbean as one of the first authors to write dialect poetry and to champion it as a medium for expressing complex and profound ideas. Although it was once popular in Jamaica, his dialect poetry is no longer performed. Not that this matters: McKay's dialect poetry has found an eternal home in successive anthologies of African American and world literature—a very different afterlife than that of most fleeting newspaper poetry, and a very different, international, audience than the local one for which the poems were intended when they first appeared in the *Gleaner*.[20] In McKay's case, our traditional associations of the rural with insularity and the urban with cosmopolitanism are belied by the politics of literary mobility, what makes one dialect poet canonical and the other merely popular. The internationally famous McKay was a rural-born Jamaican whose particular kind of dialect poetry reflects his rural origins. Only after McKay became famous as a writer of the Harlem Renaissance did critics look back to these early dialect poems. It seems fair to speculate that McKay's use of dialect in his local poetry was made to accord with his use of dialect in his "primitivist" novels, after the fact. International readers of McKay's poetry could thus assume that it was influenced by, and was part of, American artistic movements rather than the outgrowth of a Jamaica-centric interest in homegrown culture, as facilitated by newspapers, literary clubs and other popular venues.

Unlike the internationally famous, rural-born McKay, the locally famous Miss Lou was Kingston born. Her use of dialect is an amalgam of the voices of city (not country) life that she heard around her,[21] together with the folk tales and proverbs that, like Zora Neale Hurston, she collected assiduously for decades. Even a cursory look at her poems confirms their urban, street-culture focus: "South Parade Peddler" (South Parade is an area in downtown Kingston); "Rough-Ridin Tram"; "Strike Day"; "Pedestrian Crosses." Why, then, is Miss Lou associated with rural culture? Even laudatory critics refer to her poetry as being in the "traditional folk poetry" mold, implying rural origin.[22] The disdainful conflation of the "countrified and comedic" voice some writers impute to Miss Lou may be an outgrowth of the traditional contempt in which rural culture has been held by those from the more cosmopolitan cities of the Americas. The fear of appearing "bush" or "country-booky"—that is, provincial, uneducated, and "backward"—is still prevalent in Caribbean societies, apparently even among its new, young authors. The current trend toward identifying Caribbeanness with urban culture is accelerated not simply by the burgeoning of city populations in the region but also by the rejection of the supposed traits of peasant culture that are associated with racist, old images of colonialism and slavery: cheerfulness, passivity, stupidity, compliance.

On the other side of the coin are the intellectuals who romance rural peasant culture as the site of truly authentic, revolutionary Caribbean identity. McKay and other early nationalist writers, such as Haiti's Jacques Romain, typify this approach; for them it is the city that is associated with the imitative and passive colonial presence, and the country with the deeply ingrained, African-identified tradition of resistance.[23] Yet the rural-urban split has never been so strict as champions of either side would have it: many lyrics by urban ghetto dweller Bob Marley, for instance, are beholden to old folk sayings that can also be found in Louise Bennett's poetry. In particular, Marley's 1970s-era lyrics in "Them Bellyful (But We Hungry)" reproduce almost exactly Bennett's wartime-era poem "Dutty Tough" (The ground is hard), written more than thirty years earlier[24]:

"Them Belly Full (But We Hungry)"	"Dutty Tough"
Them belly full but we hungry	Sun a shine but tings no bright;
A hungry mob is an angry mob	Doah pot a bwile, bickle no nuff
A rain a fall but the dutty tough	River flood but water scarce, yaw;
A pot a cook but the food no 'nough	Rain a fall but dutty tough.
	[The sun is shining but things aren't bright
	Though a pot boils, the food's not enough
	The river floods but water's scarce, yes;
	Rain is falling but the dirt is tough.]

Whether Marley took his inspiration from the old folk proverb of "dutty tough" or from Bennett's popular poem is hard to tell, but the confluence of the two, not simply in phrasing but in meaning, suggests that the convenient oppositions of urban and folk culture distilled in the iconographies of Marley and Miss Lou are fairly meaningless.

A brief biography of Louise Bennett is necessary here. The daughter of a prosperous baker and a dressmaker, Miss Lou grew up in the black, solidly middle-class community of early twentieth-century Kingston (with some time spent in the rural parish of St. Mary). After she won a poetry contest at the age of seventeen, she started writing seriously. Her efforts culminated in two books of poetry, several books of Anancy stories for children, as well as other folklore compilations. Bennett also wrote a newspaper column, "Miss Lulu Sez," and had a local radio show, "Miss Lou's Views." She left the island to live briefly in Harlem, where she performed in plays; when she returned to Jamaica, she helped to found the modern Jamaican theater, creating and performing in the first Pantomime plays that continue to this day. As she herself pointed out, however, she was a writer long before she became a performer: her early "dulcet" verses were more or less the sort of excruciatingly bad Victorian poetry churned out by the Jamaican Poetry League (which, ironically, ignored the later dialect poetry for which she became famous).[25] An incident on a crowded Kingston tram car in the 1930s changed her forever. In an interview with critic Mervyn Morris, Bennett recalls that she wrote

GENTRIFYING DIALECT, OR THE TAMING OF MISS LOU   97

her first dialect poem, "On a Tram Car," after she boarded a packed tram car and heard a country woman say to another, "'Pread out yuhself, one dress-oman a come" (Spread yourself out, a well-dressed woman is coming). The class tensions evident in the woman's comment were the genesis for an entire corpus of dialect poetry. Miss Lou wrote the poem not from her viewpoint as a middle-class woman in a working-class public space, but rather in the voice of her working-class verbal assailant:

> Pread out yuhself deh Liza, one
> Dress-oman dah look like she
> She see de li space side-a we
> And waan foce herself een deh.
> [Spread out yourself there Liza, that
> well-dressed woman is acting like
> She sees the little space on the side of us
> And wants to force herself in there.][26]

The first-person, female voice used for "Tram Car" would become the model for Miss Lou's dialect poetry—and for that of many of her cohorts in other Caribbean countries as well. (For example, Trinidadian dialect poet Paul Keens-Douglas has a central female figure, "Tantie Merle," who appears repeatedly in his poetry and stories, similar to Miss Lou's characters "Miss Mattie" and "Auntie Roachie," whom she is always addressing in her stories and verses.) Louise Bennett had hit a central nerve of Caribbean culture: the verbal dexterity of public women. The use of amusing female characters from which to view the life of the city—there are no male characters who recur in her work—may also be a way of deflecting criticisms of her social critique, similar to the way in which cartoonists deflect ire with humor. As Denise DeCaires Narain points out:

> Following this "epiphany," Bennett will make frequent use of women speakers modeled on women like those in the tram so that, paradoxically, their recognition of *her*—as a well-dressed, middle class young woman—results in her recognition of *them:* as powerful manipulators of the word. The social distance between the poet and the people she chooses to represent does not appear to have generated similarly troubling questions to those generated by early, white, colonial writers.[27]

Carolyn Cooper also notes the genesis of Miss Lou's use of Creole but concentrates on the tram car women as the "dispossessed": "tracings [curses] and other forms of verbal abuse are essential armaments in class warfare."[28] Cooper's emphasis on the politics of women's street language is a welcome correction to the old Man-of-Words model first propounded by Roger Abrahams,[29] but DeCaires Narain astutely notes that Caribbean critics are tentative in exploring the idea that Miss Lou functions not as an embodiment but as a ventriloquist of working-class speech: certainly Cooper's analysis reflects her investment in the serious business of using Creole at all. Bennett's double-edged use of Creole is part of the problem. Her poetry reveals a form of both class ventriloquism—this is how *those* working-class Jamaicans speak—as well as class representation: this is the way *we,* middle-class, people speak too, particularly when we are at leisure.[30] Dialect poetry thus becomes ironic, an in-group acknowledgment of common cause with the masses. Even more so, perhaps, Bennett's poetry reflects a common sense of cultural identity, whether or not it is based on an ironic, middle-class reflection that "this, too, is who we are," or, as Jahan Ramazani calls it, on "a humor-based liminal solidarity."[31]

Folk Culture versus Pop Culture

Although canonical writers like V. S. Naipaul, Derek Walcott, and Claude McKay make liberal use of Creole, the writer's voice is never the same as that of the Creole speaker. Naipaul often uses Creole for satirical purposes, revealing a serious underlying social critique. McKay and Walcott use Creole speech to dramatize the intellectual depth of the folk—which perhaps explains their lack of critical regard for Louise Bennett's oeuvre. Although Bennett's work may be satirical, it is never seen as representing the profundity of folk thought or folk culture—even when it does. Louise Bennett's written work is closely associated with her role as folk archivist, and with what may be called "genteel" folklore: folklore that uncritically reinforces existing paradigms, colonial or nationalist. Some critics have suggested that Bennett's poetic voice comes out of the oral Anancy story tradition, which is mostly associated with mothers telling stories to their children.[32] Indeed, an early anthology of Jamaican writing, titled ironically *Independence Anthology of Jamaican Writing,* categorized Miss Lou's poetry under "Miscellaneous," alongside an Anancy story.[33] The feminization of the Creole voice in her poetry, together with its link to a childhood story form, may also have something to do with its perceived lack of seriousness. It could not have helped that Miss Lou also created and starred in a popular children's television show, *Ring Ding* (1970–82), which cast her in a soft maternal light rather than one of a serious national writer. In the pre- and postindependence era, the persona of the author in Caribbean literature was, even when revealing the most radical visions of Caribbean society, inevitably cast in the Victorian "gentleman of letters" model.[34] The author cast an authoritative eye on the folk and functioned as a kind of scholarly interpreter for a serious readership. Louise Bennett, by contrast, was herself a character in her own poetic narratives, the dialect-speaking female storyteller and observer.

Louise Bennett made no apologies for her dual roles as street observer and folklore archivist. Nor did she rely on her own sketchy familiarity with Anancy stories. Instead, she relied on Walter Jekyll, the English expatriate folklorist who mentored McKay and methodicly collected Anancy stories in his 1906 book, *Jamaican Song and Story*. (This association may come as a surprise to supportive critics like Kamau Brathwaite, who labored to connect Miss Lou to rural culture in order to explain her knowledge of folklore: "Miss Lou's mother's and Miss Lou's own upbringing was 'rural St. Mary': hence the Honourable Louise's natural and rightful knowledge of the folk.")[35] Miss Lou recalls in the 1966 edition of Jekyll's book that "when I was collecting Jamaican folklore for use on the stage and trying desperately to remember some of the stories I knew as a child, a friend gave me a copy of Walter Jekyll's book.... I was overjoyed to find accurate retellings of many of the stories which I had forgotten.... Now there they all were in black and white." As Denise DeCaires Narain notes, although Miss Lou had grown up with these poems, she still required the written form to remember and reproduce them, a fact that may not sit well with the romanticized nationalist vision of Miss Lou. In this view she functions as a kind of authentic Jamaican griot, embodying the oral tradition by her long historical memory. In contrast, Jekyll's love affair with Jamaica reflected the unfortunate condescension typical of his era: his book is dedicated to Jamaicans, with "their winning ways and their many good qualities, among which is to be reckoned that supreme virtue, *Cheerfulness*." If Jekyll's fascination with Jamaican dialect stories reflects the "colonial obsession with information retrieval," as DeCaires Narain puts it, it also reflects the nationalist obsession with the same: folklorists are integral to all nation-building projects because they codify the nation's cultural history.[36] Miss Lou's role as archivist displaces that of the colonial-era Walter Jekylls and is lauded by the postcolonial state, but her archive is secondary to her persona as an embodiment of that archive. In other words, Miss Lou, *as* Miss Lou, essentializes Caribbean folk culture as something native and unchanging. It is this quality of embodying tradition that is the reason for Miss Lou's canonization—as well as the reason that she is regarded with something akin to ambivalence, or worse, by many of her contemporaries in the literary world.

Derek Walcott was a student at the University of the West Indies in Kingston, Jamaica, in the 1950s at the same time that Louise Bennett was jump-starting the Kingston theatrical scene. It was during this period that she became famous for one of her most important projects, the annual Kingston Pantomime. The Pantomime is, to this day, certainly Jamaica's most popular form of theater and attracts all segments of the society.[37] Walcott was influenced by the explosion of dialect-oriented theater in both Jamaica and Trinidad (where Beryl McBurnie had been incorporating local dialect into plays at her Little Carib Dance Theatre and lecturing on the use of indigenous forms at the University of the West Indies).[38] Walcott's 1958 play, *Ti-Jean and His Brothers,* incorporated dialect, and he titled his 1978 play *Pantomime.* Yet Walcott did not seem to find common cause with Miss Lou. Jahan Ramazani argues that she was caught between two ideological poles: she mostly rejected British literary tradition for her poetry, so the champions of that tradition like Walcott may not have fully appreciated her; and her mockery of West Indian–style Afrocentrism, as evident in her poems "Back to Africa" and "Pinnicle" (a mockery of Garvey's Back to Africa movement and an urban Rastafarian community, respectively), may have put off African-oriented poets like Kamau Brathwaite. Certainly, in his withering critique of Jamaican poetry in his 1957 surveys, Walcott does not recognize Bennett as a poetic alternative to the imitative voice of the Jamaica Poetry League.[39] Ramazani is wrong about Kamau Brathwaite, however, who from the 1980s on was a champion of Miss Lou's poetry, as I have already noted. Even so, in his development of his brilliant "nation language" thesis, Brathwaite, while admiring, nevertheless regrets "the tyranny of the pentameter" in her poetry, suggesting that his problem is not so much with Miss Lou's content or her "riddim"—both of which can clearly be co-opted for their "nation-language" attributes—but rather with her colonial-era form.[40] She was, however, as much a product of the colonial period as she was a product of a parallel autonomous cultural tradition, one that defied colonial cooptation. Ironically, both are called the folk tradition.

It would be easy to mark the "problem" of Miss Lou as one that springs from the division between "folk" and "popular" in contemporary Caribbean society. "Folk" has a preservative, archival quality, implying a sacrosanct and immovable national tradition, redolent of the costumes and dances of yesteryear—a peasant tradition. Further, "folk" is inescapably connected to education, and thus to the kind of cultural institutionalization that is the preserve of the middle-class-dominated civil servant class. "Popular," by contrast, is a dynamic term, associated with the ephemeral, the new, and—in today's society—the urban working class. Popular culture is always being created, always happening, always changing—it has no unalterable ritual. It is not being produced for The Archive (although perhaps it is being "produced" for television or general commerce, but that's another matter). The problem with Miss Lou's work is the way critics—and audiences—categorize art into "folk" and "popular," with all the attendant aesthetic registers of those terms, when a work could be both. After all, aren't folk songs and stories simply the popular songs and stories of another generation that have lasted? Like her beloved Anancy stories, the poetry of Louise Bennett is, quite simply, popular. For critics, however, it is folk. The later association of what we now call folk culture with nationalist efforts at cultural reinvention in the postindependence era connects folk culture explicitly to middle-class cultural production. It is the middle class's efforts to harness peasant traditions in its own interests that produce the respectability, and the sterility, of The Archive. Folk culture thus becomes middle-class culture.

Popular culture, by contrast, is unstable, evanescent. Because of this quality, it is sometimes assumed to be innately oppositional to state interests, even if it is "just for fun," or clearly plays to state interests.[41] When Louise Bennett produced books of dialect poetry and volumes of Anancy stories, she contributed to The Archive: she is folk, a product of middle-class gentrification. When she performed those same poems in front of large, demographically varied audiences, albeit in full "national costume," she was popular—but not critically viable. I do not mean to be reductive in my reading of the interplay of folk and popular culture, because the results of both categories for Miss Lou are the same—not critically "serious." The fact that her poetry is committed to print, however, is the only reason we are even discussing it. This view is not necessarily held by every critic. Carolyn Cooper believes that popular Caribbean performance poetry will survive in canonical form, despite its inability to gain a foothold in the academy. Cooper's primary example is the way in which Miss Lou's poetry is appropriated and performed by other actors to become "a part of the communal repertoire." Rebutting Cooper's view is poetry critic Laurence Breiner, who acidly comments that Cooper "talks as if the production of performance poems were a sort of innocent folk art, pitiably vulnerable before the juggernaut of the well-oiled academic machine. (I'd hesitate to test my well-oiled machine against, say, Island Records, but let that pass)."[42] In his mocking use of the term "folk," Breiner assumes that performance poems are the antithesis of "innocent folk art" precisely because they are oppositional (not "innocent"), contemporary, popular, and commercially viable. The camps are clear: the middle-class, state-identified folk poems, and the working-class, antiestablishment performance poems. From this perspective, never shall the twain meet.

Pantomime, Poetry, and Politics in the Independence Era

Lost in this cleft between critical views of performance and written, folk, and popular poetry lies Miss Lou herself. In her many guises—newspaper columnist, radio and television personality, theater performer, screenwriter, lyricist, and poet—she trod a tightrope of mainstream respectability and progressive social views. In 1944 Miss Lou came under a volley of criticism on the eve of Jamaica's first elections under universal suffrage when she wrote a newspaper poem in the voice of an overconfident first-time voter who boasts of her voting prowess and reveals that she has no clue how to vote.[43] Readers accused her of trying to mislead the public on how to vote; the use of a first-person, dialect-speaking narrator could be read in the same vein as, say, a racist satirical depiction of blacks, from nineteenth-century European and U.S. sources, illustrating that blacks aren't educated enough to understand the apparatus of civilized society. In the Jamaica of the 1940s, dialect—usually the voice of opposition to the status quo—was threatening to the interests of the emerging nation, which did not wish to be satirized as ignorant, or to be reminded that it had never before been allowed to vote. As Julius Nyrere once remarked, nation building is an inherently conservatizing process, and laughter at that moment was unpatriotic. Suffrage was not just about poor peasants voting, after all, but about all segments of society, the middle class included, being transformed by the rights of full citizenship.

From early on, Louise Bennett learned to skewer those who would accuse her of "perpetuating ignorance in Jamaicans," as did one letter writer when what would become a monthlong controversy erupted in a local paper in the early 1970s over the supposedly "pernicious" influence of her popular radio show, *Miss Lou's Views*. Another writer complained, "In foreign countries we Jamaicans are considered the worse spoken people.... This Miss Lou Programme, is slowly destroying our young ambassadors of this great land." Even a journalist charged, "Thanks in reverse to Louise Bennett, Jamaicans of all ages and classes have forsaken good English for dialect."[44] Considering that these complaints were made in the postindependence era, when the society was flush with enthusiasm for all things native, Miss Lou's 1944 poem "Bans o' Killing," written thirty years earlier, is nothing if not prescient. As Jamaican critic Rex Nettleford points out, it illustrates her "early sense of literary purpose and courage."[45] The poem addresses the highfalutin "Mass Charlie"—a term for The Man, really—who claims that he intends to "kill dialect." Miss Lou asks, "Meck me get it straight Mass Charlie / For me noh quite undastan, / Yuh gwine kill all English dialect / Or jus Jamaica one?"

GENTRIFYING DIALECT, OR THE TAMING OF MISS LOU   103

("Let me get it straight Mister Charlie / For I don't quite understand / You're going to kill all English dialect / Or just the Jamaican one?") Arguing that Mister Charlie's revered English language is just a mass of regional dialects itself, Miss Lou proceeds, "Yuh wi haffe get de Oxford book [You will have to get the Oxford book] / O' English verse, an tear / Out Chaucer, Burns, Lady Grizelle / An plenty o' Shakespeare!" The poem concludes that Mister Charlie is a victim of self-hatred, and if he intends to kill dialect then he will have to kill himself. Her argument, Jahan Ramazani points out, although cloaked in the language of the dialect-wielding street observer, is strictly academic:[46] "Bans o' Killing" anticipates the argument that made Ngũgĩ wa Thiong'o famous decades later, when in *Decolonising the Mind* he argues that just as European fiction is founded on the European oral folk tradition, so too should African writers use as the foundation for African fiction the oral African languages and folklore and not European languages. With their radical message of language equality, Miss Lou's poems like "Bans o' Killing" are tailor-made for the postcolonial era and its concomitant emphasis on cultural parity with metropolitan centers of the West.

On the other side of the political score card, Louise Bennett's germinal work in theater was championed for fomenting another kind of nationalism. In 1949, along with Noel Vaz, she wrote the first spectacularly successful pantomime play. Called *Bluebeard and Brer Anancy,* it was the first play to bring Anancy onto the stage.[47] In the early years of the Jamaican pantomime the scripts followed the classic English pantomime formula: a children's fairy tale like "Jack and the Beanstalk," brought to life with stock characters, audience participation, and plenty of music and dancing. In this case, however, *Bluebeard* was a Jamaicanized version of the English story of the mythical pirate Bluebeard, who married and murdered several wives. In the Jamaican version, Bluebeard is an evil white plantation owner, or busha, who plots to steal the village hero's money and marry yet another innocent wife. Anancy thwarts his nefarious plan by using obeah—black magic—to turn busha into a creature whom he can dominate. Instead of English folk songs, the play mixed Jamaican songs and dialect and altogether reflected a Caribbean creolization of two mythological traditions.

Further, its inversion of the English story and the servant-master relationship anticipated the anticolonial revisionings of European classics by later, now canonical Caribbean writers such as Walcott, who would likely have been familiar with the Jamaican pantomime stories as a student at the Jamaica campus of the University of the West Indies in the mid-1950s.[48] The nationalist tinge of this lighthearted pantomime fare became apparent when Norman Manley, then radical Socialist labor union leader (and future prime minister of

Jamaica), came backstage and said approvingly to director Noel Vaz, "So I see you are trying some new things."[49] Restaged closer to Jamaican independence in 1957 and renamed *Busha Bluebeard,* the play was then taken to Trinidad as the Jamaican contribution to the first Caribbean Festival of the Arts. Its signature song, "Evening Time," with lyrics by Louise Bennett, has become so integral to the national heritage that today most Jamaicans assume it to be an old folk song, not a pantomime song written by a contemporary.[50]

The huge success of *Bluebeard,* aside from the extraordinary talent of its writers and producers, suggests that it hit a cultural nerve, and this nerve appears to be a combination of Anancy and the English tradition. One wonders if the anticolonial narrative strategy of rewriting the European text did not in some measure come out of a larger popular habit in the Caribbean of parodying or satirizing beloved English folk stories or poems,[51] a strategy Miss Lou employed at times in her dialect poetry as well as in her theater scripts. In her work, Miss Lou displays far more ease with satirizing and parodying the English tradition, or English views of the Caribbean, than with rejecting it outright, as does Garvey's Back to Africa movement or other more thoroughly Africa-centric manifestations in Jamaican culture. In this sensibility Louise Bennett may reflect the ambivalence of the nationalist-minded yet anti-Afrocentric black Jamaican middle class: an earlier pantomime, 1943's *Soliday and the Wicked Bird,* attempted what has generally been considered a more completely "Jamaican" play, based on a Maroon—or runaway slave—legend of "Bubiabo." With a screenplay by well-regarded writer Vera Bell (whose solemn ode to enslaved Africans, "Ancestor on the Auction Block," appears fairly regularly in classroom curricula), *Soliday* was part of the theater community's "African" experimentation, plumbing the nation's African roots. Whether the theater-going public had no interest in this more Afrocentric folk story, or whether the play was simply badly done, is hard to tell: nevertheless, the play was a commercial flop.[52]

Louise Bennett's work never embraced the most oppositional forms of black Jamaican identity such as the Maroon heritage or Garvey's Back to Africa movement. But then her work is Anancy-esque in the best sense: always engaging in ironic counterpoint, never in endorsement.[53] Miss Lou's political targets have a wide ideological range. For instance, if we are to read Miss Lou as socially conservative, in "Back to Africa" her rejoinder smacks of the favorite melting-pot thesis of Caribbean and Latin American societies that desire to downplay their essential blackness:

Back to Africa, Miss Mattie?	Back to Africa, Miss Mattie?
Yuh no know what yuh dah sey?	Don't you know what you're saying?

Yuh haffi come from somewhe fus	You have to come from somewhere first
Before yuh go back deh!	Before you go back there!
Me know seh dat yuh great great great	I know that your great great great
Granma was African,	Grandma was African,
But Mattie, doan yuh great great great	But Mattie, wasn't your great great great
Granpa was Englishman?	Grandpa English?
. . . .	. . . .
But de balance a yuh family,	But the balance of your family,
Yuh whole generation,	Your whole generation,
Oonoo all bawn dung a Bun Grung	All of you were born down at Burned Ground
Oonoo all is Jamaican!	You are all Jamaican![54]

Although the poem reflects a common middle-class dismissal of African heritage, it asserts Caribbean identity as primary. The poem's final lines are straightforwardly nationalistic:

But no tell nobody she	But don't tell anybody that
Yuh dah go fi seek yuh homelan,	You're going to seek your homeland
For a right deh so yuh deh!	For right there is where you are!

Despite her reputation as a champion of original dialect poetry, Louise Bennett engaged actual English texts as well, as we have seen. But whereas internationally recognized Caribbean writers revised the European classics,[55] Miss Lou, in the satiric tradition of the Jamaican pantomime, revised *popular* Victorian poems that, although well known during that period in the Caribbean, were hardly classic. (Indeed, a separate body of forgettable popular English literature functioned simply as entertainment, part of the imbalance of trade between England and its colonies.) As DeCaires Narain astutely observes, Miss Lou's poem "Independence Dignity," a celebration of the 1962 independence from Britain, at key points parallels the phrasing and meter of Charles Wolfe's "The Burial of Sir John Moore at Corunna," a mediocre poem that at one time likely was "routinely and efficiently drilled into the minds—and 'hearts'—of Caribbean schoolchildren (like Bennett herself)."[56] The Wolfe poem begins:

> Not a drum was heard, not a funeral note,
> As his corse [sic] to the rampart we hurried;

Not a solider discharged his farewell shot,
O'er the grave where our hero we buried.

The "matching" stanza in "Independence Dignity" inverts the pompous dignity of the Wolfe poem, as follows:

Not a stone was fling, not a samfie sting,
Not a soul gwan bad an lowrated;
Not a fight bruk out, not a bad-wud shout
As Independence was celebrated.⁵⁷
[Not a stone was flung, not a trickster stung
Not a soul went on bad and low rated;
Not a fight broke out, not a bad word was shouted
As Independence was celebrated.]

One can imagine the delight of those who had had to memorize the Wolfe poem in hearing that paean to English militarism skewered in a paean to Jamaican nationalism. But its pleasures, in the end, travel badly; no one remembers the original Wolfe poem, and thus the Bennett poem suffers from its "of the moment" quality, like so many topical performances of the stage. Moreover, its satirical edge would be blunted into mere comedy and read as a more conventional poem than it actually was at the time. Miss Lou's poems that endure tend to be those that are least connected to local, topical issues and most connected to the kinds of large, historically resonant themes that preoccupy academics: for example, "Back to Africa" and "Colonization in Reverse," an ironic take on large-scale Jamaican migration to England in the 1940s. Indeed, the academy cannot be underestimated when it comes to the question of how popular performers will fare in the long-term cultural memory of the Caribbean.

Canonization and Opposition

To understand how the once-disregarded Miss Lou became a Jamaican national icon, we must trace the process by which a dialect poem or performance travels from stage to book. The codifying of dialect performance provides a template for understanding the evolution—or devolution, depending on your view—of oral, popular culture into respectable culture. The social sanctioning of dialect performance followed a trajectory similar to that of American jazz, from a popular but disreputable art form to one that was inevitably archived as its prestige grew.

Miss Lou's eventual iconization by the state does not necessarily reflect a concomitant rise in scholarly respect, although it cannot be denied that it was the serious assessment of her work by two of Jamaica's most influential literary critics, Mervyn Morris in 1963 and Rex Nettleford later in 1972,[58] that coincided with increased scholarly attention in the postcolonial period. Indeed, one might argue that state-sanctioned approval is taken by the international scholarly community as a sign of critical disengagement. When in 1960 Eric Williams, the famous historian and then premier of Trinidad, invited a young V. S. Naipaul, in the early flush of success, to write a nonfiction book about the modern Caribbean, it is doubtful that Williams anticipated the caustic analysis of Caribbean societies that Naipaul would submit in *The Middle Passage*. That book, together with Naipaul's other critiques of postcolonial societies, established him simultaneously as anathema to Caribbean states and an intellectual writer of international stature.[59] Similarly, after the publication of *A Small Place* (1988), her famous critique of state-sponsored Antiguan tourism, Antiguan writer Jamaica Kincaid was not surprisingly declared persona non grata by the irate Antiguan government. ("In countries that have no culture or are afraid they have no culture, there is a Minister of Culture.")[60] Arguably this small but powerful book also launched Kincaid's international career not simply as a great novelist but as an intellectual essayist/novelist in the tradition of C. L. R. James, V. S. Naipaul, and George Lamming—a male-identified tradition. By contrast, popular dialect performers like Miss Lou *performed* their social or political critiques rather than articulate them directly in nonfictional writings. Moreover, their role as cultural archivists may well be seen as incompatible with the demands of rigorous intellectual opposition, a role that is, as DeCaires Narain points out, traditionally associated with women as "keepers of culture."[61] (Again, there is the irresistible correlation with jazz, which arguably has been "feminized" both by its association with genteel culture and by its popular reincarnation as a high school music form in the United States.)[62]

If Miss Lou is the ancestor of today's oppositional dub poets—poets who, like their Trinidadian counterparts the rapso (rap-soca) artists, work in a distinctly black, and black nationalist-oriented, working-class, and male genre, for the most part—what does it mean that one of the few female dub poets, British Jamaican poet Jean Binta Breeze, is perhaps the only dub poet to move from the oral to the written poetic form? In an essay titled "Can a Dub Poet Be a Woman?" Breeze notes that when Mutabaruka recorded her work, people thought her hard-hitting lyrics in pieces such as "Aid Travel with a Bomb" worked better with a male voice than they did when she read them aloud.[63] Defending her decision to forsake oral performance—the lifeblood of dub poetry—for the written word, she said, "I'm not screeching and shouting my poetry anymore.... I've discovered that poetry is not synonymous with preaching. My poetry has become a lot more personal."[64]

Breeze's association of "better" poetry with the "personal," and "screeching and shouting" public expressions of anger with the male-identified, Mutabarukan voice, returns us to the traditional associations of the female voice with the private, depoliticized feminine domestic space, as opposed to the public male-identified space of the performer.[65] Isn't this a step back from what an artist wants? Yet one might also argue that Breeze put her poetry into writing precisely for its staying power, its greater likelihood of being anthologized and analyzed by the academy's "well oiled machine," in Breiner's ironic phrase. (Although compact disc recordings of live dialect performances should render the question of staying power moot, it does not: recordings are still in the domain of popular culture, writing in the domain of the academy.) Miss Lou's journey from popular but critically neglected dialect poet to national icon did not initially come with the kind of critical acceptance that would propel her work into international anthologies.[66] Her performative voice is, unlike the more circumscribed world of the anthologized writer, very much a public one, reaching the widest possible demographic in a notoriously classist society. That voice, however, is not associated with the tradition of angry or otherwise more overtly political poetic discourse that is linked inescapably with serious Caribbean writing.

The "taming" of Miss Lou's social criticisms by state co-optation of Miss Lou herself does not mean the end of her work's social relevance. When asked by playwright Dennis Scott if her work was "angry," she replied, "Not *obviously* angry." Scott's association of anger with intellectual weightiness is rebutted by Bennett's implication that indirection is its own form of political subtlety, an indirection that may not have sat so well with anti-colonial-minded listeners in the feisty early years of independence. When Scott charges her with being a "professional entertainer of the middle-classes," Bennett responds, "Oh, never that," rejecting the implied triteness of the middle-class entertainer label.[67] In the end, the meaning of Miss Lou as both icon and author will elude tidy formulations from those who dismiss her and those who lionize her: a popular local author who wrote on local issues and performed in local theater; an increasingly international author who is being discussed by critics in American and English universities and whose works are now appearing on graduate school reading lists; a pleasant-faced, peasant-costumed, middle-class, maternal national icon who is yet an ancestor of today's "angry," male, working-class, dub poets.

If Miss Lou's peasant costume of yesteryear offended modern sensibilities as too accommodating to tourist desires, is there much difference between it and today's tourism-driven images of smiling, dreadlocked black male inhabitants of Jamaica playing reggae on television stations across the United States and Europe? Does this usurpation of what was once a counterculture image for commercial interests confine its meaning to the obsequiousness of a tourism pitch (and a tourist pitch, moreover, as often as not aimed at black tourists)? The famous, and famously controversial, Trinidadian calypsonian, the Mighty Sparrow, popularized calypso in England in the 1950s, helping to make calypso into a middlebrow entertainment for the genteel English classes. Despite calypso's different profile abroad, Sparrow's success there did not modify his rough-hewn, local reputation for sexually explicit and politically hard-hitting lyrics in Trinidad (nor his tough, working-class personal image).[68] Sparrow's lyrics, like Miss Lou's use of dialect, are provocative precisely because they are part of the "language of the people." Yet for this same reason, they are easily appropriated for various agendas—nationalist, academic, or otherwise.[69] In the continuing evolution of the local into the global, Miss Lou may yet enjoy another posthumous transformation, from local "professional entertainer of the middle-classes" into an anticolonial writer in her academic afterlife granted by the demands of the Western academy.

CHAPTER 4

Middlebrow Spectacle and the Politics of Beauty

> The race rises as its women rise. They are the true standard of its elevation. We are trying to produce cultured men without asking ourselves where they are to find cultured wives. We forget that cultured families constitute a cultured race and that a cultured race is an equal race. The elevation of [black] women to equality with [their] white counterparts is the Condition Sine Qua Non of the elevation of the Negro race.
>
> —Robert Love, editor of the *Jamaica Advocate*, 1895

> The obscenities, the bawdy language and the gestures of the women in the street have been pushed to a degree of wantonness which cannot be surpassed and which must not be tolerated.... The growing generation of young girls will become the curse of the country if these yearly saturnalia are allowed to continue.
>
> —*Port of Spain Gazette*, 1884

The two epigraphs describing nineteenth-century Afro-Caribbean women with which I begin this chapter contain the central ideas and images that frame my argument about the contradictory ideologies surrounding contemporary women's performance in the Caribbean public sphere.[1] The visions of black women captured in these quotations encapsulate the warring images of black femininity at the center of the debate over the place of black women in the nineteenth-century Caribbean public, images that affected, and continue to affect, Caribbean women of all ethnicities into the twenty-first century. On the one hand, black women are represented as icons of respectability, virtuous women who must be properly educated and acculturated to take their place as symbols of national progress. This image is the black nationalist ideal. On the other hand, black women are represented as the anti-woman—pathological and lascivious viragos who undermine the nationalist project. This is the historical stereotype, the nationalist nightmare against which the ideal labors. Both images spring from representations of women in popular culture rituals such as carnival, or through women's civic organizations and other vehicles of uplift.

In the Caribbean certain popular culture rituals performed by women constitute a kind of ideological "work" that both reflects and furthers the struggles for power among the various ethnicities and classes in the region. It is therefore critical that any discussion of contemporary Caribbean women in popular culture be historicized. The origins and development of Caribbean discourse on public women illustrate the historical nature of state and class interests in women's behavior in the public arena of the street, in the lowbrow arena of the dancehalls and the carnivals, and in the middlebrow venue of the beauty pageant stages. A historical lens reveals that the traditional attitude of the respectable and aspiring-respectable classes toward (usually black) women in the public sphere has been that these performances are indices of black women's innate degeneracy—a view that, I argue, has been turned on its head in the late twentieth and twenty-first centuries as modernity and cultural progress have been linked to respectable women moving into the public sphere. Here I focus on the different meanings accorded to different kinds of female public "performances," a term I use to describe women's popular culture rituals and behaviors in the public sphere. In that "performance" suggests a physical gesture made with a physical body for a passive viewing audience, it is a particularly apt term for my purposes here. "Performance" implies agency, an act meant to do particular kinds of work or make particular kinds of statements. The viewing of women's bodies in public, as opposed to the domestic space of the home, has always been framed in overtly political terms in the West (and, as far as I can tell, in the East also). It is a truism of feminist theory that if the domestic space has traditionally been marked as innately and appropriately feminine, then the public space is masculine, such that any crossing of the boundaries by women from private to public space must be interrogated and assessed as either a proper intervention that preserves the woman's femininity or a social violation that masculinizes or otherwise pathologizes her.

My argument hinges on the idea that in the Caribbean—with its history of slavery and indenturing, and the corollary of pathologizing black and other nonwhite women as nonwomen or nonsubjects—the black, brown, and Asian constituencies' desire for a publicly acknowledged respectable femininity is both overtly and covertly tied to the desire for social mobility and political or economic advancement. In that public and intellectual discourse tended, and still tends, to focus on blackness as an index of the region's progress, I maintain that the issues surrounding black women's performances tend to shape the content of the discussion about nonblack women's performances. My analysis distinguishes between the two basic categories of female popular culture performance, both of which I argue are politically determined: the transgressive, "vulgar" spectacle associated either with atavistic racial recidivism or, depending on the ethnic constituency, with taboo race-mixing, both of which are perceived as a backward step for nationalist ambitions;[2] and the socially approved, "decorous" spectacle that does the work of social uplift and thereby furthers national desires for political autonomy or socioeconomic progress.

A discussion of the politics of women's public performance in popular culture may seem beside the point in that Caribbean women, particularly black Caribbean women, continue to move into positions of power and authority with regularity. Indeed, former Dominican prime minister Eugenia Charles was the first female leader of the Americas, and former Jamaican prime minister Portia Simpson was not only the first female Jamaican leader but also came from a decidedly working-class background, in distinct contrast to the middle-class and elite men (many of them light skinned or white) who preceded her. With this kind of political progress, one might argue, why focus on the apparently less meaningful details of women's participation in calypso contests, beauty pageants, and other middle- or lowbrow cultural forms as if these constituted the sole media for women in the public sphere?

The apparent paradox of having relatively numerous Asian female leaders command societies in which large numbers of women still are bound to the home, the farm, or other traditionally female spaces begins to answer the question. In other words, political progress, as measured by the number of female leaders, politicians, corporate executives, or other professionals, does not tell the whole story. The more relevant question might then be What is the impact, if any, of the one public sphere of women—the popular, the "fun," the lowbrow—on the other? My point is that the perceptions of one are historically bound up in the other.

Female Vulgarity and Black Nationalism in the Nineteenth Century

The first epigraph that begins this chapter, black Jamaican-Bahamian editor Robert Love's exhortation to uplift black women through education so that they can become the cultured wives of cultured black men, is intensely nationalist in spirit, if problematic to our twenty-first-century views of the role of women in society. What is important to us here is his vision of black women as central to the black nationalist agenda; at the close of the nineteenth century, with the rise of an educated black middle class in the still-colonized Caribbean, there was much public debate about the possibility of future black rule of the islands. Much of the debate among English intellectuals and leaders centered on the fitness of black people—black men—to rule, and as black professional men sought to be recognized as civilized and therefore capable of self-rule, their focus—as well as the focus of white Englishmen—turned to their women. Black male leadership qualities were judged by the ability of black men to rule their women, and in this respect they were found sadly wanting. As nineteenth-century Oxford historian Anthony Froude put it, "If black suffrage is to be the rule in Jamaica, I would take it away from the men and give it to the superior sex.... They would make a tolerable nation of black amazons, and the babies would not be offered to Jumbi."[3] Froude's and other English male travelers' supposed admiration for the self-sufficiency of black women cannot be taken at face value, however, since the purpose of these observations was really to point out the insufficiencies of black men. Englishmen's observations of black Caribbean women, when not a comparison with the men, were far more critical: black working-class women were usually described as loud, lewd, and not respectable because they were too strong to be protected by black men and also because they were always "in the street." In Trinidad in particular, black women were constantly compared to the "delicate"—and less publicly visible—East Indian women.[4]

These English perceptions of the pathological masculinity of black Caribbean women, highlighted against other racialized femininities such as those of white and Asian women, were—and arguably still are—the basis for black (and later, Indo-Caribbean) nationalists to police the public images of their women, and this policing meant scrutinizing their public behavior. The second epigraph, taken from an 1884 editorial in the Trinidadian newspaper *Port of Spain Gazette*, refers to the "yearly saturnalia" of carnival and exhorts the respectable classes not to tolerate the "wantonness" of the young girls, known as jamettes, who participated in it. The term "jamette" refers to black women in nineteenth-century urban Trinidad who were associated with the barracks yards, gangs, and the streets. (Originally the term referred to female stick fighters; stick fighting is considered a male sport.) These disreputable women, these thorns in the sides of lawmakers and the respectable classes, were also active as "chanterelles," or calypso singers, and their "carisos," songs, were habitually castigated as lewd and erotic, and for allegedly instigating obscene dancing.

The criticisms levied by both English travel writers and black newspaper editors at the public behavior of black Caribbean women were taken from their observations of women specifically of the working class or peasantry.

Yet these images circumscribed the behavior of all black women, across class lines. Given the historical stereotypes of black women perpetuated under slavery, it is not surprising, then, that members of the relatively small emergent black middle class, barely a generation out of slavery at the end of the nineteenth century, should feel the need to distance middle-class black women from these images in order to make social and political progress. Because respectable middle-class black women could not create physical differences between themselves and working-class women—to the nonblack observer, black was simply black—it became imperative to create notable and distinct differences in habit, speech, and style. This essentially political need to establish difference is, I believe, at the root of modern anxiety about black women's performances in the public sphere, an anxiety that requires decorous spectacles of black womanhood as its antidote. If black working-class women had heretofore defined black womanhood, then, in the postcolonial era of globalization and positive indigenous symbols, the traditional need to identify different classes of black women is indistinguishable from the modern need for middle-class women to participate equally with—or, perhaps, to *replace*—working-class women in the public sphere, with parallel yet distinct rituals that are at once authentically Caribbean and identifiably modern.

I submit that, in the Caribbean, modernity is generally associated with whiteness in the sense that it represents the First World, a technologically advanced and therefore supposedly superior culture. The symbolic positioning of brown women provides some insights into how the nationalist project has attempted to fuse the indigenous and "primitive" with visions for national progress in the postindependence era.

Brown Women, Sensual Spectacle, and Erotic Nationalism

Although black women's public performances in carnival and in general were decried as shameful images that kept the nation from being viewed and from viewing itself as civilized and therefore worthy of political equality, English travel writers displayed an undercurrent of consistent admiration for brown women's physical appeal in carnival and other public rituals.[5] The seemingly more benevolent images of brown women displayed in the pages of English travel narratives—always with an emphasis on physical beauty—laid the groundwork for the different treatment accorded brown women in the public sphere today. In the contemporary Caribbean, images of brown women are ubiquitous: they adorn tourism posters and newspaper advertisements for glamorous items such as jewelry, and for most of the postindependence era the women themselves were the habitual winners of the region's innumerable beauty contests (except in the Hispanophone Caribbean). Vera Kutzinski remarks that the images of brown women were central to the construction of Cuban nationalist discourse in the nineteenth century. Brown women, as symbols of the intertwining of the two dominant ethnic groups, were seen to be peculiarly apt images of Cuba's revolutionary *mestizaje,* or mixed, vision of itself, far more so than were brown men.[6] Even today, one of the ways in which communist Cuba advertises itself in Europe and Canada is through the images of its brown women, whose bodies are used to showcase the carnival, the exciting nightlife, and, as some have suggested, the unofficial sex trade.[7]

Since the traditional race-mixing image was the combination of the nonwhite woman and the white man, the brown woman's body was overtly sexualized as the means by which racial progress, or racial devolution (depending on the political viewpoint), came about. Consequently, there are far more references to brown women than to brown men in nineteenth-century European travel literature about the Caribbean. The values accorded to black, brown, Asian, and white women's bodies in Caribbean societies have thus remained more or less constant for over a century. These values are by no means equal, nor do they necessarily reflect the multicultural utopia that the states promote. In Caribbean societies in which the black population is a plurality or a majority, there seems to be an almost visceral desire both to emphasize the society's multicultural nature and to deemphasize its blackness, at least where middle- or highbrow culture is concerned. The Spanish-speaking Caribbean nations are notorious for their undercount of the black population, notably because much of the population does not identify itself as black on the census. And in years past in English-speaking nations like Jamaica, where the population is 90 percent black, the brown and nonblack members of society have been featured so prominently in public spaces like the national newspaper, beauty contests, and tourism posters that they have given the impression of a more ethnically diverse population than is actually the case. One might assume that, in this context, the obsession with brownness is linked to the politics of the dominant brown or white elites of the region, who would clearly have reasons for promoting this particular vision of the nation. But not so. The black populations of the Caribbean also have had a concerted interest in promoting the image of the brown nation, it seems. Traditionally, the most vociferous supporters of the brown-identified beauty contests have been the members of the heavily black audience.

Moreover, as has been noted more than once, Jamaica's most famous dancehall queen was a brown woman; her decade-long reign was unheard of in a contest in which the queens do not usually last longer than a few months and a queen's tenure is usually determined by the approval of the black working class.[8] Despite the overwhelming disapproval expressed by the respectable classes toward female dancehall participants, Queen Carlene was chosen to make an appearance in a tourist oriented video. In later years she became cohost of *Our Voices,* a radio talk show (modeled along the lines of the popular American television show *The View*); the other cohost was a former Miss Jamaica who won the Miss Universe contest in 1993, Lisa Hanna.[9] It is hard to imagine a black, working-class former dancehall queen making the transition from working-class icon to respectable professional in quite so routine a manner. Thus the "vulgar" spectacle of black working-class dancehall women dancing obscenely in lewd outfits is transformed into "decorous" spectacle when performed by eroticized brown women. The dancehall moves of black working-class women, descendants of the nineteenth-century jamettes, can therefore mean something entirely different, depending on who is performing them, and to what purpose. Part of the problem of female public performance is that there are different registers of signification accorded to different racial types, even as the society continues to underplay race and overplay class as the criteria by which such distinctions are made.

Caribbean Nationalism and the Racial Politics of Beauty Pageants

The brown ideal for Jamaica and other Caribbean societies has been nowhere more apparent than in its beauty pageants, where brown women have more or less predominated in the last forty years. Beauty pageants in the Caribbean are something of a regional obsession. As a mostly state-approved form of female spectacle, pageants are particularly relevant to any discussion of femininity in the Caribbean. A study in contradiction, they function as middlebrow popular entertainment, featuring the physical charms of middle-class women of apparently highbrow tastes who then are used as national icons and spokeswomen at nationalist-tinged events.

Interestingly, Jamaica's desire to be represented as a brown nation has not always meant a de facto flight from blackness or an alignment with elite white interests. One of the more bizarre moments in the history of beauty pageants occurred in Jamaica in 1986 when, amid a sea of brown contestants, Lisa Mahfood, a white upper-class Jamaican of Middle Eastern descent, won the Miss Jamaica title and was stoned off the stage by the outraged black audience.[10] The violent public rejection coincided with the increasing unpopularity of the Jamaica Labour Party, the capitalist-oriented party in power at the time, a party headed by the then prime minister Edward Seaga, himself of Middle Eastern descent. Moreover, the government was publicly aligned with U.S. political and business interests on the island. Possibly Lisa Mahfood's connections to the business community and her membership in the white merchant community (an important distinction in the types of whiteness on the island) were the main reasons the partisan crowd rejected her victory, feeling it to be part of a larger political "fix." At a time when the increasingly corporate nature of beauty pageants demanded that all the contestants have sponsors from the business community, and when the contests were (and still are) fixated on picking a winner who was perceived to have a better chance of going on to win a more internationally recognized title such as Miss World or Miss Universe, Lisa Mahfood's connections to the business community were not unusual, however. The other white beauty queen of note, Cindy Breakespeare, who became Miss Jamaica 1976 and later Miss World, also came with corporate sponsorship and was from an elite white family. Unlike Mahfood, however, Breakespeare was a wildly popular queen and at a time when Jamaica had reached the apotheosis of its black consciousness movement, with a socialist government in power, black nationalist figures such as Marcus Garvey iconized as national heroes, government ministers eschewing Western business suits in favor of the "cariba jackets" or guayaberas, and the rise of reggae, previously scorned by the respectable classes as black ghetto music, to national and international acclaim. Why the difference?

Perhaps the answer is that Breakespeare, though white, was perceived to be part of the new cultural order, a woman who embraced "roots," or popular Jamaican culture, and who had a public relationship with Jamaica's (inter)national black working-class icon, the reggae superstar Bob Marley. It is not merely race alone, then, that determines the meaning of the beauty queen's appeal but also whether she is seen to represent the interests of the country at large. In the mid-1970s the socialist Jamaican government actually took over the running of the Miss Jamaica beauty pageant, placing an emphasis on "cultural awareness, talent and community development," to public chagrin.[11] The beauty portion of the pageant was removed to a private sports club. The beauty pageant survived and thrived as a privately sponsored event, however, whereas the more socially conscious version of the pageant withered away. What Jamaica's disastrous experiment in enlightened pageantry heralded was the now-common view that beauty queen contestants should reflect an intrinsic Caribbeanness. In the postindependence years, with the increasing acceptance of the postcolonial philosophy that indigenous Caribbean culture is as good as the "superior" cultures of Europe and the United States, and that a showcasing of state-sanctioned totems of Caribbean culture is in fact the very sign of modernity, beauty queens who were not born in the region or who could not sufficiently perform Caribbeanness by using a local accent or by identifying key local items were publicly scorned and ridiculed. Witness, for instance, the lyrics to the calypso hit "Miss Barbados" (1985) by calypsonian Mighty Gabby:

> [For the beauty queen crown]
> It's big prizes they offer
> Jewelry and trips galore
> Things they never give calypso
> The beauty queen
> Will get a limousine
> . . . .
> When they announce this Caucasian as the winner
> If you hear the boos that night
> Some say she get it because she white
> But they didn't know
> That she wasn't Bajan at all,
> And when they find out the truth
> They hold down they head and bawl.
> [Chorus]
> Miss Barbados never hear 'bout ackee tree!
> Miss Barbados never hear 'bout Sir Gary
> or even me
> Miss Barbados never hear 'bout bul-jol and ackee, so
> when she get she Bajan citizenship, lemme know!
> Miss Barbados, she don't know 'bout cassava
> Miss Barbados, I don't want she portrayin' us.

The framing of this critique of the white Canadian-born Miss Barbados is particularly noteworthy for the contrast it offers between the pampered pageant winners, showered with expensive gifts, and the calypsonians, who are almost exclusively black, male, and working class.[12] The implication behind the contrast is that calypsonians, as popular and more authentic representatives of Barbadian/Caribbean culture, are unfairly treated by the establishment in favor of an inauthentic foreign white woman who is supposed to perform the all-important task of representing Barbados to the world even as she is unable to identify key items of "Bajanness": ackee, bul-jol, and cassava, which are vegetable dishes indigenous to the region; Sir Garfield Sobers ("Sir Gary"), the famous Barbadian cricketer and regional icon of black Caribbean respectability and nationalism; and even the calypsonian Mighty Gabby, himself a cornerstone of Barbadian popular culture. The result is that the beauty queen does not fulfill the requirements of nationalism that are intrinsic to this particular form of decorous female performance, hence the calypsonian's pronouncement, "I don't want she portrayin' us."

Despite popular black outcry, the white winners of the Miss Barbados and Miss Jamaica contests were clearly the choices of the business establishment, which saw them as appropriate models of Caribbeanness to showcase to the world, if not to the majority in their own societies.

Times have changed. The increasingly vociferous protests of inauthentic representatives of culture during the 1980s dovetailed with the increasing number of black women entering and placing at the top of regional beauty contests. Also a significant number of black women—dark-skinned black women—in recent years have won such major First World titles as Miss America, Miss Italy, and Miss Universe. Nor is it a coincidence that the more recent Miss World and Miss Universe pageants have been held in developing countries: India, Namibia, South Africa, and Trinidad and Tobago, to name a few. The global beauty industry now apparently recognizes black and other kinds of "ethnic" beauty, added to which the mores of what constitutes a desirable, "modern," professional young woman have shifted. Not surprisingly, the result is that the nature of the racial, if not the class, politics of Caribbean beauty pageants has indisputably changed. Given the intimate relationship between international beauty pageants and American corporate finance, however, it may be closer to the mark to suggest that it is not racial progress per se that is changing the face of pageant winners but rather a strategic move to open Third World markets to First World business by embracing Third World nationalist symbols.

In a parallel move, Caribbean pageants are more open to, even encouraging of, dark-skinned black women entering the contests. Recent dark-skinned winners include Zahra Redwood, Miss Jamaica Universe 2007, the first Rastafarian to win any Caribbean beauty pageant. When asked how she intended to improve the nation's chances of winning the international Miss Universe competition, Redwood wrapped herself in the mantle of Marley, responding that "Bob Marley has long been synonymous with Jamaica and with all the attributes I possess."[13] Redwood's Rastafarian faith, combined with her university degree and her interests in solidly upper-middle-class pursuits—including "parasailing and horseback riding"—provided the capstone that marked her as essentially Jamaican yet professional. Indeed, Redwood claimed that "the Rastafarian culture and beauty pageants have a great deal in common because they both promote decorum in the attitude of the female and the female as a role model in society."[14] The putative political significance of the occasion was not lost on the general population: "Marcus Garvey must be smiling in his grave," exclaimed one admirer in a letter to the editor.[15]

Perhaps. But the crowning of a beauty queen who is a Rastafarian, that is, a member of what was once the most despised and marginalized of communities in Jamaica, signals not so much a radical shift in Jamaican race and class politics as it signals the way in which Jamaica's constant pulse-taking of global culture affects its own view of the local. The comments of one of Miss Jamaica's organizers, veteran Mickey Haughton-James, are instructive:

> There was a time when people like light-skinned, pretty girls could win. The girls you see entering now...they would not have entered previously because they didn't think they stood a chance. They didn't think they had a chance against light-skinned, long-haired girls. When you have [dark-skinned] pretty girls with height, stature...they have a better chance of winning. *Miss World expects a beautiful black girl from Jamaica.* We weren't having a lot of girls with university degrees, but now there are beautiful girls with intelligence.[16]

In other words, Jamaican society now recognizes that, in the age of black supermodels and the ubiquitous Oprah Winfrey, dark-skinned black women are visible as international icons of beauty and professionalism. It is only now that the affirmation can be made, without irony, that the international image of Jamaica is a dark-skinned, black woman. (Was it ever otherwise?) Accordingly, professional, dark-skinned black women are more likely to apply to and win beauty pageants. There is a certain amount of defensiveness in the comment that the contest was not attracting a lot of "smart," or university-educated, women; coming on the heels of the remark that in the international arena black women were expected to be representatives of Jamaica, it seems to suggest that the reason dark-skinned black women had not won in previous years was that they were not educated enough. Apparently smartness was less of a problem when white- and brown-skinned women were winning.

As the beauty pageants change, so may the conventions that govern the contestants. One of the more absurd aspects of pageants is the requirement that the contestants not be pregnant or married. This requirement implies that "respectable" contestants are virgins, an anachronism for today's professional woman, for whom an active sexual life does not detract from her class status. This bit of hypocrisy was laid bare in the 2007 Miss Jamaica controversy when the 2006 winner, the dark-skinned Sara Lawrence (who had advocated for safe sex and had placed sixth in the international contest), resigned after she announced she was pregnant. Amid the commingled choruses of outrage and support, the organizer criticized Lawrence for harming the pageant's reputation and for not choosing "another way out of the predicament" (that is, deciding not to have an abortion).[17] Similarly, when the popular former Miss Trinidad and Miss Universe Wendy Fitzwilliam announced—at a Catholic girls' school, no less—that she was pregnant out of wedlock, the announcement caused a commotion in Trinidad.[18] The dark-skinned Fitzwilliam is iconic in her home country: a lawyer and local celebrity who has a hospital named in her honor, Fitzwilliam represents all the virtues of black professional women as models of nationalism. Ironically, the Miss Universe pageant held in Trinidad in 1999 anticipated the moment when sexuality and professionalism would clash in the pageant. The final three candidates were asked the same question: "If you become pregnant during your reign as Miss Universe, what would you do? Would you continue to reign?" All three candidates answered in the affirmative. The eventual winner, Miss Botswana, responded that "Having children is a celebration of womanhood for all females, including beauty queens." Clearly, the right answer was the one that was seen as the most socially progressive, most in keeping with the vision of an autonomous professional womanhood that the pageant itself courted, even as its requirements suggest a more Victorian sense of female virtue. Caribbean society, in its zeal to embrace the black beauty contest winner as representative of black progress, still struggles with these clashing images of the modern that echo the vulgar spectacle of promiscuous black womanhood from the colonial age.

Asian Caribbean Women and the Politics of Public Performance

Beauty contests are not considered a vehicle for social mobility and social visibility by all ethnicities of the Caribbean. As Natasha Barnes notes, although the first woman of color to win the Miss Jamaica title in the preindependence era was a Chinese Jamaican, in the immediate postindependence era of the mid-1960s virtually no white or Chinese Jamaican women dared to enter because of black nationalist interests; the Chinese, as part of the merchant class, were perceived to be aligned with white interests, while Indo-Jamaicans, who had come to the Caribbean as indentured laborers, continued to enter the contest along with brown women.[19] By contrast, even to the present day Indo-Trinidadian women are not particularly visible in the Miss Trinidad pageant, which is primarily a creole arena,[20] and none has ever won the contest, although an Indo-Trinidadian contestant has placed second.

In recent years, as Indo-Trinidadian women have entered beauty contests in ever increasing numbers—one recent winner was an Indo-Trinidadian woman—there has been increased criticism from the Indo-Trinidadian community about how Afro-Trinidadians dominate the contest. As if to underscore the competition between Afro- and Indo-Trinidadians over such national symbols, Indo-Trinidadians, in the 1999 Miss Universe contest held in Trinidad, were accused of being unpatriotic because they cheered for Miss India, not for the black Miss Trinidad.[21] The relative absence of Indo-Trinidadian women in the pageant may have something to do with the politics of Indian nationalism in Trinidad, where conservative Indo-Trinidadian nationalists perceive the entertainment arena to be a degraded creole space. The prevalent fear among the cultural nationalists is that "douglarization" of Indo-Trinidadian culture will occur.[22] As if to counter the growing participation of Indian women in the creolized space of the national beauty pageants, the Indo-Trinidadian community organizes an annual, televised Miss Mastana Bahar pageant, in which contestants wear saris—there is no bathing suit competition—and answer questions in Hindi. Their Indianness is gauged by whether they can identify the names of Indian movie stars or Indian songs, and in this way a parallel national Indo-Trinidadian space is evoked and preserved. It therefore should have been no surprise that when female Indo-Trinidadian calypsonian Drupatee Ramgoonai brought chutney soca—the distinctively Indian version of creole-derived soca music—to the annual calypso competition, she was vilified by a chorus of outraged Indian nationalists for her sexually suggestive lyrics and for throwing away "her high upbringing and culture to mix with vulgar music, sex and alcohol in Carnival." As Shalini Puri points out, although chutney soca is seen by many conservative Indo-Trinidadians as authentically Indo-, not Afro-, Trinidadian, it is only valid as an Indo-Trinidadian art form when performed in the contained, female space of the traditional all-women's gatherings during Hindu wedding festivities.[23] Outside that space, the same art form becomes debauched, creolized. The public sphere of Trinidad remains, for the Indo-Trinidadian nationalists, innately black.

Calypso and its accompaniment, the steel band, are still overwhelmingly black working-class male preserves. The encroachment of nonblacks, in particular privileged white and brown Trinidadians as well as Indo-Trinidadians, into this domain has caused some anxiety about the black hold on national symbols, however. Especially the election of an Indo-Trinidadian, Basdeo Panday, as prime minister, from 1995 to 2001, increased the fear among the black population—which is slightly smaller than the Indian population—that it was losing political, and with it cultural, power. The initial reception of

Denyse Plummer, a white Trinidadian female calypsonian who first ascended the stage in 1990 during the annual carnival's Calypso Monarch competition and was pelted with oranges and rolls of toilet paper, parallels that of Lisa Mahfood and the white Miss Barbados. Although Plummer has gone on to become one of the most successful female calypsonians ever, she was seen initially not as an inauthentic Trinidadian but as an inauthentic calypsonian in *that* Trinidadian context. As the antithesis of the black working-class male, she was an interloper come to take away one of the only acknowledged forms of black working-class male authority on the island.

Global Desires: Caribbean Nationalism and Miss Universe 1999

In an interesting contrast to the scorn displayed by Indo-Trinidadian cultural nationalists toward women who engage in public performances, the Indo-Trinidadian government leaders had a concerted interest in promoting the 1999 Miss Universe pageant. Seeking a chance to create economic opportunities for Trinidad by showcasing the country's rich cultural heritage, the government hoped to introduce the country as a desirable tourist destination to the "international" (that is, First World) audience. Also, the large and small business communities desired to make money from the event and to build business contacts with the likes of Donald Trump, who owns the Miss Universe franchise. Added to this aspiration was the feverish hope among the general population that another Miss Trinidad and Tobago would win the title yet again. The Miss Universe franchise holder in Trinidad dreamt that Miss Trinidad placed as a second runner-up, and a newspaper rushed to print the story on the front page.[24]

In a bizarre move to marshal public support for the pageant, the Miss Universe Pageant Company sought to exploit national desires for international recognition by declaring May 6, 1999, as Red Day and by "call[ing] on all citizens to wear red in solidarity with the Miss Universe show and also in recognition of indigenous beauty."[25] Red Day was supposed to meld the opposing poles of postcolonial modernity: it would satisfy the need to indigenize the pageant as well as to "globalize" the populace by connecting it to the wider world. The show itself was filled with spectacular displays of every conceivable Trinidadian cultural symbol. African-style dancers, complete with feathers and loin cloths, performed on the stage, and stick dancers perched on stilts; African drumming was featured alongside Indian tassa drumming; a limbo exhibition took place during the bathing suit competition; and huge dancing puppets from carnival were brought on to gyrate wildly while a steel band played as the finalists took center stage, escorted by local cricketers (the athletic equivalent of respectability in the popular culture sphere). The suited and bejeweled audience members were given white handkerchiefs to wave in the air, carnival style, in an imitation of wild and sweaty carnival abandon.

Newspapers commented that Red Day had succeeded in highlighting the country's charms: "There were some especially proud moments [in the pageant] for citizens of this country," swelled one commentator.[26] The spectacle of Caribbeanness on parade at the Miss Universe pageant was generally a proud moment for the local audience and did not appear to be viewed as akin to the mindless caricaturing of local culture that is the usual entertainment at tourist resorts, despite the similar financial aims of both endeavors. Beauty pageants are a curious combination of lowbrow culture with highbrow pretensions at best; who has not heard the snide jokes about beauty queens in bathing suits and high heels laboring to illustrate their erudition on questions of world peace? Nevertheless, in the Caribbean, where contestants of whatever ethnicity are inevitably from the relatively small, relatively well-educated middle class, the display of the region's educated brown and black women in competition with (and not in service to) the world's "best" before an international audience is an indication of the region's entry into modernity, into the value systems of the industrialized West. The display of local culture in this context transforms it from the "backward," or the merely local, into a global culture.

Regional newspaper stories, such as the one that appeared in the *Jamaica Gleaner,* extolled the appeal of first-time African winner Miss Botswana and appeared to underscore the perceived link between victory in the Miss Universe contest and economic progress in the Third World: "Botswana has the Prettiest Girl in the World—and One of the Fastest Growing Economies as Well."[27] Because of this general perception of a link between beauty pageants and economic progress, Caribbean beauty queens are ideal spokeswomen for nationalist sentiments. The region's queens can frequently be heard issuing sound bites on the need to celebrate indigenous culture. A similar conflation of nationalist sentiment with global ambition can be seen in the beauty contests of Latin America, in particular those of Venezuela, where the Miss Venezuela pageant is close to a national industry, a precious natural resource, like oil, to be developed and sold abroad for the enrichment of the nation.

The desires of nineteenth-century black nationalists like Robert Love to raise Afro-Caribbean women from the bawdy spectacles of street life to the enclosed respectability of educated society would find an ironic end in today's beauty pageants, where genteel black women are sanctioned precisely by being on display, thus raising the image of black women from the "incondite," vulgar spectacles of the carnival and the dancehall to an eroticized yet decorous vision of a peculiarly Caribbean modernity. By rendering black womanhood visible in this space, the tainted racial meanings of stick fighting or other black-identified cultural forms are divested of historical meaning and become just another marker of authenticity. Nonblack Caribbean women have helped demarcate the public space in various ways: white and brown women have legitimized the movement of respectable femininity from the private, domestic sphere to the public space and the public gaze by performing a sanitized eroticism for public pleasure. The link between white women and corporate finance has in large measure validated spaces such as the beauty pageants and the carnival competitions. Brown women made nonwhiteness, in the form of hybridity, into an acceptable nationalist symbol. Asian women remain both within and without the public gaze: they are Asian when they are confined to private, Asian spaces, and creole or Caribbean when they step into the public domain. The entry of brown, white, and Asian women into the "vulgar" public spaces of black working-class culture is also a performance of a perceived authentic Caribbean subjectivity, because blackness itself marks the Caribbean space in both the national and international gaze.

At the core of these various responses to women's public performances is a series of negotiations over, and a desire to transform the image of, the "authentic" Caribbean subject. These negotiations are as true for black women as they are for nonblack women. Black middle-class women in beauty pageants defuse the very idea that a real West Indian is a vulgar black "street" woman, who is herself the very essence of the antimodern, or to put it in Paul Gilroy's words, the very counterculture of modernity. In this way, a class discourse helps to erase an overdetermined race discourse in the establishment of blackness as a legitimate cultural signifier. It is then possible to replace the entrenched images of blackness as backward and primitive with these new icons of a black(ened), creolized modernity.

CHAPTER 5

Organic Imports, or Authenticating Global Culture

The distinction between folk and popular that I have made thus far contrasts the "purity" of sterile, stable traditions of the past with the dynamic, unstable proclivities of the present. The former is associated with the cataloguing impulses of the state and the latter with its antithesis. The distinction is not, however, entirely workable. Such a distinction presupposes that the state has no interest in contemporary popular culture. Quite the contrary. Caribbean states have an investment in popular culture in much the same way that the region's corporate sector has. As Nestor García Canclini has noted, the embrace of the popular is required to legitimize a democratic secular government.[1] Moreover, what is popular is generally profitable, and in a region characterized inevitably by its poverty on the global stage, one aspect that elicits something other than hand-wringing or neocolonial desires for tradition is the Caribbean's assertive popular culture.

When reggae and its metonymic idol Bob Marley gained international recognition, for instance, reggae finally became respectable—and profitable—at home. In Marley's honor the government of Jamaica commissioned a statue of the reggae singer for Independence Park, home to statues of national icons. Jamaica was arguably the first to jump-start the "festival tourism" trend with the creation of the now-extinct Reggae Sunsplash in 1978, formulated as vehicle for developing tourism during the dormant summer season.[2] Reggae and carnival have now come to symbolize what is known internationally as

Caribbean culture. There is some irony that these formerly maligned forms of working-class popular culture have allowed Caribbean states and business interests to reimagine the Caribbean as an international player on the world stage in ways that building a respectable civil service and relatively prosperous workforce has not. Consider that, despite the relative prosperity of British colonies such as Bermuda or the Cayman Islands, or even of independent nations such as the Bahamas or Barbados—the latter, in particular, with its well-educated citizenry, protectionist government, and solid economic standing—their international images remain mired in colonial-era images of able servants on a plantation paradise. This dynamic has something to do with their overwhelming dependence on tourism, of course, but with one or two exceptions all of the Caribbean countries are. Economic prosperity and political stability, then, do not go hand in hand with enhanced international stature.

Popular culture, however, has allowed not so much a reimagining so much as a reestablishment of the same colonial dynamic: eager servants, albeit dreadlocked and reggae loving; native gaiety in the service of the European or American tourist. One might even argue that increased international visibility has an inverse relationship to economic progress. As the economy declines at home, it becomes incumbent upon regional governments to point to international markers to validate the idea that the nation is progressing. Koningsbruggen points out that, in Trinidad, "one need only peruse the country's largest daily newspapers in order to observe what are frequently considered newsworthy reports from North American or European sources that the country has ranked highly in activities such as sports, the economy, the arts, beauty contests, and so on."[3] If such international recognition tends to focus on popular practices, then these practices fulfill both a local and a global function. In this chapter I examine popular, frequently middle-class-oriented cultural practices that are simultaneously tourist oriented or state-identified. In particular, I excavate the "importing" and staging of cultural practices, whether from other Caribbean countries, the United States, or Europe, as a key component of native cultural development. To this end I examine Trinidad carnival and its various reproductions alongside popular jazz and literary festivals of the region.

A truism of both globalization and postcolonial theory that has yet to be applied to the Caribbean context is that the "authentic" versus "external" model of culture is illusory. It was Arjun Appadurai who first observed that cultural homogenization and globalization are two separate phenomena:

> The globalization of culture is not the same as its homogenization, but globalization involves the use of a variety of instruments of

homogenization (armaments, advertising techniques, language hegemonies and clothing styles) which are absorbed into local political and cultural economies, only to be repatriated as heterogeneous dialogues of national sovereignty, free enterprise and fundamentalism.... In general, the state has become the arbitrator of this *repatriation of difference* (in the form of goods, signs, slogans and styles). But this repatriation or export of the designs and commodities of difference continuously exacerbates the internal politics of majoritarianism and homogenization, which is most frequently played out in debates over heritage.[4]

In other words, the argument that globalization—by which is usually meant U.S. consumer culture—overwhelms the cultural singularity of developing nations ignores the fact that the deployment of the artifacts of global culture often highlight that very singularity through their different context and meaning. Even so, the question of what is "really ours" is still asked in the Caribbean, where its economic dependence on tourism conflicts with its independence-era sensitivities to imported goods, imported labor, and imported culture. A platitude is worth repeating here: even the most unimpeachably authentic practices have roots in another culture. There would be no reggae, for instance, without American rhythm and blues, or Indian ragga rhythms. Therefore the questions I ask are, given the hybrid origins of almost any cultural practice, how are commercially viable practices consciously authenticated by corporate and state interests, and what are the social politics that play out around that authentication process? Authentication is an issue that has come to bedevil the region's most famous festival, the annual Trinidad carnival, which has now become a huge production involving both the state and the commercial sector.

Mimicry Begins at Home: Trinidad Carnival and Its Copies

Carnival is not unique to Trinidad. It is associated with Pan-Caribbean culture precisely because of its ubiquity in the Catholic-identified Caribbean, from the Caribbean coastal regions of South America to St. Lucia, from Cuba, to Haiti and the Dominican Republic. Further, the emancipation day and harvesting festivals in the region's non-Catholic countries such as Barbados, Antigua, and Jamaica reveal similar masking and parading traditions. Outside of Brazil, however, of all the regional carnivals the Trinidad carnival is the most famous and the most influential; its costumes and set pieces are admired as art and have traveled the world over.[5] The Trinidad carnival has long and storied roots, going back to the eighteenth century. Its history has been chronicled by innumerable scholars, but it was Trinidadian scholar Errol Hill who in 1972 first consciously linked it to state interests by suggesting that it provided the basis for a national theater tradition.[6] First brought to the island by French settlers, its early incarnation followed the European prototype: a Catholic pre-Lenten celebration for the white elites that ended with the asceticism of Ash Wednesday. (The Latin phrase *carne vale* means "farewell to the flesh.") Over the centuries, carnival evolved into a spectacularly Caribbean ritual as the island's nonwhite majority took it over and made it primarily a working-class street spectacle, synthesizing African masking traditions and religious practices with European masking traditions and religious practices. Today's carnival has its roots in the nineteenth-century version, called *cannes brûlées* (or "burning cane"), which commemorated the emancipation from slavery of the island's blacks, giving the carnival an oppositional edge and linking it more profoundly to the emancipation festivals of the non-Catholic countries. By the mid-nineteenth century, however, carnival was moved to *dimanche gras,* or the Sunday before Lent, and took on a less oppositional character. More recently, as the Indo-Trinidadian population has become more urban and more state-identified, carnival now reflects the popularity of Indian musical traditions as well.

Predictably, as Trinidad's carnival became identified with black and brown working-class people, the respectable classes came to scorn it. Nineteenth-century accounts of carnival from Port of Spain drip with disdain: as the ruling class withdrew from the event, the leading newspaper, *Port-of-Spain Gazette,* began a campaign to abolish the street masquerade, declaring it to be a "wretched buffoonery [tending] to brutalize the faculty of the lower order of our population."[7] The black masqueraders would blacken their already black skin to heighten their social visibility, a form of ethnic self-assertion that must not have been lost on the ruling class.[8] By the 1930s, however, the creole middle class began to participate in carnival. It became associated with a newly politicized black consciousness from the 1950s, when Eric Williams and his black-identified People's National Movement (PNM) came to power in 1956 and virtually co-opted the festival. Williams's government set up a Carnival Development Committee, which further strengthened the link between the government and the carnival and neutralized any dissent against the running of carnival, which, as Richard Burton notes, would be construed as a protest against the government.[9] The 1970 Black Power revolts in Port of Spain put an end to the government's encouragement of politicized Afrocentrism, however. A popular uprising against poverty and the underclass status of poor black youth, the uprisings seriously threatened Eric Williams's

PNM government and revealed the depth of social unrest in the country. Since then, Trinidad's carnival has become less overtly political and more of a reflection of government commercial interests. Most critics argue today that the event has turned 180 degrees from the politicized carnival of years past to become primarily a middle-class event.[10] Some go further, insisting that it is longer Trinidadian, as "true true Trinnies" have withdrawn in the face of massive contingents of overseas "salt-water Trinnies" and foreigners overtaking the proceedings. Richard Burton succinctly summarizes this view:

> In short, as carnival mutates from a popular national festivity into an international postmodern extravaganza, the active masquerader of old is giving way to the passive spectator-consumer of today. Carnival has been exoticized and commodified for foreign consumption, and Trinidadians allegedly confront it as tourists in their own land, estranged from the very festivity that is supposed to embody the quintessence of what it is to be Trinidadian or even of what it is to be West Indian, or black.[11]

Although the alienation thesis overstates the case, it is nonetheless true that carnival has been "commodified for foreign consumption"—as well as for local, middle-class consumption. The question is, who counts as "foreign"? The "saltwater Trinnies" who live abroad but embrace carnival as a lodestone of Trinidadian authenticity? The Jamaicans, Barbadians, Guyanese, and other Caribbean nationals who participate in large numbers? The African Americans who are curious to see the carnival of which they may have heard from their Caribbean friends and neighbors and which is advertised heavily on Black Entertainment Network (BET)?[12] Or the more conventional, Euro-American tourist who has limited knowledge of the region and limited contact with West Indians? In 2007, the majority of the visitors to Trinidad and Tobago during the carnival season were from North America—63 percent, compared to 21 percent from Caribbean, Caricom, and neighboring nations.[13] The number of "North American" tourists is deceptive: just how many of these are Trinidadians and other Caribbean immigrants? Certainly, as Koningsbruggen notes, "the number of whites among the audience is negligible," suggesting that carnival's tourists are a Pan-Caribbean—or at the most, African diaspora—population.

Critics of today's superficial, "wine and jam" variety of carnival decry that it is the appeal to foreigners that has diluted the complexity of the "old-time" carnival. "Wine and jam" refers to the gyrating and body rubbing that occurs as part of carnival dancing. Although from all accounts carnival has, from the nineteenth century, always involved overtly sexualized dancing, the expansion of the joyous sexual dancing of "pretty mas'" (pretty masquerade) to encompass the carnival as a whole has, in the minds of many critics and "old-time" masqueraders, trivialized the meaning of carnival. That is, it has reduced the festival's ability to reflect on the society as a whole. Pretty mas' and ugly mas' represent a kind of yin and yang of carnival aesthetics. The pretty mas' represents characteristics of our world that are associated with the positive: beauty, harmony, laughter. Ugly mas' represents the opposite: ugliness, sin, discord, and violence. In her fascinating essay on *jour' ouvert* (or, in Creole, *jouvay,* meaning "carnival morning celebrations"), Patricia Alleyne-Dettmers notes that the most African aspects of carnival reside in the traditional ugly mas' of jouvay.[14] Jouvay represents the spiritual aspect of carnival, and it is in jouvay that we see the representations of African instruments, the enactments of the fights of enslaved ancestors, the use of mud on the body, and many of the African musical and masking traditions that the Europeans derided as ugly or dirty. Indeed, traditionally ugly mas' has been the venue to critique social ills or present political satire. Take away this aspect of carnival and the festival's ability to comment widely on the spectrum of Caribbean life is indisputably diminished.

What is left is pretty mas'; if jouvay is carnival's interior, pretty mas' is its exterior. The diminution of ugly mas' and the expansion of pretty mas' suggest a de-Africanizing of the festival, to conform to a more multicultural, middle-class sensibility that is both more appealing to tourists and less historical, less threatening—in both symbolic and actual terms. In particular, the heightened presence of certain kinds of women—middle-class, brown and nonblack women—"wining and jamming" on the streets has become a marker of three, not altogether compatible, views of Caribbean progress—or lack thereof. In the first view, the physical presence of professional and elite women on the streets signals the advent of women's liberation and social progress, as "respectable" women move from the invisible space of the home to cultural ownership of the streets. (Not coincidentally, one of the monster carnival hits of 2006 was "Roll It" by female soca artist Alison Hinds, whose lyrics are a paean to female independence.)[15] In the second, their presence signifies carnival's success as a safe, profit-making event that guarantees the participation of those who can pay: in other words, it signals economic progress. In the third, the presence of professional, nonblack women signals a kind of neocolonial mimicry: they are presented in an inverse relationship to the dynamism and creativity of the "original" carnival. As their presence intensifies, carnival becomes a degraded tourist spectacle that reduces Trinidad to the same banal tourist culture of other islands from which it had so long distinguished itself. In this view, the presence of brown-hued women half naked on the streets exemplifies the carefree sexual paradise of the neo-colonial tourist brochure—a servant culture.

This last view is the one that is the most troubling, even for those who are modern carnival's most active participants. The white Trinidadian carnival set designer Peter Minshall, famous for his elaborate pieces, nevertheless bemoaned that carnival's costumes are now so big and extravagant that they are no different from those of "Las Vegas showgirls": "We have sold our soul," he said recently, "as we pay homage to the cheapest of the cheap: American standards of entertainment."[16] Peter van Koningsbruggen sees it not so much as pandering to tourist sensibilities as part of a larger internalization of the tourist brochure, of the tourist ideal. Trinidad has a relatively small tourist industry, and unlike the other islands, it is oil, not tourism, that is its economic mainstay. Why, then, the profound investment in Americanization and what "they" think of "us"? The idealized tourist image is important because it allows Trinidadians to reimagine themselves as global citizens, as agents of a modern, transnational world. As Koningsbruggen puts it, "Trinidadians din into themselves by constantly trumpeting their own praises that they belong to the 'most beautiful people of the world' and live in a carefree and cheerful 'tropical paradise of sand, sea and sun.'"[17] It is an image of Trinidadianness that is cultivated not only by Trinidadians "at home," but also by "saltwater Trinis" and, I argue, by middle-class Pan-Caribbean nationals who attend, all of whom are equally invested in the federated Caribbean image of public harmony, modernity, and multiculturalism.

The touristification of carnival is assumed to bring an increasing modernity, exemplified by an expanding economic autonomy and social progress. Yet if such modernity is signified by a public female presence, it is one of the ironies of modern carnival that, in an inversion of the men outside/women inside paradigm, women's increased presence on the street has meant a concomitant retreat of men to the interior. According to Koningsbruggen, until the 1950s men were overrepresented in the carnival bands; by the 1990s that figure had turned on its head, with the annual average female composition of the bands estimated at 80 percent.[18] The feminization of carnival has been much commented on in Trinidad, and as I have indicated, has been variously attributed to women's increased autonomy as they work outside the home and earn their own money, and to the changing social ideal for "ladylike" women.[19] (Judging from anecdotal reports, I suspect that the majority of tourists who come from other islands also appear to be women.) It is less clear what began the trend toward pretty mas': the ever-increasing presence of women in the carnival such that the event now reflects the culture of middle-class Caribbean women or a state imperative to attract

ORGANIC IMPORTS, OR AUTHENTICATING GLOBAL CULTURE 133

more tourists with "safe," female-identified themes. Regardless, some critics identify women with carnival's decreased sense of agency and creativity, and increased exclusivity.[20]

Women buy their costumes, they don't make them, as did previous generations of men. Further, women congregate in bands that reflect their own social class. "Pan men"—the primarily working-class men who create and play in the steel bands, which are the sound of carnival itself—are now to be found primarily in the pan yards,[21] the last bastion of masculinity and "traditional" mas'. One might argue that men are even being "imported" into Trinidad carnival through the state-sanctioned traditional mas', given that a large number of the "living history" bands—the sailor bands, for example—are populated by older men from Brooklyn and other parts of North America who either played in these bands in their youth or, if they didn't, associate them with a lost cultural heritage.[22] In other words, if elite women's participation is associated with modernity, nonelite men's is associated with authenticity.

The government of Trinidad appears ambivalent toward carnival. On the one hand, it promotes the event as a centerpiece of its tourist economy and as its main contribution to global visibility. Carnival makes a lot of money for Trinidad. It makes even more money after the event is over, when carnival costumes and bands make the rounds of transnational carnivals, from Jamaica's April carnival celebration to Toronto's Caribana festival in August to Brooklyn's West Indian Day parade in September.[23] Further, Philip Scher argues, "as revenues from oil and other traditional sources dwindle the state sees increasingly professionalized carnival as a strategy towards catering to a demanding and competitive tourist consumer."[24] The evidence that the state controls the format and presentation of the event is as obvious as a Google search: type in "Trinidad carnival" and the searcher is linked immediately to a number of government-sponsored sites. The National Carnival Commission (NCC) is a state-sanctioned governing body that oversees carnival, and to this end it has encouraged carnival's academicization by sponsoring conferences and journals on the festival.

On the other hand, the state wishes to preserve the "true" carnival, which it believes to be in danger of extinction.[25] To that end the NCC issues periodical lamentations over the "excesses" of the wine and jam carnival, which it links to the disappearance of traditional mas'. This decline it has attempted to correct with the deliberate reinsertion of traditional mas' into the carnival. In 1994, when traditional carnival characters had been resurrected for a performance out of their original context, the NCC's official anthropologist argued that this was a valid move: they "add to the uniqueness of the National Festival which . . . create(s) a differentiation of the product as Trinidad and Tobago

Carnival claims a niche in the world economic market."[26] The emphasis on carnival as product and its place in the world economic market undermines the argument made by the defenders of tourism that, in Orlando Patterson's words, "tourism enhances residents' awareness of indigenous cultures."[27] Or, in a neat twist, the natives learn about their own culture from tourism. From the government's point of view, however, the interest in traditional carnival is in furthering the tourism "product."

Meanwhile, the "wine and jam" version of carnival that now dominates Trinidad is, save for its large scope, virtually indistinguishable from its simulacra in the other Caribbean islands. It is the banality of sameness that is the greatest threat to the essential Trinidadianness of carnival. As Trinidad's Las Vegas–style carnival diffuses across the Caribbean, Trinidad's government, following Jamaica's example, has pursued the possibility of copyrighting certain aspects of the festival to prevent their "theft, degradation, or misappropriation by both locals and foreigners."[28] But here's the problem. It is precisely to experience this feminized, overly eroticized spectacle that tourists flock to the island, but the state wishes to preserve a nostalgic version of carnival that no longer reflects the realities of Trinidad's transnational, intraregional culture. Further, other festivals in Trinidad are more compatible with the state's emphasis on authentic local practices, but these are Indo-Trinidadian festivals, such as the Muslim festival Hosein and the Hindu Ramleela, both of which feature male creole "unbelievers."[29] The creole-identified state, despite its increased acknowledgment of the Indo-Trinidadian influence on Trinidadian culture, is not apparently ready to throw its weight behind these all-too-local, non-creole-identified traditions, which do not lend themselves to a global vision of what Trinidad is "supposed" to look like.

In the meantime, the Trinidad's pretty mas' carnival has been reproduced across the Caribbean and beyond, transforming emancipation and harvest celebrations to resemble a festival that is, in an ironic doubling, itself connected to these festivals by its origins in the emancipation/harvesting celebrations of *cannes brûlées*. In some ways, the American and English versions of carnival may be partially responsible for the growth of Trinidad-style carnival in the region, as Caribbean migrants to London, Toronto, and Brooklyn encounter the festival as a Pan-Caribbean affair and reintroduce it into their homelands. More to the point, however, the different versions of Trinidad-style carnival among the nations of the Caribbean all have one thing in common: an overarching commercial interest in promoting carnival as an authentic national experience. The carnival copies include the Jamaica carnival, consciously imported from Trinidad in the early 1990s by a few wealthy Jamaicans; Barbados's August Crop Over, a traditional harvesting celebration from Barbados's more agrarian past which was deliberately resuscitated to attract tourists during the slow summer season of 1974; both the British and the U.S. Virgin Islands' carnivals (held at different times of the year), nominally based on older festivals and updated to conform to a Trinidadian format; Antigua's carnival, originally a celebration of emancipation that incorporates Trinidadian forms with traditional Antiguan ones, such as Junkanoo; and the Aruba carnival, possibly the oldest Trinidad copy in that it was Trinidadian oil workers who brought the festival to that island, and in so doing transformed Arubian culture.[30]

Trinidad's carnival, as the largest, most spectacular, most organized, and most visible celebration in the Caribbean, provides a template for other Caribbean nations on how to put themselves on the tourist map. Beyond the obvious interest in tourist dollars, however, the diffusion of carnival supplies other potential benefits: a sense of regional identity that the failed West Indies Federation began and that the West Indies cricket team is struggling to maintain, for one; and local appreciation of native traditions that are inscribed with the modern and the global. As Frank Manning notes, as early as the 1970s Antigua made a point of chartering flights from other islands for carnival, and radio personalities would remind their listeners that arrangements had been made to carry broadcasts to neighboring islands. Despite its origins in the 1950s as a tourist draw, the Antiguan carnival evolved independent of the tourism promotion plan. The imagined white tourists never arrived; instead, the carnival audience consisted entirely of Antiguans, other West Indians, and a significant number of African Americans, the latter no doubt interested in the overt displays of Afrocentrism evident in the music, styles, and displays of Antiguan carnival.[31] In other words, the imported carnival became indigenized and performed a kind of black-identified "revitalization," in Frank Manning's phrase. A similar phenomenon, albeit from the bottom up, is observed by Victoria Razak in her study of how the Trinidadian carnival became a symbol of Arubian identity, managed and controlled by the native—not immigrant—Arubian middle class. Given the distinct differences in Trinidadian and Arubian identity, this development is no mean feat: Trinidadian immigrants to Aruba are overwhelmingly black and English speaking, whereas Arubans are primarily mestizo and Dutch speaking. Moreover, when Trinidadian workers first brought carnival to Aruba's streets in the mid-1940s, the local Arubans called them "noisy rabble" and "a bunch of monkeys."[32] Sixty years later, however, the highly popular ritual serves simultaneously to associate colonial Aruba with an independent national culture of the Caribbean while maintaining a rigorously policed Arubian vision of itself as prosperous, orderly, and mestizo.

The Jamaican version of the Trinidad carnival is arguably more artificial than the Arubian or even the Antiguan version. Jamaica's carnival has no relationship to its indigenous Emancipation Day celebrations, or to its African-derived Junkanoo[33] masking celebrations. It was not initiated by Trinidadian migrants or Jamaicans who had lived in Trinidad. It is completely imported. The Antiguans have closer ties with Trinidad because of their relative proximity, history of migration to Trinidad, and tradition of producing outstanding calypsonians. Jamaica, by contrast, is perhaps the most notoriously culturally chauvinist nation in the English-speaking Caribbean. Jamaicans as a group see themselves at the vanguard of Caribbean identity and have traditionally patronized the "small islanders" of the leeward islands. Given all this, the insertion of Trinidad-style carnival into Jamaica's aggressively nationalistic cultural landscape seems like a nonstarter, but the Jamaican investment in Trinidadian carnival is a profoundly classed one. It was a group of wealthy Jamaicans who organized the first Jamaican carnival in the early 1990s, and its classed antecedents frame the carnival to this day, despite recent attempts to retroactively "indigenize" it. Middle-class and elite Jamaicans of various ethnic designations—brown, white, black, Chinese—can experience the mirage of multiracial classlessness on the street in Trinidad in a way that Jamaica's starkly unequal, violent urban culture cannot allow.

The suburbs of middle-class Kingston increasingly resemble fortresses under siege, as the professional classes barricade themselves in gated communities with elaborate burglar bars and high walls to protect themselves from the violence of those living in the poor, black streets. By contrast, the importation of Trinidad's myth of a multiracial utopia supports Jamaica's desire to believe its own, bullet-pocked motto, "Out of Many One People." Even as the violence rages on Kingston's gritty downtown streets, organizers hold out hope that by including ghetto dwellers in the uptown event, carnival can transform the area. "Downtown can be a positive place," said one, sounding not altogether convinced, "and maybe this carnival can change how the city is seen and bring people in the area together. Maybe."[34] Striking a similarly defensive note, one carnival Web site proclaims that despite all of the "negative critics," it is "creating a positive force that brings Jamaicans together": "[The carnival] is becoming very local with the emergence of the local designers and Mass [*Mas'*] Camps. Carnival has done the same for the Jamaican population as it has done in all other countries, united the population, created jobs and is also increasing the Tourism industry."[35] Still, despite the determinedly positive reviews, there is now some acknowledgment that the Jamaica carnival cannot survive without "Jamaicanizing." Whereas in years past dancehall was kept resolutely out of Jamaica carnival in an effort to maintain its distinctively different cultural order—dancehall performances, like those of rap and hip-hop in the United States, are inescapably associated with violence—in an effort to attract a wider cross-section of the population the two major promoters of carnival in Jamaica have now injected a number of dancehall acts into their events. And in the spirit of civic responsibility, carnival organizers set up a free health clinic at the mas' camp.[36] If the soca music of Trinidadian carnival is still not altogether satisfying for the larger Jamaican population, it is worth pointing out that, apart from carnival season, in Trinidad the radio stations play Jamaican dancehall far more than they play the indigenous soca.

In sharp contrast to Jamaica, Barbados's version of the Trinidad carnival started out as an effort to reintroduce Afrocentric traditions into Barbadian society. The original Crop Over was a harvesting celebration from the slavery era, imbued with the familiar carnivalesque mythologies of multiracial, classless unity. ("All authority, and all distinction of colour ceases; black and white, overseer and bookkeeper mingle together in dance," wrote one admiring observer in 1832.)[37] The festival had died out but was resuscitated in 1974 by the Yoruba Foundation during an era of fervent postcolonial nationalism. Barbados's only indigenous music, spouge,[38] was playing on the rediffusion, and, like Antigua, Barbados looked for black-positive indigenous images with which to reflect the nation's new, modern, African-descended identity. The concept was taken over in later years by the Barbados Tourist Authority in an effort to improve tourism during the slow summer season. Now administered by the National Cultural Foundation, the festival has morphed into the commercially profitable "wine and jam" tourist spectacle that it is today. Still, Crop Over maintains many of the rituals of the original festival, so it retains an essential "Bajanness."[39] This "Bajan" identity is evident in various ways, from the continuing emphasis on Crop Over's origins in the sugar industry ("sugar is still important in Barbados")—despite the fact that tourism supplanted the sugar industry a long time ago—to the Tourism Board's proclamation that Crop Over is "more than a Carnival," even as the board's Web site is filled with traditional, Trinidad-style images of scantily clad women in carnival dress.[40]

The original Crop Over died out in the 1940s as the sugar industry declined and Barbados's society moved from an agrarian to a service-oriented one. Around this time, as the island became more exposed to U.S. and metropolitan culture, residents began to see the festival as a gauche anachronism. In an effort to fill the cultural gap left by Crop Over, the chamber of commerce staged an annual carnival on the Trinidadian model from 1958 to 1964.[41] Erected around the time of the failed West Indies Federation, this version of Trinidad carnival, like its political prototype, never gained real traction and was soon abandoned. It is tempting to speculate as to why the first incarnation of Trinidad carnival failed and the second is thriving; perhaps the answer lies in Barbados's more comfortable modern national identity. To emulate Trinidad's signature cultural motif during the late 1950s and early 1960s, at a time when the federated identity of the Anglophone Caribbean was still a theoretical ideal not grounded in the reality of distinctive national cultures, would yield no cultural dividends for the nation. It was merely emulation. In the twenty-first century, however, immigration, regionalism, and globalization have ensured that individual Caribbean nations now have a distinct sense of both national as well as regional identity. Expressions of an essential "Trininess," "Bajanness," or "Yardie-ness" (Jamaican identity) have proliferated as the societies have become increasingly similar, as attested to by the constant circulation of e-mail "jokes" detailing the difference between Trinidadians and Bajans, or the difference of either from Jamaicans.[42] In these humorous stories, the stereotypical image of Barbadian personality is of a dull but dependable efficiency: stolid but solid. Barbados's reputation in the English-speaking Caribbean is that it is the most "English," and therefore the most colonial minded, of the independent nations, despite its history of vigorous nationalism and anticolonial policies.[43]

Crop Over allows a different projection of Barbadian identity. Whereas the original Crop Over reaffirmed, at least in the minds of Barbadians, that the nation was embarrassingly plantation bound, the new Crop Over is associated with an assertive Caribbean identity. Carnival-style Crop Over becomes the cultural capstone that highlights Barbados's economic prosperity and decidedly non–Third World status. With few resources, Barbados has thrived more so than its oil- and bauxite-rich neighbors. It has done so even as Barbados has moved from a plantation economy to a service one, making tourism its most powerful asset. Whereas formerly highly educated populations such as those of Jamaica and Guyana saw educational levels plummet in the postcolonial era, Barbadians remain among the most highly educated populations in the world. Yet, unlike similarly prosperous, tourism-oriented Caribbean neighbors like Bermuda, the British Virgin Islands, or the Cayman Islands, Barbados is an independent nation resolutely connected to the cultural community of the independent Caribbean. Barbados thus straddles the two Caribbeans: the prosperous but dependent colonies, and the fiercely nationalistic but struggling independent nations. Crop Over does the cultural work of welding together the two images of a prosperous and independent Barbados.

In summary, for Trinidad and its Caribbean neighbors, Trinidad's carnival performs various forms of cultural work. In particular, its various manifestations exude the discourse of professionalism, from the copyrighting of cultural "product" in Trinidad, to the civic-minded goal of social unity professed by Jamaica's organizers, to the expressions of a prosperous "Bajan-ness" in Barbados.

Modern Blackness: Jazz in the Caribbean

The reengineering of the cultural folk festival of yesteryear to today's commercially savvy jazz festivals is another generating point for the discourse of professionalism. Several islands in the Caribbean, most notably St. Lucia, Barbados, and Jamaica, have instituted a series of jazz festivals to attract tourists during off-season. These are modeled on prominent African American jazz festivals such as the Essence Festival in New Orleans, and at least one—St. Lucia Jazz—is underwritten by Black Entertainment Television and heavily advertised among African Americans and West Indians in the United States, as well as within the Caribbean. The percentage of West Indians attending the festival from other islands is as high as the percentage of Americans attending. As Kirby Allain, public relations manager for the St. Lucia Tourist Board explained in an e-mail message: "St. Lucia Jazz does encourage intra-regional travel, economic support and on a wider level regional integration. We believe it helps us as West Indians, understand the importance of appreciating what is ours." According to Allain, Caribbean tourists accounted for 33 percent of the arrivals for St. Lucia Jazz, compared with 34 percent of Americans and 22 percent of Europeans. Curiously, Allain distinguishes between "calendar events" such as St. Lucia Jazz and "cultural festivals" such as carnival and Jounee Kweyol (Creole Day), which are "rooted in our colonial/slavery past and depict our traditional dances, creativity... and other traditions."[44] The audience, whether African American or Caribbean, is heavily, perhaps mostly, women. Why does this conspicuously imported model of culture speak so powerfully to Caribbean middle-class desires for cultural ownership?

First, it must be owned that this is not the first time the Anglophone Caribbean has displayed an interest in jazz music. Its middle class was taken with jazz in the 1940s and 1950s, when jazz was still considered popular music. The American influence was especially heavy in Trinidad, where the United States military kept a base during the war years. Just as U.S. servicemen's enthusiastic patronage first elevated calypso to a respectable national art form, so too did the calypsonians pay attention to American, particularly African American, musical forms.[45] It was during this time the famous calypsonian Lord Kitchener incorporated bebop phrasing and instrumentation into his calypsos. American films shown in Caribbean theaters often showcased film "shorts" of American jazz bands such as those of Count Basie, Duke Ellington, and Dizzy Gillespie.[46] African American legends like Billy Eckstine toured Jamaica, and these images of cosmopolitan, stylish black men made an indelible mark on the emergent black middle classes of the region.[47] Many Jamaican musicians who would later go on to become legends in reggae music played jazz for tourists in the island's hotels, and thus jazz became associated with tourism, even as it was a symbol of a powerful, black, masculine modernity.

In the independence era of the early 1960s, jazz took on a distinctly organic tone as the Caribbean middle class attempted to indigenize the musical form. Class affiliation merged with independence ideology as members of the black middle class, now in positions of authority, sought cultural forms that expressed their class status and cultural origins. Accordingly, jazz in the Caribbean of the early 1960s was only to be found at the most expensive venues that required a dress code and a cover charge; for example, Barbados's fashionable Belair Jazz Club was a "hub of middle class nightlife."[48] In later years, jazz was elevated to a position of symbolic preeminence as an expression of cultural identity and newfound Pan-African ideology, according to musicologist Warren Pinckney Jr. Trinidadians tried to indigenize jazz by creating the hybrid genre of calypso jazz, which is still around today. In Barbados, at the first Barbados/Caribbean Jazz Festival in 1985, the director of the National Cultural Foundation announced that the festival's aim was to promote "a meaningful, relevant...kind of music in Barbados and throughout the Caribbean."[49] As if to bear out this emphasis on "relevance," virtually every ensemble on the program emphasized Afro-Caribbean and African influences on the jazz idiom. In later years the organizers of the festival tried to indigenize jazz by underscoring the historical connections between African Americans and West Indians, arguing that Caribbean people have been practitioners of jazz "almost from [its] birth" and that "jazz...is not new in the Caribbean." The hope was that the music produced from the Barbados/Caribbean Jazz Festival of the 1980s would produce a distinctively Caribbean brand of jazz that "reflect[ed] the cultural influences of the various countries in the region."[50]

If jazz is not new in the Caribbean, neither is its connection to high-class status. What is new, however, is, first, the focus on creating a proletarian following for jazz; and, second, the visibility of its marketing. The working class is essential—more important, is *perceived* to be essential—to almost any modern cultural production of Caribbean identity. In addition, as we have already seen with the Trinidad carnival, Caribbean ideas of cultural authenticity are being reconstituted in such a way that the marketing and importing aspects of culture are no longer an invisible part of the process. Rather they suggest a self-conscious, visible integration of what West Indians understand to be true Caribbean culture. Just as commercialized carnival highlights the middle-class ideal of a particularly modern, global form of Caribbean culture, so too is the jazz festival symptomatic of the same desire. The jazz festivals are up front about their link to commerce and tourism, and they highlight that link with lots of industry jargon: the Jamaican jazz festival Web site defines itself as "an effort to redefine the Jamaican musical landscape and enhance the Tourism product by providing an atmosphere that whole families [can] share and enjoy," and as "a complete jazz vacation."[51] This statement is more than a tourism ploy, however. St. Lucia's jazz festival proclaims itself "second in Caribbean festivals, eclipsed only by Trinidad & Tobago's carnival," indigenizing itself by the link to carnival via intraisland tourism. Further, in both Jamaica and St. Lucia, the festival organizers promote free concerts around the islands, which emphasize local jazz talent. In St. Lucia, the free concerts were known ironically as "the fringe," deployed mainly to give economic opportunities to St. Lucians who had no interest in the jazz acts, free or no. In recent years, however, "the artistic dimension of the fringe has evolved away from [the jazz] mainstream and towards a musical style which is clearly Afro-Caribbean. The organisers are hopeful that a uniquely St. Lucian sound could evolve from this and take its place on centre stage in the Jazz world."[52]

Clearly the hope for a "uniquely St. Lucian sound" is inextricable from the commercial aim to increase tourism, given the desirability of a marketable culture for the "upscale" cultural consumer. The integration of local musical acts underscores the association of Caribbean culture with a prestigious African American jazz heritage. Many of the headline acts, however, often hardly qualify as jazz: R & B singers figure prominently on the main stages, and the 2005 lineup for the St. Lucia jazz festival included the famous Jamaican dancehall deejay Beenie Man.[53] The jazz festivals' canny promotion of a combination of American R & B laced with local Caribbean music and validated by a star jazz act is intended to, as the St. Lucia Jazz Web site phrases it, "put us on the map."

When one considers that the English-speaking Caribbean, certainly in the postcolonial era, has had little interest in jazz, the blending of jazz with R &B, reggae, or soca acts has the effect of indigenizing jazz and making it palatable to the large regional Caribbean audience, which already knows where to locate St. Lucia and therefore presumably is not just being introduced to the delights of a country roughly similar to its own. In the Caribbean and the larger world, modern jazz is widely seen as "difficult" in the same way that modernist literature or modern art is, requiring specialized, ivory tower, "insider" knowledge. The Caribbean jazz festival retains the idea of insider knowledge, but only by association: to be present in the audience suggests that one has an understanding of the language of jazz, even if one does not. But every West Indian "understands"—or feels she understands—the language of Beenie Man (or feels no shame in not knowing).

As if to underscore the Caribbean link to jazz, Sonny Bradshaw, the Jamaican jazz band leader, in arguing for more sponsorship of the Jamaican jazz festival, observed in the local newspaper that jazz "is our music. We the black people invented it and it is a part of our culture.... We would like to encourage sponsorship for the product, which is one of the safest, cleanest and family-oriented." The emphasis on the implicitly respectable milieu of jazz is continued in a letter to the editor titled "Jazz Festival of Class": "No expletives were heard, no bottles were thrown, no gunshots were fired... instead patrons were entertained with the sound of great music brilliantly performed by the world's best musicians both local and international.... The Jamaica Tourist Board should take note.... Class or crass; that is the question."[54] Thus is the transformation of highbrow jazz accommodated to middlebrow tastes through the discourse of "family friendly" professionalism.

In his classic 1967 essay, "Jazz and the West Indian Novel," Caribbean critic Kamau Brathwaite called on Caribbean writers to establish a jazz

FIGURE 4. Mostly women and several children are in the crowd at the 2004 St. Lucia Jazz Festival. Photo taken by Chris Huxley. Permission granted by the St. Lucia Tourist Board.

ORGANIC IMPORTS, OR AUTHENTICATING GLOBAL CULTURE

aesthetic in Caribbean literature, arguing that unlike calypso, jazz as a black idiom is the music of protest, one that is "best interpreted by Negro artists." "There is no suggestion of alienation, no note of chaos in calypso," Brathwaite lamented. His wish for an indigenous Caribbean music with outsider status was thoroughly realized with reggae in the 1970s, of course, but at the time, Brathwaite considered jazz the ideal outsider music for black diaspora people. He further advocated for jazz as a black diaspora genre by insisting that "jazz is an example of a living, active expression on easy terms with all the world. While retaining its basic blues idiom, it is also, at the same time, capable of exploiting the extremes of contemporary sophistication." In the end it was jazz's global acceptance, its "easy terms with all the world," that made it particularly fitting for the Caribbean artist—more so than what Brathwaite derided as the "modern folk" expressions of highbrow writers and artists. These expressions he saw as a "desperate effort of the overurbanized to escape 'civilization'": "We must try to find the high ground from which we ourselves will see the world, and towards which the world will look to find us. An 'international' tradition by all means for those that wish it. *But a creole culture as well.* And a creole way of seeing, first."[55]

Brathwaite's call for a Pan-Africanist, global jazz aesthetic—one rooted in a regional, creole, working-class, "basic blues idiom" yet with a highbrow, international reach—is in essence a call to create a highbrow international aesthetic out of a lowbrow local one. The jazz aesthetic was to be a natural outgrowth of the folk tradition, whose culmination Brathwaite saw operating in novels such as Jamaican Roger Mais's 1954 folk novel *Brother Man*. Mais's novel, as well as other intellectual efforts at writing the folk such as Orlando Patterson's *Children of Sisyphus,* never achieved the international stature of Brathwaite's hopes. His desire to re-create jazz in the Caribbean based on its combination of outsider aesthetic and global appeal finds an ironic response in today's tourism-driven Caribbean jazz festivals. Jazz in today's Caribbean signifies insider, not outsider, status. Jazz signifies not alienation and chaos, but rather the antithesis: group identity and order.

Tourism and the Making of a Local Literature

The blending of the serious and the popular at the jazz festivals is mirrored in the marketing of both serious and popular Caribbean literature at the annual Calabash Literary Festival, the creation of Jamaican author Colin Channer. The savvy marketing of Calabash is not accidental: the Brooklyn-based Channer has, as he has noted on his Web site, an extensive background in marketing, and owns a branding and design firm. Channer founded Calabash in 2001 with the support of two friends, Jamaican poet Kwame Dawes, who is the program director, and film producer Justine Henzell, daughter of Perry Henzell, who directed the iconic Jamaican film *The Harder They Come*. The first director of the festival was the renowned Jamaican literary critic Carolyn Cooper, who founded reggae studies at the University of the West Indies and, like Perry Henzell, is an intellectual champion of working-class Jamaican culture. The festival's stated aim is "to create a world-class literary festival with roots in Jamaica and branches reaching out into the wider world" and "to transform the literary arts in the Caribbean by being the region's best managed producer of workshops, seminars and performances. We will achieve these goals by focusing on our *audiences,* managing our budget, creating a community of supporters in the media, government, business, the performing arts... and by becoming the festival of choice for the world's most gifted authors."[56]

Although, like the jazz festivals, the Calabash Festival is clearly modeled on an American idea, its concerns are as much local as international. Aimed as much at the local and regional audience as the foreign "cultural" tourist,[57] the festival is similarly positioned during the beginning of the low tourist season and is meant to be a "happening." The prominence within the festival's administration of cultural personalities such as Cooper and Henzell, whose names are synonymous with the celebration of black Jamaican ghetto culture, further serves to underscore the festival's aim to transform literature into the people's culture. The mission statement's emphasis on a plural audience, rather than on a singular one, signals the dual aims of culture and commerce. The desire to create a community of supporters among the multiple—and often competing—constituencies such as the government, the private sector, and the arts communities suggests efficiency and economy, hallmarks of the professionalist discourse that the festival literature deploys. Also like the jazz festival, Calabash combines the local and the international by showcasing locally or regionally popular authors such as Jamaican comic writer Anthony Winkler alongside internationally renowned authors such as John Edgar Wideman and Amiri Baraka. Calabash also features music and "other forms of storytelling," intermingled with readings; according to the Web site, the *New York Times* applauds the festival as both "a mini-Woodstock on the Caribbean" as well as a "world-class Caribbean literary festival." Music and "other forms of storytelling" again link the apparently highbrow form of literature to the more populist forms of music, singing, and oral poetry.

Calabash—again, like the jazz festivals—makes a point of holding free events as a way of bringing in the community. Channer states that "when

ORGANIC IMPORTS, OR AUTHENTICATING GLOBAL CULTURE   145

you read at Calabash you're reading to upwards of 2000 of the most appreciative people you'll ever meet, some of whom are fishing folks and farming people."[58] A recent visit suggested that the audience for the readings was overwhelmingly composed of upper-middle-class Jamaicans from the cities (with the exception of the final night's dance, which drew a large number of young locals); the festival's soundtrack was the ubiquitous music of Bob Marley, which imbued a relentlessly nostalgic ambience that would appeal to the well-heeled, mostly over-thirty, patrons. One might argue that the community becomes a mere backdrop for the staging of authenticity, but that would be reductive and fundamentally untrue. The festival format is a way to literally blend literature, like jazz, into the Caribbean landscape, and thereby naturalize it as Caribbean. Even as the nearby north coast beaches are increasingly privatized for the use of foreigners or the elite, free access to the public space where these cultural events take place is a way to reinscribe that public space as "of the people." The fisherfolks and farmers are in fact more than backdrops: they invoke authenticity not simply by being present but by their *approval* of the culture on display. As its Web site proclaims, not money but "passion is the only price of entry" to Calabash. In other words, the active participation and approval of *all* classes is seen as a prerequisite for authenticity by the festival's middle-class producers.

Beyond the showcasing of Jamaica as a stage for international erudition, the organizers have made an effort to use the festival to launch a specifically local literary culture. Through the Calabash International Literary Festival Trust, a nonprofit organization dedicated to the literary arts, they have set up the Calabash Writer's Workshop in Kingston, which is open to all. Short stories from the first workshop were read at the 2006 Calabash Festival, and one of its writers, Jamaican author Marlon James, won international acclaim for his debut novel, *John Crow's Devil*.[59] *Iron Balloons,* a volume of the participants' writings, was published in 2006 with an introduction by Channer. Despite the volume's local emphasis, the publisher is an independent U.S. company with a taste for the unusual. Channer defends his choice by noting the paucity of publishers in the Caribbean for creative fiction: "There is almost no book publishing industry to speak of in Jamaica today, outside the specialized areas of education and law. Today, I cannot think of ten established, active, home-based novelists, memoirists, or poets below the age of sixty-five. Those who I can identify are the remnants of a small group that came of age before independence... yet Jamaican music is increasing its local and global relevance every single day."[60]

The festival's aim, then, is to produce local Caribbean writers whose creative output mirrors the global relevance of Caribbean music (here read as singularly Jamaican). In concert with this local focus, Channer describes the workshop as being in consistent counterpoint to an elite, or foreign, perspective. The writers meet "in a house without a roof," in contrast to the American vision of an exclusive writer's hideaway, "a nicely renovated farmhouse with its own organic garden and a pond." Pushing the ghetto image of Jamaica favored by most West Indians, he offers up this depiction of the workshop's island home, "a big polluted harbor, the water macho gray in blunt refusal to assume the sissy turquoise of the tourist traps that dot the Caribbean Sea."[61] (Channer notes subsequently that the workshops were actually held in "what today is quite a spiffy mansion right behind Vale Royal, the Prime Minister's Official home, a gabled eighteenth-century home": one no doubt as romantic as any renovated American farmhouse.) The inference is that the unvarnished Jamaican literature produced therein will be tough, hard, "real." The extraordinary efficiency, canny marketing, and international pull of Calabash, then, have set the wheels in motion for a conscious revitalization of a local literature that is already positioning itself as a standard of Caribbean literary authenticity.

If it seems I am suggesting that these festivals are inauthentic only because they are reproductions, or because they are Americanized, or because of their canny marketing strategies or conscious deployment of working-class people and culture, let me emphasize again that that is not my point. Academic discourses of globalization focus mostly on the deleterious effects of our closer world, the obvious neocolonial aspects of "multinationalization," in which formerly exploited colonies become currently exploited markets.[62] Channer and the festival organizers understand something obvious that scholars are only now acknowledging: globalization includes not just markets but culture in its widest sense, and culture is not always an imposition in the ways that we understand colonial culture to be. The Caribbean middle class takes its models from an international middle class of which it is also a part. The middle-classing of the Caribbean is not an economic reality—the societies are as poor and unequal as ever—but rather a process reflected in the discourse and products of the international professional class. The cultural festival is not meant to appeal particularly to the outdated model of the wealthy white Euro-American tourist, who arrives with no knowledge of the Caribbean. It is the black tourist who is the target. She may be African American, Caribbean American, or Caribbean European; she may be middle class or working class with aspirations; she will, however, undoubtedly see the festival as one of "our" events.

In the Caribbeanist lexicon, "mimicry" and "importation" are two key words that are so intimately aligned that they have become indistinguishable.

The field of Caribbean studies has in some sense been founded on the belief that to import an idea is to reduce it to mimicry. There have always been cultural imports coming in and going out of the Caribbean, but it is particular kinds of imports that have been understood to be problematic: those that come with the weight of imperial or economic power behind them. Thus to write like Charles Dickens is to be inauthentic, but to scat like Cab Calloway is to have influences. But something in the regional ether has changed. To copy an idea can also mean to exchange an idea; in the case of the commercial carnivals and festivals of the Caribbean, it is perhaps the idea of blackness itself that is being copied, transformed, and exchanged, reflecting the tendency toward homogenization and synthesis that is so much a part of Atlantic history.

Chapter 6

Transnational Communities and the New Pop Fiction

Popular fiction has always been a staple of the Caribbean entertainment diet. As we have seen, however, most of the popular fiction of one hundred years ago was relegated to small daily or weekly doses, published in the columns of a "serious" newspaper, or to the odd volume published either in London or locally, and paid for out of the author's pocket. Today's popular fiction, by contrast, is a burgeoning industry, spurred on by desktop publishing and the innovations of the Internet. Globalization has meant the expansion of local popular fiction to international markets to serve the wider Caribbean immigrant populations of Europe and North America. These Caribbean diaspora readers have become the most critical factor in the creation of modern Caribbean literature, "popular" or not.[1] It is *their* experiences, *their* desires for a memory of "home," that shape most of these stories. Many if not most authors themselves are immigrants to North America or Europe, and reflect, to a greater or lesser degree, their new community. It is their more malleable sense of cultural identity as both Americans (mostly) and West Indians that has opened up the possibilities of genre and expanded the capacity for what constitutes Caribbean fiction.

Still, the Americanization of the Caribbean poses a dilemma for writers and readers. For some Caribbean writers, the lure of the American market evokes contradictory desires: they wish *not* to be pigeonholed as black writers, yet they crave access to the lucrative African American reading market, which buys primarily black-authored books. For immigrant readers, Caribbean popular fiction does similar double duty. It reinforces their Caribbean identity by allowing them to participate in an imaginary community of Caribbean readers, all linked to an understanding of "home." Yet it does this task while acknowledging the readers' status as North Americans. Popular fiction creates a more cosmopolitan diaspora identity through the Caribbeanizing of forms most associated with American popular culture: the "summer reading" romance novel, for example, or science fiction, or the television soap opera. These products of an American leisure sensibility reflect a changing model of middle-class identity for the Caribbean. The popular images of Caribbean characters they generate are not simply recognizable local archetypes—ah yes: the planter, the Rastafarian, the market woman—but also reconstituted archetypes: the Rastafarian playwright who lives in both London and New York; the Midnight Robber transformed into a futuristic female rebel; the "liberal" planter who falls in love with his slave. As these examples indicate, the new popular fiction often depends, literally, on readers' familiarity with an old "type" of Caribbean character, which it then subverts or otherwise transforms.[2]

The authors of today's popular fiction are a diverse lot: they range across genres, united only by a common Caribbean identification: Colin Channer's urban relationship novels; Nalo Hopkinson's science fiction; Anthony Winkler's rural comedies; and Valerie Belgrave's romances. In this chapter I examine the "new" fiction through two basic premises: that the rise of African American popular fiction has been the central agent in the rise of recent Caribbean popular fiction; and that local popular fiction—that is, fiction written or published within the Caribbean—itself functions as part of a diasporic exchange that consolidates Caribbean identity abroad. New Caribbean fiction is being shaped by two parallel yet paradoxical forces: the (African)Americanization of Caribbean immigrants in the United States,[3] and the insistent re-Caribbeanization of those same immigrants through the global circulation of local popular fiction and local typologies.

Globalizing Local Fiction

Local Caribbean fiction and internationally circulated Caribbean fiction have long been confined to separate critical spaces. Local fiction has been relegated to the category of unserious public fare, as we have seen. It is leisure reading and emphatically not for "outside" consumption. In contrast to its local relative, internationally circulated Caribbean fiction was, until recently, insistently highbrow, presupposing an erudite non-Caribbean audience as much as an erudite Caribbean one. When critics turned to their attention to popular culture in literature, their take was inevitably sociological, not aesthetic. Critical references on popular culture tended to be taken from internationally circulated novels that argued either that Caribbean popular culture functioned as a form of political resistance or that it was subject to co-optation by elites.

For example, discussions of carnival and street culture inevitably reference Trinidadian Earl Lovelace's 1979 novel, *The Dragon Can't Dance*. This novel promotes the argument made by Caribbean intellectuals that the culture of popular resistance has been co-opted by neocolonial forces. At another level, however, the novel satirizes such intellectual discourse as irrelevant. Lovelace's working-class protagonists reveal that it is they, popular culture's creators, who must ultimately determine and control the meaning of the popular if they are to exert any real power, an idea taken up by another critically acclaimed writer, Jamaican Michelle Cliff, in *No Telephone to Heaven (1987)*.[4] Today's popular Caribbean literature, however, illustrates there is no such dissonance between the producers and the consumers, or creators and interpreters. Popular literature reflects completely the global desires of the Caribbean's aspirational class without the mediating critical apparatus that controls and determines meaning. Intellectual discourse over neocolonial appropriation has given way to a popular discourse predicated on common class identification: we produce our own culture, we consume our own culture, we interpret our own culture. Whereas a previous generation associated the international bourgeoisie with alienation from the local, today the distinction has little relevance, if ever indeed it were true. Saskia Sassen argues that globalization is not separate from the national but rather partly inhabits it, and indeed it is this national dimension that is illuminated in the global dimensions of popular Caribbean literature. Although a feature of the existing scholarship on global classes is, as Sassen says, "its prevalent tendency to equate the globalism of the transnational professional and executive class with cosmopolitanism," this equation is not necessarily accurate. Just as the professional class "remains embedded in thick localized environments," so too does the aspiring class seek a connection to a larger global class in its desires and tastes, tastes that nevertheless remain emphatically local, national, and regional.[5]

Old School versus New

The Anglophone Caribbean does not have a large audience for published fiction. Half of all book sales are from school textbooks, testifying to the population's utilitarian view of books typical of many developing countries.[6]

Even the once-solid academic market for fiction is threatened by changing attitudes in the high schools, where there is mounting skepticism toward literature as a subject of compulsory study.[7] Although the study of English language remains compulsory for most, the subject of literature is left up to individual high schools to determine its relevance to the core curriculum, leading some schools to cut the subject altogether. Jamaican writer Marlon James reports that "at my old high school the teachers recently took a vote to decide if literature should remain a compulsory subject. It was the literature teachers who voted no."[8]

The declining interest in serious fiction is compounded by the unstable economics of the book trade. Still a local affair, the trade is controlled by individuals and families dominant in the local industries for generations. The lack of profitability in the book trade has been a problem not just for Caribbean writers but also for publishers of Caribbean fiction, both local and foreign, who must carefully calculate the purchasing power of each novel that they sell. One British publishing magazine summarized it thus: "The total English-speaking population across the region is barely four million. The countries are stubbornly independent and fractious, and their aspirations are very different. The influence of the nearby US is invasive, and literacy rates are problematic."[9]

The view from inside the region is even more critical. Norman Rae, a Jamaican theater director, believes that the dearth of publishing houses in the English-speaking Caribbean is not so much a problem of money as of culture. He cites the relatively prolific publishing industries of Latin America and the Hispanic Caribbean as evidence that in those societies,

> writers and artists help create the nation and its thinking and...their contribution is as vital as bread and wine. In Kingston, the metropolis of the English-speaking Caribbean, you can count on less than one hand the bookshops that offer the equivalent or even attendants who know anything about books (unless they're schoolbooks).
>
> The University Press, for example, tries hard to produce elegant, well-designed books, but who reads them?[10]

There are, to be sure, outposts of optimism: one of the more promising ventures aimed at a mass market reading audience is the Trinidad-based *Caribbean Review of Books,* which writes lengthy reviews of both scholarly and popular books for the educated lay audience. The large number of academics and intellectuals on the editorial board, however, suggests that the readers themselves reflect a fairly narrow demographic, and indeed, the *Review* started out as a university-based journal.

Popular author Colin Channer, who wields considerable influence in the Jamaican publishing industry because of his commercial successes there, is similarly critical. Contrasting Jamaica's book industry with its robust music industry, Channer argues that Jamaican fiction is floundering because it is elitist, whereas Jamaican music is flourishing because its music industry is more inclusive.[11] Channer believes that most of the good writing in the Caribbean is not published, and with that in mind his model for instituting a dynamic literary scene is Trinidad's calypso tent, or Jamaica's proliferating music scene, where even in the early 1970s almost anyone could produce a recording cheaply.[12] This more democratic vision of the Caribbean publishing industry, as articulated through Channer's Calabash writing workshops and publications chronicled in the last chapter, is fundamentally linked to the "new" Caribbean literary aesthetic elaborated by Channer and his Calabash collaborator, fellow Jamaican and poet Kwame Dawes. In various writings and interviews—including, in Dawes's case, a work of literary criticism—they contrast the "new" Caribbean writing, a genre they aver is inspired by a globally positioned "reggae aesthetic," to what they view as the more insular, anticolonial yet "genteel" writing of the past.[13]

In this view, the "old school" of Caribbean literature was essentially produced by British publishers such as Heinemann, which published books for an English or Caribbean school audience and cherry-picked the themes: hence colonialism, mimicry, and the other thematic signposts of Caribbean literature were established by decades of rote inculcation. If England represents the dreary past of colonial conformity, America represents the fulfillment of Caribbean singularity and difference. Says Channer, "the Caribbean novel is still for the most part engaged in dialogue with its colonial past, a conversation that is now of little interest or relevance to the rest of the world and even the people of the Caribbean, who overwhelmingly prefer American books. I am an American citizen, and this country gave me the opportunity to be a writer."[14] Positioning himself as a sort of America-inspired literary rebel, Channer takes as his creed the Bob Marley lyric "I want to disturb my neighbor": in other words, literature should provoke.[15]

Provoke what, though? It is hard to see any, save erotic, provocations in his oeuvre, most of which derives from the popular African American "urban relationship" genre, despite his insistence to the contrary. (Indeed, the "new" aesthetic in Channer's work seems to consist mostly of a tendency toward explicit depictions of sex.) On an earlier version of his Web site, the New York–based Channer aligned himself with young, "serious" Caribbean authors, and claimed to be puzzled by the comparisons of his novels to those of popular African American writers such as Eric Jerome Dickey and

E. Lynn Harris. "You can count on them for a book a year," he says. "They are very clear about their ambitions: they write *entertainments*. And people turn to them for that. My ambitions are different.... Anyone who's ever really read my work will understand that these are not my natural peers."[16] Indeed, Channer takes a swipe at formulaic African American romances in his novel *Passing Through,* in which one character, himself a Caribbean writer, tells his African American girlfriend that "after Terry McMillan, babe, the constitution of your country says that there is a book that every negress has to write... four sister-friends in Atlanta, D.C., or L.A. Places where they get to drive expensive cars.... There you have the recipe. Go cook the people's book."[17]

The recipe appears to be one that Channer himself uses. His early novels feature main characters with obvious appeal for young black readers with professional aspirations: sexy, well-read black bohemians with glamorous occupations who move easily between the metropolitan centers of North America and the Caribbean. Channer invites his reader to see herself through the romantic filter of the jet-setting black professional class, a view not lost on reviewers. "Channer woos the ladies with searing, sex-filled romps peopled by rich black folk armed with killer bodies and Ivy-League degrees," notes one. Another refers to him as one of the "testosterone-influenced practitioners of black chick-lit."[18] Certainly the marketing team for his first two novels projected his audience to be young black women, the same audience that E. Lynn Harris (whose endorsement appears on the cover of one novel) and Eric Jerome Dickey pursue. All three novels feature covers with attractive young black women at their center. The banner at the top of Channer's first novel, *Waiting in Vain* (1998), proclaims it a best seller "as featured in *Essence*," the African American women's magazine. The cover image is a recipe for black erotica: a close-up photograph of a young, hip, Afroed black woman wearing dark glasses in whose lenses are reflected the image of a dreadlocked, naked, heavily muscled young black man. The gaze is hers, not his—a concrete indicator of the book's main demographic. These basic elements are repeated on the cover of Channer's sophomore effort, *Satisfy My Soul*.[19]

Still, these images are not necessarily of the Caribbean professional class so much as of the international black professional class. The international black professional class is a grouping much more palatable to a readership that encompasses both Caribbean residents and immigrants. Caribbean diaspora readers might wish to see themselves as socially mobile and cosmopolitan, but not as African American—a group they constantly imitate but with whom they do not ultimately identify—nor as stolidly, laboriously "immigrant" or "Third World," with all of the associations of poverty and the cultural rearguard.[20] How the reader positions herself through her desires is clearly important to authors like Channer. In describing his readership he both flatters his audience and acknowledges that he provides an element of social fantasy: "My existing fans are smart and worldly. They support my work because my books are filled with smart and worldly people just like them.... still I write with a kind of mindfulness that most people who read my work are not from my world."[21]

What is more interesting than the actual substance of Channer's texts, then, is his insistence on his difference as a "glocal," popular/serious, phenomenon. (Indeed, Channer has found literary success in both the Caribbean and North America—no mean feat.) At Channer's 2006 Calabash Literary Festival, the deejay spun a relentless cycle of "golden oldies" reggae records from the 1970s, almost all of them Bob Marley tunes, and none of them the infamously "offensive" dancehall tunes that dominate Caribbean airwaves today. The vendors in the booths that rimmed the festival sold T-shirts that proclaimed "The Cuban Revolution" and even "Castro." The ambient nostalgia for Jamaica's most politicized, most overtly anticolonial era was everywhere evident, reflecting perhaps the coming of age of the festival's predominantly middle-aged patrons. It seems that Channer's proclamation of a "new" literary aesthetic is simply a way to call academic attention to a younger generation of writers whose aims are, for the most part, less overtly political than those of their predecessors.[22] The "new" writing is presented in a format that is both modern—the efficiency and elegance of the well-run Calabash festival—and traditional, anchoring the works in an atmosphere that suggests the "old" themes. The "new" aesthetic is, in actuality, implicitly invested in the "old" tradition: the organizers have worked to reissue out-of-print works by respected colonial Jamaican writers from the 1940s and 1950s, in collaboration with Macmillan Publishing and other stalwarts of the book publishing industry.[23] In 2007 they arranged for the venerable Commonwealth Prize to be awarded during the Festival.

The strategy is a winning one. The director of Jamaica's Novelty Trading Company, the primary distributor of books on the island, reports that Channer's novels outsell every other novel except, ironically, H. G. de Lisser's perennial best seller, the plantation gothic *The White Witch of Rose Hall*. Fame has something to do with this: Channer's *Waiting in Vain* was a best seller in both the Caribbean and the United States, and listed as a Critics' Choice in the *Washington Post*. Apart from his writing, Channer is a minor celebrity in Jamaica and the larger Anglophone Caribbean for his work with the Calabash festival. According to one publisher, it is Channer's canny marketing of his novels rather than their good reviews that has propelled them to the top of the lists: his first two novels are named for Bob Marley tunes. Jamaican and other Caribbean readers are immediately flagged to the book when the title is taken from a "text" that they recognize. For the same reason, the publisher speculates, Guyanese Canadian science fiction writer Nalo Hopkinson's novel *Brown Girl in the Ring,* whose title is taken from a traditional children's song popular in Jamaica, sold well in Jamaica; her second effort, however, titled *Midnight Robber* after the traditional carnival figure from Trinidad, did not.[24]

Racial Ideology and the American Market

These canny title formulas suggest that the authors themselves are consciously tailoring their literary products for the market, and as I've mentioned, Channer has a background in brand marketing. Hopkinson, however, vigorously denies that marketing has anything to do with her titles or indeed with the concerns of her work:

> Marketing is not what drives me. Originally I wanted to title *Salt Roads* "Griffonne" [a pejorative term for light-skinned blacks, used in New Orleans and the French-speaking Caribbean]. I knew it wouldn't mean much in the English-speaking Caribbean, maybe in the French. My editor said that she was overruled by the marketing team, who said my main audience would not understand what the word meant, and that they would be too embarrassed by not knowing the word to pick up the book.[25]

By "main audience" Hopkinson believes her editor meant American. It appears the editor probably meant African American; the novel was marketed not within Hopkinson's genre, science fiction—which has a mainly white, mostly male audience—but as a mainstream release.[26] Hopkinson, like most authors, has little control over the titles and covers of her books. Given that several of Hopkinson's novels have titles that echo a well-known phrase from some part of the African diaspora (*Mojo* is yet another black-identified title), and that all of the paperback covers feature renderings of black people, a black diaspora readership has clearly long been a main focus of her American marketing team's strategy. Certainly without the large and voracious readership of African American women who purchase the works of Terry McMillan and other popular African American authors, neither Hopkinson nor Channer, nor any of the Caribbean authors who publish in the United States, would likely have been published by mass market publishing houses such as Warner and Random House (the latter's One World and Strivers Row imprints were created to showcase multicultural and African

American fiction, respectively). Acknowledging the power of African American women readers, Brooklyn-based Trinidadian writer Elizabeth Nunez, herself a recipient of an American Book Award, asserts that it is the opinion of African American women's reading groups, like the Go On Girl! Book Club, that matter more to her than the opinion of critics and writers, because it is the members of these reading clubs who buy her novels and keep them relevant.[27]

In the late 1980s the major American publishing houses "discovered" black readers, in particular black women readers, after Terry McMillan singlehandedly turned her "serious" novel, *Mama,* into a bona fide best seller by marketing it herself.[28] Although metropolitan publishers now acknowledge the power of African American readers, the Caribbean reading public is perceived to be too small to have its own marketing niche. Nalo Hopkinson's editor observed that, although she saw Hopkinson's novel *New Moon's Arms* as a Caribbean novel, "if I were to label it as 'Caribbean' I'd lose readers and I don't want to do that. We can target Caribbean readers by branching out but keep the message as broad as possible for 'black readers.'"[29] Accordingly, most of these new Caribbean novels are marketed as African American or distributed under an African American imprint. Readings and book signings at African American–owned bookstores and book fairs, like the Harlem Book Fair and the Hue-Man Bookstore and Café, are essential stops now for any Afro-Caribbean author who hopes for sales in the United States. Nalo Hopkinson informed me that a significant number of members of her marketing team are black women of African American and Caribbean descent.[30] Because, in the larger sense, Afro-Caribbean immigrant readers in the United States are black Americans, from a socioeconomic perspective it makes sense to categorize their literature with that of the native-born African American population.

The problem is the categories themselves. Just as Channer complains of being pigeonholed in the "urban relationship" genre (a genre to which critics do not pay much attention, he rightly notes),[31] an Afro-Caribbean science fiction writer like Hopkinson can become trapped by the conventions of that genre. Although gothic fabulist tales have been popular and ubiquitous in Caribbean popular literature since the nineteenth century,[32] science fiction in the conventional sense is not. Hopkinson's novels do not mirror the images typically associated with American-style science fiction: white men pioneering in space, à la *Star Trek,* meeting aliens, and utilizing far-out technology. Like science fiction's core white American readers, African diaspora readers expect to see themselves reflected in the story. So West Indians most likely read Hopkinson's novels not because they mirror a futuristic society of indeterminate ethnic and national origin, but because they mirror their own cultural history and traditions, however recombinative. Caribbean folk tradition is consciously and lovingly evoked in almost all of Hopkinson's work, from the folkloric titles to the use of a Pan-Caribbean Creole and a Pan-Caribbean glossary of place-names and associations.[33] Yet if Caribbean readers will be drawn to a novel positioned as science fiction because of these familiar associations, the conventional science fiction reader probably will not be.

When asked how well black-authored science fiction sells, science fiction editor Jaime Levine commented bluntly, "They don't. [Black] titles split markets. White sf [science fiction] readers think, oh, this is not for me, and black readers from what I've seen don't read sf, they don't think it's for them."[34] Science fiction, as a popular genre, is inevitably published by mass market publishers. For a mass market publisher to recoup costs, the book must appeal to the widest common denominator, far beyond the 2,000 to 4,000 book sales that a small publisher would consider a success. Levine went on to say that although Hopkinson had been taken on by Warner Aspect Books purely on the strength of her writing submission, the company had already published famous African American science fiction writer Octavia Butler and detective novel writer Walter Moseley, and it had seen an opportunity to strengthen its offerings in black-authored fiction. And certainly Hopkinson's first two books had sold relatively well. Still, even though black-identified issues are central to both Hopkinson's and Butler's work, Levine asserted that "the successful black-authored sf book is marketed as sf rather than as 'black.'" Still, she believes that *Dark Matter*, an anthology of black science fiction to which Hopkinson contributed, was "political" by its very nature as an ethnically identified text. Hopkinson's novel *Salt Roads* was her "turning point book" as a science fiction writer. Although marketed as science fiction, it did not conform to the expectations of the genre. The novel—moving back, not forward, in time—is set in late eighteenth-century Haiti, entangling Caribbean history with its supernatural legacies. After the novel's poor sales, the decision was made to transform Hopkinson from a science fiction writer into a writer of women's fiction, specifically of black women's fiction, which is how her current fiction has been marketed and in which slot she remains.

Mass market publishers like Warner Aspect are not shy about their commercial interest in subsuming Caribbean fiction into one of the prescribed categories. Smaller publishers, on the other hand, can afford to be more eclectic and less market driven in their preoccupations. Or, at least, they can afford to concentrate their marketing efforts on a smaller demographic of readers who are less invested in genre categories. This narrower demographic appears to be the future of one segment of Caribbean book publishing, as Caribbean authors across the board eschew the school-catalogue-oriented Caribbean Writers Series formula of Heinemann for a more eclectic, and ultimately more profitable, audience. If Caribbean literature is difficult to position outside the African American genre for publishers like Warner Aspect and Ballantine, it may be because the Caribbean still has no firm place in the American imagination. Yet that feature, its un-place-ability, may be precisely what makes it attractive to independent publishers who cater to readers looking for the "unusual" or exotic. For example, the Brooklyn-based independent publisher Akashic Books has positioned itself as a publisher of new Caribbean fiction, which it markets much the same way as its other popular fiction, aimed more or less exclusively at young white American college students with a taste for "underground" themes. Akashic's founder and publisher is Johnny Temple, a relatively young man who tours with his own rock n' roll band. Temple became interested in publishing Caribbean fiction as a result of his youthful adventures at the now-defunct Reggae Sunsplash as well as a fortuitous Brooklyn meeting with Colin Channer in his role as Calabash organizer.

Temple says that Akashic's catalogue is not market driven, as illustrated by the small number of books (twenty-four) that it publishes each year. Further, he emphasizes that he has a personal passion for the books he publishes. "In some ways we are a typical left-wing company," he observes, in that his books themes often converge with left-of-center values such as opposition to racism and homophobia; his efforts to publish Cuban writers in Cuba has threatened to violate the Trading with the Enemy Act. Akashic's motto is "Reverse Gentrification of the Literary World," a sentiment in neat accord with Channer's stated view of Caribbean literature. "We never look at it that the audience is limited to Jamaicans or any other group," said Temple, who observed that Channer didn't want to be "reduced" to the category of "black writer." Accessing Akashic's core audience is insurance against such reduction. They, in Temple's view, are well-educated "young white hipsters in cities who listen to independent rock music," cultivate a rebel image— "dyed hair, pierced nose and stuff"—and have a taste for the subversive. Akashic's catalogue is ripe with books that explore provocative—Temple calls them "taboo"—themes, such as AIDS, punk rock, and religious fanaticism. The implicit assumption is that most popular literature does not challenge the status quo, and to this end Akashic positions itself as counterculture fiction for the urban reader. "Akashic challenges the happy-ending theory or women's writing or whatever," elaborated Temple, distancing his catalogue from the predictable inanities of "chick lit."[35]

Male pop lit clichés, however, are taken more seriously. Akashic's first Caribbean acquisition, Uruguayan Cuban author Daniel Chavarría's *Tango for a Torturer,* is billed on the publisher's Web site as a "sexy political thriller"; the volume's cover features a vintage dime-store-novelesque image of a brown-skinned woman with a heavy bosom spilling out of her red dress.[36] The prominent blurb on another edition—featuring yet another brown-skinned beauty with a heaving bosom—quotes an endorsement from a Scottish newspaper: "Sex is something Latin American writers such as Chavarría do so much better than us Brits." Chavarría himself is described on the Web site as having two passions: classical literature and prostitutes, as if to consciously reject the division between highbrow and low. The deliberately kitschy cover art similarly elides the division by relying on its viewers' ironic sense of vintage camp. It was their mutual admiration for Chavarría that drew Channer and Temple together. Temple's vision of Channer's audience appears to be the one that a new generation of Caribbean male authors seeks: one that is educated but not tied to the academy's approval, one with no investment in maintaining the distinctions of "good" and "bad" literature, "high" and "low" culture—and one that is not *presumed* to be female, even if it is. (It would not be the first time that ambitious male writers who seek a "serious" audience have wished to avoid the perception that their work is tailored to female readers: American author Jonathan Franzen worried that male readers might be put off reading his acclaimed novel *The Corrections* after it was chosen for Oprah's Book Club.)[37]

Akashic Books published Jamaican writer Marlon James's first novel, *John Crow's Devil,* to critical acclaim. James believes that Akashic's primary readership of white college students worked in his favor

> because it [*John Crow's Devil*] went to the mainstream white media first—it didn't get labeled as a genre. Cuz you don't want to get labeled with the Caribbean Writer Series type thing, cuz then they ghettoise you. They lock you in somewhere and go "Oh! He's a Caribbean writer, oh, we don't cover Caribbean fiction full stop. So it did, in its own way, work well—I wouldn't have gotten a *New York Times* review if it was the other way around.[38]

James's anxiety about being ghettoized by a genre implies that there are books that have no genre. The real issue, of course, is that the genre in question—Caribbean literature—is too small to hold an American publisher's interest. By contrast, the "genre" of American fiction—or mystery fiction, or science fiction, or romance fiction—is capacious enough to elicit commercial interest, because it means, in essence, white readers, America's ethnic majority. James's belief that it is the white college readership that propelled his book to a *New York Times* review does not mean, however, that it is white college students who are the publisher's expected primary readers. Both *John Crow's Devil* and the Calabash anthology *Iron Balloons* are listed under "African American Interest" on Akashic's Web site. (This categorization does not mean, on the other hand, that it will be African Americans or even West Indians who will actually read any of the books so classified, only that the problem of genre persists even for independent booksellers.) Despite Temple's claim not to focus on a nationally specific audience, *John Crow's Devil* sold well in Jamaica. Meanwhile, Temple acknowledged that he is still trying to tap the Caribbean audience in the United States, in part by targeting Caribbean-focused book fairs among other strategies. "We bust our asses to sell these [Caribbean] books," he said.

In the end, it may be African American readers who "find" the Caribbean readership for Akashic and other American publishers. African Americans have a powerful presence in the publishing industry, as well as a long and continuous history of reading clubs. The choices made by African American book clubs influence the larger community to a significant degree.[39] By contrast, although literary societies existed in the Caribbean from the nineteenth century into the mid-twentieth, they are no longer a part of the popular culture. Caribbean readers of today are influenced by two main venues: the classroom and the American best-seller lists.[40] Given the influence of African American professional culture on Afro-Caribbean professional culture through middle-class venues such as *Essence* magazine, it seems fair to surmise that African American reading habits to some degree shape Caribbean ones. Indeed, African American interest in fiction with "black" themes, regardless of the black authors' national origin, guarantee that black authors from outside the United States have an opportunity to sell books.[41] Marlon James himself acknowledges the power, even the centrality, of the African American female reading audience's commercial influence and its ability to keep afloat black novelists across the diaspora:

> The first time I went [to the United States] I really did not want to be known as a black novelist. But somebody pointed out to me that yeah, but you know something though, all those organisations like Mocha Moms [a support group for mothers of colour] and the black reading groups, and the Sistas this and so on, they are supportive and they're loyal and they'll be the best friend you can have. And I've seen it. I've seen the same people come out for my Harlem book reading and they bring their friends. When other people see that they say, "Oh, this is a

writer we can work with because he has a community." Because you don't really have a sense of community here [in the Caribbean].[42]

This lack of a literary community in the Caribbean, which James laments, points to a fundamental problem for publishers of Caribbean fiction. Readers tend to buy books that reflect their own community, however they see that community. Despite their large numbers in a few American metropolises, Caribbean people living in the United States are largely first- and second-generation immigrants. They do not have the cultural presence to justify their own genre category in the United States. (Nor, perhaps, do they have the purchasing power: Caribbean populations in the United States and Canada are also largely working class.) The Caribbean audience for popular Caribbean literature is an amorphous entity, situated anywhere from the Caribbean to the metropolitan centers of North America and Europe. As James ruefully claims, "It's been hard just getting [my] books into the Caribbean." By contrast, in England, with its large and multigenerational Caribbean population, black popular literature presses such as Black Amber and X Press emerged in the early 1990s and have achieved commercial success because they can market directly to a large buying public of Caribbean—particularly Jamaican—origin. To do so they have spawned their own working-class genre—"yardie" fiction—and cater to "the black person in the street."[43] Their audience is, unlike that for most black popular literature in the United States, heavily male. The advocacy of reading as an oppositional activity for working-class black British men is such a constant presence in the black British pop fiction that Curdella Forbes wonders "if the authors are instructed to insert such statements as a kind of advertising manifesto."[44] Further, X Press has set its sights on deconstructing the highbrow/lowbrow division in Caribbean fiction by reissuing Claude McKay's canonical *Banana Bottom* with yet another dime-store-type cover featuring its heroine as a sexy young beauty.

The complex interplay of marketing with perceptions of ethnic difference (or sameness) is at the heart of how, and where, Caribbean fiction is published outside of the Caribbean. Although the Caribbean has its own history of popular fiction, it never had a popular fiction *industry*. It has always had, however, a taste for American popular fiction. As the didactic purpose of literature wanes in the Caribbean, American consumption patterns become more central to determining how the Caribbean sees the purpose and utility of literature. It comes as no surprise, of course, that marketing and sales play so prominent a role in determining what constitutes Caribbean fiction. Fiction is, in its broadest sense, part of the entertainment industry, not the academy. It begs the question of how critics interpret the *Caribbeanness* of

Caribbean literature, however, when even the most general overview of the industry reveals the far extent to which American conceptions of ethnicity, reading audience, and reading culture are now determining that literature's content and audience.

On the one hand, Caribbean *difference* from African American culture creates a niche market, or the perception of one, for independent publishers in the United States who trade on the image of Caribbean radicalism or cultural otherness. On the other, the elision of Caribbean with African American culture guarantees that Caribbeanness becomes a variant of an (African) American norm, a widening of the parameters of the globalized African American subject. Even the X Press series, the British version of popular Caribbean literature, is arguably little more than a London-based version of African American "ghetto lit" from earlier trailblazers such as Iceberg Slim and Donald Goines. This inevitable bifurcation of the Caribbean subject mirrors a similar split between the local and the international readers of local popular literatures.

Revisiting the Plantation: History, Tourism, and Local Pop Fiction

The plantation is an archetypal image of the Caribbean, but it is a paradoxical archetype. It evokes a brooding legacy of slavery and violence, which hovers over the present like a miasma. It also evokes a tropical paradise, complete with "quaint" and friendly villagers. The paradisiacal associations are, Krista Thompson informs us, the result of a concerted effort in the late nineteenth century by an assortment of elites—hoteliers, colonial administrators, rich local whites—to refashion the poor image of the islands, which were regarded as death traps by the British because of their high mortality rates from malaria, cholera, and a host of other tropical diseases. The birth of the Caribbean's modern tourism industry lay in the dissemination of picturesque postcard images of Jamaica and the Bahamas around the United Kingdom and the United States. What the white viewer saw were reassuring portraits of barefoot black peasant women in an untouched, "natural" landscape. Images of black men were relatively scarce.[45] Many of the traditional images of the Caribbean stem from these originary images of exotic, yet disciplined, subjects of the British Empire.

The tourist gaze, as emblematized by the tourist brochure, has thus been essential to the way the Caribbean has looked at itself. Modern Caribbean writers have tried to dislodge the tourist gaze by utilizing the paradisiacal image for oppositional purposes. From Derek Walcott's vengeful vision of the fallen British Empire in his poem "Ruins of a Great House" (1956), to Margaret Cezair Thompson's allusively titled novel of war-torn, dystopian Jamaica in *A True History of Paradise* (1999), Caribbean authors have argued that the grandeur of the plantation image is a form of historical deracination, obscuring an ugly Caribbean reality under its appealing facade. And indeed this is true. Still, it is easy to understand the appeal of the plantation ideal for white tourists seeking fun in the sun, served by a subservient native population.[46] What is less easy to see is the continuing appeal of the image for Caribbean peoples themselves. The plantation image, along with its iconic types, inhabits much of the region's popular fiction, particularly fiction that is locally produced (not to mention its presence on local television soap operas such as Jamaica's *Royal Palm Estate,* which chronicles the extended family ties of an old planter family). The deployment of the plantation is varied: it ranges from Anthony Winkler's piquant depictions of Jamaican villagers in his most famous novel, *The Lunatic,* which features a local busha (or planter); to Valerie Belgrave's plantation romance, *Ti Marie;* to Colin Channer's *Passing Through,* which uses an old planter to tell a history of the imaginary island of San Carlos.

Some of these images are directly linked to what a tourist would expect to see. Indeed, Channer is frank about how he pitched his book to American readers: "A lot of the characters are American travelers, so American readers will be able to relate," he says on his Web site. Nevertheless, he indigenizes the paradisiacal association by claiming that "San Carlos is magical because it's in the Caribbean—and all the islands of the Caribbean began as creations of an Amerindian god of leisure and taste."[47] The main demographics of Channer's readers are African American and Afro-Caribbean women, so it appears that African American readers also find appeal in the escapist fantasies and paradisiacal images of the Caribbean, despite their own history with oppressive plantation economies.

As Ian Strachan has noted, African American tourists are a courted demographic in the tourist industry, and they are just as susceptible to the "plantation paradise" imagery as their white counterparts.[48] The tropical winter vacation, so long a privilege of the white rich, is now more accessible to African Americans, who are flocking to these majority black islands, where they feel at home as part of the ethnic majority as well as "special" because they are a coveted commodity. They are, after all, American tourists—with American dollars to spend. *Essence* magazine has long promoted travel in the global locations of the African diaspora and showcases the Caribbean regularly in its pages. Terry McMillan's best-selling novel and film *How Stella Got Her Groove Back* (1998) is about a middle-aged professional African American woman who is romanced on a trip to Jamaica. She meets her love match, a younger black Jamaican man from the professional middle class (his parents, we discover, are doctors). The role of the Jamaica Tourism Board in the film's making cannot be understated in that the clichéd images of the island's beauty play out as an extended advertisement for the island paradise. *How Stella Got Her Groove Back* revamps the paradise association by both sexualizing and modernizing the Caribbean. Certainly the photograph on the cover of *Passing Through* evokes exactly this kind of vacation paradise: a slim black woman in the tropical wear of the well-to-do—a wide-brimmed hat and a colorful tropical-print bathing suit and wrap—against a backdrop of Spanish colonial architecture.[49] The black female professional subject is thus repositioned in Caribbean history. No longer an ethnographic subject— the peasant woman on a country road who functions merely as part of the scenery—the black woman is now the subject of the frame: the quintessential First World traveler, consuming the "romantic" colonial history evoked by the architecture. Although Caribbean history continues to be a staging ground for tourist desire, this time the tourist could be Caribbean or African American—*all* black professional women of the diaspora are invited to insert themselves as main actors into the historical romance of the Caribbean. The black woman's painful subaltern past in the slave economy is replaced by a revised version of the story where she is triumphant.

The plantation paradise is even more powerfully evoked on the cover of Belgrave's *Ti Marie*. Taken from batik created by the author herself, the cover features a brown woman in a white billowing dress and a flower in her hair embracing a white man in eighteenth-century dress amid a profusion of tropical color, with a red and white gingerbread-style colonial mansion in the distance. No reader would guess, to look at the picture, that the two lovers are master and slave. The couple is indistinguishable from the glorious landscape: at once historicized and dehistoricized. The reader is thus cued to see the novel as a historical romance and *not* as a novel about slavery.[50]

Slavery is not a very romantic subject. But inasmuch as it is an inescapable part of Afro-Caribbean history, for any historical romance featuring a black or brown heroine the slave experience needs to be transformed by the powers of escapist literature. Or so the author thinks. In an interview she elaborated on why she chose the genre of the historical romance:

> I think it's time for us to have books that are also for pleasure.... I write for people what I think the people like.... Rather than criticise people for liking soap operas, foreign entertainment, etc., I look and see what is it that attracts them. If you like romance or you like to deal with

FIGURE 5. Cover of *Ti Marie*, by Valerie Belgrave (1988 ed., published by Heinemann International, Kingston). Courtesy of Valerie Belgrave.

the aristocracy, I'll deal with it. But what I'll do is to bring it down to our level. I'll show you what truly sympathetic white aristocrats would have been like if it belongs to us, if it was in our control or circumstances.[51]

So, for Belgrave, it is the local setting, and local "control" of the story, that is necessary to transform the historical romance into one in which black subjects can be actors. To be sure, the historical romance is an old genre in the Caribbean—H. G. de Lisser, as I have mentioned, made a small industry out of plantation romances. Belgrave's explanation, however, suggests that it is not so much the story as who is telling it—in her case, black women—that gives it validity in the postcolonial era. Elsewhere she says that she wrote the novel because she wanted to recognize "middle-class contributions to Trinidadian culture rather than focusing on barrack yards and poverty," and "she was tired of waiting for someone else to tell this story."[52] The elevation of poverty in Trinidadian literature as represented by "yard literature" is an attempt by Trinidadians to write "like the British" and "for a foreign audience," she concludes.

Yard literature is the genre more or less begun by C. L. R. James with the publication of his novel *Minty Alley,* whose protagonist is a middle-class black man living in a working-class yard. As an example of Trinidad's early realist fiction, the novel sustains a realism that is inauthentic because of its downward gaze. By contrast, *Ti Marie* moves its gaze upward by removing the sting of history: coercion and exploitation become seduction and a happy ending. Belgrave sees her improbable romance of a black slave and a white slaveholder as a more authentic sample of Trinidadian literature, as well as a showcase of actual middle-class "contributions." What her comments reveal more particularly than their surface judgments, however, is the view that an authentic Caribbean literature does not examine poverty and other social embarrassments that put the reader in one of two personas: the detached foreign analyst or the humiliated object of that analysis. If, as one is tempted to argue, nothing could be more objectifying than slavery, the response might be, Not so if the black reader *wishes* to identify with the slave when she is beautiful and desirable. Not so if the black reader can be assured that the black or brown subject will ascend upward, not downward. The popular genres allow the Caribbean reader to be the socially mobile subject, and indeed the publisher of *Ti Marie* marketed the novel as a "Caribbean *Gone with the Wind,*" ensuring that local readers will understand the heroine as Caribbean while giving international readers a familiar prototype for an epic romance.[53] The novel was successful enough that Belgrave went on to write a number of shorter romances for Heinemann's now-defunct Caribbean Caresses series.

Like Belgrave, white Jamaican writer Anthony Winkler wrote his popular rustic comedies *The Painted Canoe* (1983) and *The Lunatic* (1987) for a local Jamaican audience and published them in Kingston. Yet they also appeal to a tourist sensibility and have been reissued in Britain by Macmillan Caribbean for the British market. As one British reviewer enthused, they "offer a reviving antidote to midwinter gloom." Although Winkler's memoir of socialist 1970s Jamaica, *Going Home to Teach (1995),* reveals a viciously unequal and exploitative society, the reviewer found that "Winkler's fiction magics the island into a place of rough-edged enchantment."[54] It is easy to see the appeal for the British market: Winkler's stories play up "old West Indies" archetypes familiar to both British and Caribbean readers, so his work is now hugely popular in the larger Caribbean immigrant communities of North America and Europe. (*The Lunatic* was even made into a movie in 1993.) The stories elicit nostalgia for a bygone Caribbean village life where bushas still rule and Junkanoo dancers dance in the streets for Christmas. Winkler does not try to subvert the plantation image: he revels in the idea of Caribbean exoticism and difference. Although the busha is an anachronism in today's Caribbean, and although his stories are set in Jamaica's late twentieth-century present, Winkler writes as if these types are still present in the time-capsuled villages of the Caribbean.

The humor of the stories often comes from the clash between modern and traditional Jamaica. In *The Lunatic,* for example, Winkler's description of the busha emphasizes the character's local importance by contrasting him with an implied American norm, suggesting a kind of time warp: "The very title of 'Busha'—a slave corruption of 'overseer'—spoke of ancestry, wealth, land, striking the local ear with the same galvanic ring that initials such as ITT, IBM, GM have on Americans."[55] Of course, the names of American industries strike the local ear with precisely that galvanic ring, but no matter: Winkler's point is made, and cultural difference is established.

In *Coming Home to Teach* Winkler reveals that during the heady days of the socialist Manley era, when black pride was part of a formal government position, he felt he had "'internalized' a black identity just as many of his upwardly mobile black peers were ingesting a white one."[56] Even so, Winkler's novels are clearly aligned with the old planter stories of the premodern era, suggesting that, for Winkler and his audience, the plantation past holds more romantic possibilities than the present. If the "black" romance of the plantation paradise is to revise history so that blacks are agents within it, perhaps the "white" popular romance of the plantation is to return to a "simpler" time when whites still had a visible and important cultural role to play, and a recognizable type.[57]

It is not hard to understand why this idea would appeal to white West Indian readers. Yet it clearly holds appeal for the nonwhite ones who constitute Winkler's main demographic, and in particular the ones who live outside of the Caribbean. Plantation typologies are an insistent reminder of "home," a way of plugging into a community of shared mythologies. Immigrant Caribbean populations must insistently remind themselves of their Caribbean difference in order to maintain their sense of a permanent and immutable Caribbean identity. That difference from an omnivorous North American or European identity is sharpened by such devices as the constantly circulating online "jokes" among Caribbean people that feature an interchangeable Caribbean national whose more primitive but practical cultural sensibility clashes with the supposedly more sophisticated machinations of the American or European.[58] Plantation typologies are a part of that difference, requiring insider knowledge of Caribbean histories and mythologies. The readers for the plantation stories might be assumed to be a different demographic than those who read "urban relationship" novels or science fiction stories, but on closer inspection they constitute part of the overlapping communities of local and "foreign" Caribbean readers, who trade books as well as goods across the Atlantic. *Passing Through* begins almost one hundred years earlier as the story of a white planter and ends in the present with his black descendant, a New York–based writer much like the author himself. The busha, along with other Caribbean typologies, becomes yet another commodity whose circulation confirms the cultural authenticity of those writers and readers even as they migrate, ascend, Americanize.

Notes

Introduction

1. See S. Harris, "Dreadlocked Beauty a Bold Step," Letters to the Editor, *Jamaica Gleaner* (online ed.), March 28, 2007.

2. "Redwood, an Ideal Jamaican Mix," *Jamaica Gleaner* (online ed.), March 25, 2007.

3. Malcolm Page, "Review Essay: West Indian Writers," *Novel: A Forum for Fiction* 3, no. 2 (Winter 1970): 167–72, quotation at 167. In this article, Page reviews *The Islands in Between: Essays on West Indian Literature* by Louis James and *Caribbean Writers: Critical Essays* by Ivan Van Sertima.

4. George Lamming, *The Pleasures of Exile* (London: Allison and Busby, 1960), as quoted in Leah Rosenberg, *Nationalism and the Formation of Caribbean Literature* (New York: Palgrave Macmillan, 2008), 3.

5. The Beacon group of Trinidad was the first organized, and by far the most influential, writers' group in the Anglo-Caribbean. The quotation is from a lecture given by C. L. R. James in 1959, published as "The Artist in the Caribbean," *Radical America* 4 (1970): 62–63.

6. The attitude that the Caribbean did not produce authentic art was not confined to literature: Harvey Neptune observes that in 1944, white Trinidadian critic and local musician McDonald Carpenter dismissed the calypso as merely entertainment and not art, a distinction confirmed by the fact that the Americans, known not to have any interest in "real" art, were enthusiastic fans of the calypso. What is noteworthy here, however, is that it is a middle-class musician and critic who is dismissing the calypso. See McDonald Carpenter, "Calypsos Not Art," *TG,* February 8, 1944; and Carpenter, "Europe's Culture Cast Our Own," *TG,* February 25, 1944; both quoted in Harvey Neptune, *Caliban and the Yankees: Trinidad and the United States' Occupation* (Chapel Hill: University of North Carolina Press, 2007), 154–56.

7. V. S. Naipaul, *The Middle Passage* (New York: Vintage 1981), 69.

8. Colin Channer, "Q & A with Author," http://www.colinchanner.com (accessed 2007).

9. See Helen Tiffin, "The Institution of Literature," in *A History of Literature in the Caribbean,* vol. 2: *English and Dutch-Speaking Regions,* ed. A. James Arnold (Philadelphia: John Benjamins Publishing, 2001), 58; and Bradford F. Swan, *The Spread of Printing (Western Hemisphere): The Caribbean Area* (Amsterdam: Vangendt, 1970).

10. See Edward A. Cordle, *Overheard: A Series of Poems Written by the Late Edward A. Cordle* (Barbados: C. F. Cole, Printer and Publisher, 1903). Clearly this is not true for the working-class version of dialect poetry, written by the so-called Dub poets

of Jamaica, whose serious, overtly political commentary found a much larger international audience than did the dialect poetry of the earlier generation.

11. Sean X. Goudie, *Creole America: The West Indies and the Formation of Literature and Culture in the New Republic* (Philadelphia: University of Pennsylvania Press, 2006).

12. The *New York Times* carried an account of the Jamaican exhibit at the 1893 World's Columbia Exposition in Chicago. Headed by Colonel C. J. Ward, founder of Jamaica's Ward Theatre, the exhibit was intended to showcase Jamaica as the "winter island par excellence of the West Indies" ("What Jamaica Will Show," May 1, 1893). See also Krista Thompson, *An Eye for the Tropics: Tourism, Photography and Framing the Caribbean Picturesque* (Durham: Duke University Press, 2006), for an account of the origins of Caribbean tourism.

13. See Neptune, *Caliban and the Yankees*, 109.

14. It is Karl Marx's fundamental conceptualization of bourgeois society that provides the engine for almost any scholarly analysis of middle-class culture, and this analysis is no different. I owe a debt to Marx for his powerful insight that middle-class society is omnivorous and co-opting, a point that anchors my thesis on middlebrow culture. Yet it is this Marxian formulation that is, in another sense, the problem. Marx saw bourgeois society as fundamentally omnivorous and parasitic. In his view, the cultural production of the working class (or any other social formation) always means absorption by the middle: "Bourgeois society is the most developed and the most complex historic organization of production. The categories which express its relations, the comprehension of its structure, thereby allow insight into the structure and relations of production of all the vanished social formations out of whose ruins and elements it built itself up, whose partly still unconquered remnants are carried along with it." See Karl Marx, *Grundrisse: Foundations of the Critique of Political Economy* (London: Penguin Books, 1973), 105. I thank Natalie Melas, whose paper "Modernity and Untimeliness" (Society for the Humanities, Cornell University, April 2007) drew my attention to Marx's formulation here.

15. I owe this example to Gabriela Vargas-Cetina, "Music, Silence, Noise and the Uncomfortable Scribe: Studying Trova Music in Yucatan, Mexico," paper presented at the Society for the Humanities, Cornell University, Fall 2006, which influenced my thinking here.

16. There have been countless discussions of African American modernism, and a significant number on Caribbean modernism. For some of the more influential examples, see Simon Gikandi, *Writing in Limbo: Modernism and Caribbean Literature* (Ithaca: Cornell University Press, 1992); and Michael North, *The Dialect of Modernism: Race, Language and Twentieth Century Literature* (Oxford: Oxford University Press, 1994).

17. See Chris Bongie, "Exiles on Main Stream: Valuing the Popularity of Postcolonial Culture," *Postmodern Culture* 14, no. 1 (2003): 3.

18. The popular dialectical tradition in Anglophone Caribbean literature probably begins with Augustus Matthews, *The Lying Hero, or an Answer to J. B. Moreton's Manners and Customs of the West Indies* (St. Kitts [St. Eustatius]: Edward Luther Low Printery, 1793), a response by Matthews, of Montserrat, to J. B. Moreton's critique of Caribbean society. See Tiffin, "Institution of Literature."

19. I am referring here, in chronological order, to the various covers of *Children of Kaywana:* the 1976 Corgi paperback edition, the 1952 Nevill Day mass market paperback edition, and the 1955 New English Library edition. The novels of H. G. de Lisser have been packaged in similarly sexualized ways, notably Sangster's edition of Lisser's historical adventure *Psyche,* which features a young black woman, head wrapped and exposed bosom heaving, watching a white couple embrace.

20. I am thinking in particular of the various statements made in Kwame Dawes, *Natural Mysticism: Towards a New Reggae Aesthetic* (London: Peepal Tree Press, 1999), esp. chap. 6, "'Stir It Up': The Erotic in Reggae"; and by Colin Channer in his essay "I Am Not In Exile," in *Catch Afire: New Jamaican Writing,* ed. Kwame Dawes, special issue of *Obsidian III: Literature in the African Diaspora* 2, no. 2 (Fall/Winter 2000–2001): 43–56, as well as on his Web site and in various interviews that emphasize graphic sexuality as part of a postcolonial "reggae" aesthetic. Certainly contemporary Caribbean novels employ graphic sexual scenes in ways that their predecessors did not. We see similarly "graphic" sexual scenes emerging in African literature, from young novelists such as Yvonne Vera of Zimbabwe and Calixthe Beyala of Cameroon, which begs the question of whether such graphic sexuality has more to do with generational differences than with a specifically Caribbean aesthetic, "reggae" or otherwise.

21. Sydney Olivier, friend of Bernard Shaw and governor of Jamaica from 1907 to 1913, functioned as a patron of sorts for both de Lisser and McKay. Errol Hill's detailed account of Jamaican theater reveals the central role that white Jamaicans played in that country's dynamic theater scene up to the early twentieth century, from building influential venues such as the Ward Theatre to acting in early plays. See Errol Hill, *The Jamaican Stage, 1655–1900: Profile of a Colonial Theatre* (Amherst: University of Massachusetts Press, 1992).

22. Kenneth Ramchand gives a scathing account of "popular" education in the nineteenth-century Caribbean that underplays the central role of literature in popular culture: "The basic facts about popular (mainly Negro) education in the nineteenth century, and those broad effects of concern to the literary historian are only too well known: popular education was elementary education; it began out of public funds with the Emancipation of the slaves, but it was neither sufficiently extensive nor deep enough to create a public able to read and write—even by the least demanding criteria; the system, such as it was, produced a few distinguished Negroes for the professions (mainly Law and Medicine, with the Church a poor third), but literary Negroes in the nineteenth century were exceptions among exceptions." See Kenneth Ramchand, *The West Indian Novel and Its Background* (London: Faber and Faber, 1970), 19.

23. James Pope-Hennessy, *Verandah: Some Episodes in the Crown Colonies, 1867–1889* (New York: Knopf, 1964), as quoted in Naipaul, *Middle Passage,* 57.

24. See Shalini Puri, "Beyond Resistance: Notes toward a New Caribbean Cultural Studies," *Small Axe* no. 14 (vol. 7, no. 2) (September 2003): 24; Richard D. E. Burton, *Afro-Creole: Power, Opposition and Play in the Caribbean* (Ithaca: Cornell University Press, 1997), 267, as quoted in Puri, "Beyond Resistance," 24.

25. The most influential examples of the oppositional popular culture argument are those made by Jamaican critic Carolyn Cooper, who consistently reads dancehall

and other working-class Jamaican cultural practices as defying of Jamaican state interests. See Carolyn Cooper, *Sound Clash: Jamaican Dancehall Culture at Large* (New York: Palgrave 2004). On the subject of cultural hybridity, Shalini Puri takes a more nuanced tack, identifying what she calls "douglarization"—or the synthesizing of Afro- and Indo-Trinidadian culture in Trinidad—as both "canonized" and "resistant." Nevertheless, the dougla as an ethnic symbol tends to stand in for an oppositionality to orthodox Indian identity. See Shalini Puri, "Canonized Hybridities, Resistant Hybridities: Chutney Soca, Carnival, and the Politics of Nationalism," in *Caribbean Romances: The Politics of Regional Representation,* ed. Belinda Edmondson (Charlottesville: University Press of Virginia, 1999).

26. Peter van Koningsbruggen, *Trinidad Carnival: A Quest for a National Identity* (London: Macmillan, 1997), as quoted in Gerard Aching, *Masking and Power: Carnival and Popular Culture in the Caribbean* (Minneapolis: University of Minnesota Press, 2003), 76. Aching notes that van Koningsbruggen draws his conceptualization of middle-classization from the work of S. B. MacDonald, *Trinidad and Tobago: Democracy and Development in the Caribbean* (New York: Praeger, 1986); and Gordon K. Lewis, "The Contemporary Caribbean," in *Caribbean Contours,* ed. Sidney W. Mintz and Sally Price (Baltimore: Johns Hopkins University Press, 1985).

27. See, for some of the more famous examples, Peter Stallybrass and Allon White, *The Politics and Poetics of Transgression* (Ithaca: Cornell University Press, 1986); and Dick Hebdige, *Subculture: The Meaning of Style* (London: Methuen, 1979). For an insightful look into how Shakespeare is transformed from populist to polite culture in the United States, see George Levine, *Highbrow, Lowbrow: The Emergence of Cultural Hierarchy in America* (Cambridge: Harvard University Press, 1988).

28. Deborah Thomas, *Modern Blackness: Nationalism, Globalization, and the Politics of Culture in Jamaica* (Durham: Duke University Press, 2004); and David Scott, *Refashioning Futures: Criticism after Postcoloniality* (Princeton: Princeton University Press, 1999).

29. See Leah Rosenberg, "Modern Romances: The Short Stories in Una Marson's *The Cosmopolitan* (1928–1931)," *Journal of West Indian Literature* 12, nos. 1–2 (November 2004): 170–83.

30. See Natasha Barnes, *Caribbean Conundrums: Gender, Race, Nation, and the Making of Caribbean Cultural Politics* (Ann Arbor: University of Michigan Press, 2006); Aching, *Masking and Power;* as well as the novel by Earl Lovelace, *The Dragon Can't Dance* (Port of Spain: Longman, 1977).

31. "Wine and jam" is a popular Caribbean phrase for gyrating ("wining") and body rubbing ("jamming").

32. Tony Becca, "The Missing Cricket Fans," *Jamaica Gleaner* (online ed.), April 1, 2007; for a discussion of Portia Simpson's political use of cricket, see Marc Lacey, "In Jamaican Politics, Just about Everything Is Cricket," *New York Times* (online ed.), April 2, 2007.

33. The only male-authored Caribbean fiction that I found reviewed in science fiction journals was, ironically, Edgar Mittelholzer's novel *My Bones and My Flute* (1955), which is reviewed by Dennis Lien in the journal *Fantasy and Science Fiction* (Hoboken) 109, no. 6 (December 2005): 162. The reviewer referred to Mittelholzer's homeland, Guyana, as "British Guinea." Moreover, it seems that science fiction may become a female genre as well: witness the popularity of black women science fiction

writers such as Octavia Butler or, more recently, Guyanese-Jamaican writer Nalo Hopkinson.

34. "Jamette" is a term originating in early Trinidad for public women, usually black, who danced in the street during carnival; later it became a general phrase for a virago. "Streggeh" is a Jamaican term for a promiscuous, loud woman.

35. See Carla Freeman, *High Tech and High Heels in the Global Economy* (Durham: Duke University Press, 2000), 214.

36. Freeman is not the first critic of globalization to notice strategic ambiguity. See Barbara Ehrenreich and Annette Fuentes, *Women in the Global Factory* (Boston: South End Press, 1985), for a similar observation of Asian and Latin American global workers.

37. Frantz Fanon, *The Wretched of the Earth* (New York: Grove Press, 1965), 153.

38. For example, see Aching, *Masking and Power*, 98, quoting Frantz Fanon.

39. Look, for example, at the large number of American evangelical preachers making regular forays into the Caribbean for both healing and profit, who are instrumental in the changing religious landscape of the region.

40. See, for example, Mike Alleyne's discussion of the "refining" of the Bob Marley sound and image; Alleyne, "Positive Vibration? Textual Hegemony and Bob Marley," in Edmondson, *Caribbean Romances*.

1. Early Literary Culture

1. "Nancy Story Competition," *Daily Gleaner,* December 23, 1899, 11, emphasis added.

2. Race was then, as now, a notoriously slippery category in the Caribbean, with many brown people who could do so opting to pass for white. When categorizing mixed-race writers of this period, therefore, we run into problems. Thomas MacDermot, founder of the All Jamaica Library, refers to himself as a white man in "The Present Conditions of Jamaica and Jamaicans," *Canadian Magazine,* October 1899, 503–4; yet as Rhonda Cobham notes, elsewhere he is described as octoroon, or one-eighth black. See Rhonda Cobham, "The Creative Writer and Jamaican Society, 1900–1950" (Ph.D. diss., University of St. Andrews, 1981), 61n24. Similarly, Jamaican author and editor H. G. de Lisser started out brown and "became" white as he rose up the social ranks. See n. 44 in this chapter for more on de Lisser's racial transformation.

3. The historian Hilary Beckles, writing of Barbadian society at the end of the nineteenth century, observes of cricket (then, as now, Barbados's favorite sport): "From the 1870s, the game was ... an index by which social classes could be clearly distinguished during this time of unprecedented restructuring of the social order. While merchants were rapidly becoming planters, and some coloured and black men were emerging as merchants and politicians, the still dominant traditional planting families sought to maintain their class distinctions within the area of social culture." Later, Beckles notes that these same respectable lodges and societies would provide the breeding ground for the Pan-Caribbean black nationalism of Garvey's Universal Negro Improvement Association to take root in Barbados among the black working and middle classes. See Hilary Beckles, *A History of Barbados* (New York: Cambridge University Press, 1990), 149–53, 154–55.

4. W. P. Livingston ascribes this phenomenon to the increase in literacy among the black population: "There is as yet no popular literature in the country, but the taste for reading is spreading rapidly. At the reading room of the Institute of Jamaica during the 4 years ending 1896, the attendance was augmented by 200%. The circulation of the principal newspapers has recently been doubled, the new subscribers being largely those negroes who are rising up from the mass. The value of books imported in 1885 was 8,374 [pounds]. By 1894 it had risen to 20,651 [pounds].... The white community has been but slightly augmented, and the increase must, therefore, to a large extent be attributed to the growing intellectual appetite of the blacks." W. P. Livingston, *Black Jamaica: A Study in Evolution* (London: Sampson, Low Marston, 1899), 204, as quoted in Cobham, "Creative Writer and Jamaican Society," 65.

5. Gordon K. Lewis, *The Growth of the Modern West Indies* (New York: Monthly Review Press, 1968), 28, 254, 188.

6. Kenneth Ramchand's seminal book, *The West Indian Novel and Its Background*, was the first sustained analysis of this period that I know of. He writes: "Few Negroes in the nineteenth century cultivated the art of reading imaginative literature, and fewer attempted to write it. The period appears to have produced no novelists, only a handful of minor poets. Their poems reveal the alienation of the insecure and embryonic black middle class from the uneducated and illiterate groups to which they or their parents had belonged" (31).

7. Claude McKay, *Banana Bottom* (New York: Harcourt Brace Jovanovich, 1932).

8. See Swan, *Spread of Printing*, 14, as quoted in Tiffin, "Institution of Literature," 58.

9. Examples of the early dialectical tradition include *Froudacity: or, West Indian Fables Explained* by black Trinidadian John Jacob Thomas (1889), a response to Oxford historian James Anthony Froude's *The English in the West Indies* (London: Longman's Green, 1888); and Augustus Matthews's *The Lying Hero, or an Answer to J. B. Moreton's Manners and Customs of the West Indies* (1793), published in St. Eustatius (St. Kitts).

10. The first printing press in Jamaica was established in 1718, and although longer works such as histories and novels were published outside of the country, Jamaica has a long history of publishing pamphlets and monographs. Jamaica also had a theater scene from as early as the mid-seventeenth century. See Cobham, "Creative Writer and Jamaican Society," chap. 2; and Hill, *Jamaican Stage;* as well as Frank Cundall, *A History of Printing in Jamaica* (Kingston: Institute of Jamaica, 1935).

11. Editorial, *Jamaica Telegraph*, November 29, 1898.

12. See Cobham, "Creative Writer and Jamaican Society," 63, 66. I am indebted to Cobham's extraordinary diligence in hunting down these details of Jamaican publishing history. See also G. F. Judah, *The Newspaper History of Jamaica* (1899; reprint, Mona Jamaica: University of the West Indies Library Studies, Working Papers on West Indian Printing, ser. 1, no. 9a, 1975), 5, which lists twenty-seven newspapers on the island from 1822 until 1898, as quoted in Cobham, "Creative Writer and Jamaican Society," 63.

13. Robert Love, editorial page, *Jamaica Advocate*, December 15, 1894.

14. Robert Love, "Study Your Business" (editorial), *Jamaica Advocate*, December 15, 1894, 3.

15. Tony Martin discusses the literary competitions and beauty pages of the *Negro World*, in chap. 3, "Garveyism and Literature," in *Literary Garveyism: Garvey, Black Arts, and the Harlem Renaissance* (Dover: Majority Press, 1983), esp. 41.

16. "Welcoming *The Jamaica Times*" (editorial), *Daily Telegraph,* November 29, 1898.

17. See Cobham, "Creative Writer and Jamaican Society," 69.

18. "Winkler's Choir Leader," *Jamaica Times,* December 17, 1898, 5.

19. Charlotte, Daily News Letter sec., *Daily Telegraph,* November 29 1898.

20. "Nancy Story Competition," *Daily Gleaner,* December 23, 1899, emphasis added.

21. "The Amusements of the People," *Jamaica Times,* July 22, 1899, 13. Another example is H. G. D., "A Peculiar Love Scene," Amusements of the People sec., *Jamaica Times,* July 1, 1899, 5, where the author veers between "us" and "them": "our laughter-loving people have their own way of making themselves happy.... We may look forward with hope to the day when, climbing the steep path of progress, they will have a better, truer view of the realities of life. And this can only be when those who are 'set over them'... and those who are their social, moral and intellectual superiors, will undertake this labour, by slow prudence to make mild a rugged people, and thro' soft degrees subdue them to the useful and the good." Yet another example is the first-person account of "The Revival Balm Station of Mother Ackinson"—the balm yard being a popular healing place in Jamaican peasant life—where the author opines, "Like many another thing to which one looks forward with that keen interest that invests the new, the strange, the unknown, with enchantment" (*Jamaica Times,* December 10, 1898, 5).

22. "Is Novel-Reading Injurious?" (editorial), *Jamaica Times,* December 10, 1898, 9.

23. Weekly Prize Story, *Jamaica Times,* July 22, 1899, 13.

24. See, for example, an editorial in the December 24, 1898, edition of the *Jamaica Times,* describing the move of a junior clerk to director of his firm: "His record is one that every Jamaican should strive to emulate."

25. For a more detailed assessment of gender and authorship in the English-speaking Caribbean, see chap. 2, "Literary Men," in Belinda Edmondson, *Making Men* (Durham: Duke University Press 1999).

26. Bridget Brereton, *Race Relations in Colonial Trinidad, 1870–1900* (Cambridge: Cambridge University Press 1979), 46.

27. Bridget Brereton, Rhonda Cobham, Mary Rimmer, and Lise Winer, introduction to *Rupert Gray: A Study in Black and White,* by Stephen Cobham, ed. L. Winer (Kingston: University of the West Indies Press, 2006), xxi.

28. Brereton, *Race Relations,* 96.

29. The anti-Asian (by which is meant anti-Indian more so than anti-Chinese) aspect of official Trinidadian nationalism continued—and some might say, continues still—well into the mid-twentieth century, prompting comments like this one found in the January 12, 1957, edition of the *Clarion* (Port of Spain): "Indians can't be loyal Trinidadians if they take off their shoes to go to their Muslim Temple." For more references to Indians and Portuguese in nineteenth-century Trinidadian newspapers, see Tian Uddenberg and Karen Vaucrosson, "Lists from the San Fernando Gazette Trinidad West Indies, 1865–1896" (National Archives, Port of Spain, 2002), 7–8.

30. For a detailed account of early Trinidadian nationalism in the context of Thomas's writings, see Faith Smith, *Creole Recitations: John Jacob Thomas and Colonial Formations in the Late Nineteenth-Century Caribbean* (Charlottesville: University of Virginia Press, 2002).

31. Many Anglophone Caribbean newspapers founded publishing companies, through which the newspapers' editors often published their own novels. Examples include the early Guyanese novel *Of Those That Be in Bondage* (1917) by Trinidad-born, Guyana-based A. R. F. Webber, editor of Guyana's *Daily Chronicle*, and the many novels of the prominent editor of Jamaica's *Daily Gleaner*, H. G. de Lisser, which appeared first in that newspaper.

32. See Bridget Brereton, Rhonda Cobham, Mary Rimmer, Karen Sanchez-Eppler, and Lise Winer, introduction to *"Adolphus, A Tale" (Anonymous) and "The Slave Son" (Mrs. William Noy Wilkins)*, ed. L. Winer (Kingston: University of the West Indies Press, 2003). See also Maxwell Philip, *Emmanuel Appadocca, or Blighted Life* (1853; reprint, Amherst: University of Massachusetts Press, 1997).

33. See "Local Fiction" (editorial), *Beacon* 1, no. 10 (January–February 1932). Another editorial of this ilk is "A Commentary," *Trinidad* 1, no. 2 (Easter 1930), as quoted in Reinhard Sander, introduction to *From Trinidad: An Anthology of Early West Indian Writing*, ed. R. Sander (London: Hodder and Stoughton, 1978).

34. Reinhard Sander, *The Trinidad Awakening: West Indian Literature of the 1930s* (New York: Greenwood Press, 1988), 7.

35. In *The Overcrowded Barracoon*, Naipaul observes that the alternative to English novels "was provided by some local short stories. These stories, perhaps a dozen in all, never published outside Trinidad, converted what I saw into 'writing.'... Every writer is, in the long run, on his own; but it helps, in the most practical way, to have a tradition. The English language was mine; the tradition was not" (27, as quoted in Sander, *From Trinidad*, 151).

36. Sander, *Trinidad Awakening*, 31. This last group is particularly noteworthy because criticism of early Caribbean literature concludes that Asians, as recent arrivals and "outsiders" to the creole establishment, were more anxious to preserve their own heritage than they were during the anticolonial political ferment taking place on the island in the early twentieth century, a phenomenon that occasioned multiracial, multiclass collusion. See Sander, *From Trinidad*.

37. As quoted in Sander, *From Trinidad*, 2. The Trinidad Awakening is the popular term, coined by Sander, for the flowering of creative literature out of the *Beacon* group that spawned the now-classic writings of C. L. R. James and others.

38. See Sydney Olivier, *Jamaica the Blessed Island* (London: Faber and Faber 1936), 54, as quoted in Cobham, "Creative Writer and Jamaican Society," 27. Olivier was popular among the Jamaican upper and middle classes for his criticism of official colonial policy toward Jamaica, which suggests again the inchoate nationalism of even the island's elite.

39. There are several sources on debating societies in the Anglophone Caribbean, especially those in Jamaica, Trinidad, and Barbados in the late nineteenth and early twentieth centuries. For a discussion of Jamaican debating societies, see Cobham, "Creative Writer and Jamaican Society"; for a discussion of Trinidadian debating societies, in particular the Trinidad and Tobago Literary Club founded in 1925, see Anson Gonzalez, "Race and Colour in Pre-Independence Trinidad and Tobago

Novel" (Ph.D. diss., University of the West Indies, St. Augustine, Trinidad, 1982). Although I found no discussion of debating societies in Barbados, I found a telling headline in the *Barbados Advocate* (January 4, 1930, 4): "Mr. Bernard Grant Addresses Literary Society." (Grant was on the staff of the *Daily Mirror*, which was founded as a women's paper.)

40. Many of the intellectual arguments about the place of literature in the Caribbean echo those taking place in the United States around the same period, as indexed by E. Franklin Frazier's *Black Bourgeoisie* (New York: Collier, 1957), which indicted the African American middle class for rejecting any representation of "the masses" in the quest to produce art. It is hard to calculate just how influential African American thinking is on this subject, given that this view tends to be a Marxist perspective that influenced any number of societies; nevertheless, given the historical connection between African American intellectuals and Caribbean cosmopolitans, it is worth considering.

41. Editorial, *Spotlight,* December 1951, 12.

42. See Winston James, "Becoming the People's Poet: Claude McKay's Jamaican Years, 1889–1912," *Small Axe* 7, no. 1 (2003): 17–45, 33.

43. Reinhard Sander makes a similar claim for the work of V. S. Naipaul and Samuel Selvon, arguing, for example, that Naipaul's *Miguel Street* has its roots in newspaper features. See Sander, introduction to *From Trinidad*.

44. De Lisser was technically a "brown," or mixed-race, man—a light-skinned brown man, but brown nevertheless. De Lisser was not attempting to pass as white when he worked as an editor for the middle-class, brown-identified *Jamaica Times,* but by the time he became editor in chief of the *Gleaner* he had apparently "whitened." Rhonda Cobham suggests that he "became" white through his friendship with a British viscount, a friendship that gained him entry into Jamaica's elite white circles, which had otherwise been closed to him. His own racial and class anxiety may account for his excessive snobbery. See Cobham, "Creative Writer and Jamaican Society," 61n31, in which she cites Ansell Hart, "Colour Prejudice in Jamaica," *Jamaica Journal* 4, no. 4 (December 1970).

45. The *Jamaica Times* notes that McKay's consideration for the Musgrave silver medal had to be postponed because of the absence of H. G. de Lisser, who had nominated him. See *Jamaica Times,* January 22, 1912, as quoted in Cobham, "Creative Writer and Jamaican Society," 72 and n. 32.

46. Sander, *Trinidad Awakening,* 5.

47. Regarding MacDermot's race, see n. 2. The quotations are from text that appeared in the beginning of all the books in the All Jamaica Library.

48. MacDermot, writing in the preface to his second novel, *One Brown Girl And*—(1909), as quoted in Cobham, "Creative Writer and Jamaican Society."

49. See Henry Fowler, "A History of Theatre in Jamaica," *Jamaica Journal* 2, no. 1 (1968): 54. See also Richardson Wright's accounts of early American actors on the Jamaican stage, wherein he specifically details the influence of the American Company of Comedians; Wright, *Revels in Jamaica* (1937; reprint, Kingston: Bolivar Press, 1986). Errol Hill further explores the influence of this company on the local, active Jamaican theater scene and notes that Jamaican actors were well known in New York (Hill, *Jamaican Stage,* prologue).

50. See Hill, *Jamaican Stage,* 90.

51. A study of the January 1930 issues of the *Barbados Advocate* revealed, other than "hard" news, only cricket scores and serialized pulp fiction, inevitably a romance, from American newspaper services.

52. Marlon Downing, "Libertas C, or Died for Cuba," *Jamaica Times,* May 27, 1899, 7.

53. Examples of African American literary culture of the nineteenth and early twentieth century are far more commonly known than are those of the Caribbean, so just a few examples suffice here. For a complete discussion of African American literary societies, see Elizabeth McHenry, *Forgotten Readers: Recovering the Lost History of African-American Literary Societies* (Durham: Duke University Press, 2002); examples of early "middle-class" African American literature include popular writer Frances Watkins Harper's *Iola Leroy* (1892) and Charles W. Chesnutt's *The Wife of His Youth, and Other Stories of the Color Line* (1899).

54. V. S. Naipaul, *A Turn in the South* (New York: Vintage, 1989), 19.

55. Governor Edward Eyre to Newcastle, July 5, 1862, "Despatches from the Governor of Jamaica," in "Correspondence respecting the Emigration of Free Negroes from the United States to the West Indies. Confidential," CO 884/2/15, National Archives, Kew, England; cited in Tim Watson, *Caribbean Culture and British Fiction in the Atlantic World 1780–1870* (Cambridge University Press, 2008), 188–89n7.

56. B. P. Wynter, "A Negro's Christmas Message to His Race in Jamaica," *Bocas del Toro,* December 4, 1899, printed in the *Daily Gleaner,* December 23, 1899, 12, emphasis added.

57. Wong Chin Foo, "The Mandarin's Daughter: A Romance of Chinese Life, ch. 1," *Jamaica Times,* July 8, 1899, 13, emphasis added.

58. Carlisle Fonseca, "Carvalho," *Jamaica Times,* May 6, 1899, 13.

59. Alexander MacGregor James, "The Mysterious Murder," *Jamaica Times,* December 17, 1898, 13. MacGregor James later published "Soul's Sacrifice" as part of his anthology, *Four Stories and a Drama of Old Jamaica* (Kingston: Gleaner Co. Ltd. Printers, 1921), as well as a novel titled *The Cacique's Treasure*. Although MacGregor James grumbled about the lack of money from the government-sponsored contests through the Institute of Jamaica, the *Times*'s competition, like the *Gleaner*'s, offered five-shilling prizes for winning its literary competitions of the 1890s.

60. Jamaica's Jewish population was active in the creation of many institutions of middle- and upper-class culture on the island, from the founding of Jamaica's premier newspaper to the construction of Kingston's famous Ward Theatre.

61. Delia Jarrett-Macaulay, *The Life of Una Marson* (Manchester, UK: Manchester University Press, 1998), 151. Similar developments transpired in Trinidad, where Audrey Jeffers founded the Coterie of Social Workers in 1921. Veronica Gregg, introduction to *Caribbean Women: An Anthology of Non-Fiction Writing, 1890–1980,* ed. V. Gregg (South Bend, IN: University of Notre Dame Press, 2005), 74.

62. Gregg, introduction to *Caribbean Women,* 73.

63. Author's interview with Suzanne Lee, director of the Novelty Trading Company and great-granddaughter of Novelty's founder, May 27, 2006, Calabash Literary Festival, Treasure Beach, Jamaica.

64. H. G. de Lisser, "The Fair Daughters of Jamaica: Characteristics," *Planter's Punch* 1, no. 6 (1925–26): 4–5.

65. Cobham, "Creative Writer and Jamaican Society," 81, 81n43. Cobham relays that, from personal interviews with former readers, many black and brown people

could recall their families reading *Planter's Punch* out loud for Christmas. It is not inconceivable that members of the brown and black middle class, striving to solidify their class position, may well have sought identification with the magazine's aristocratic tone.

66. De Lisser's "The Jamaica Nobility; Or, The Story of Sir Mortimer and Lady Mortimer" begins with a sarcastic note about Marcus Garvey's title of president of the African Republic. See *Planter's Punch* 2, no. 1 (1926–27). See chapter 2 of this volume for a more detailed analysis of de Lisser's Garvey fears. See also Joseph Husband, "The Citadel or The Ring of Dessalines," 1, no. 6 (1925–26): 31.

67. See Sander, *Trinidad Awakening,* 32. The magazine's frank sexual expression and attention to miscegenation was pronounced "obscene" by respectable constituencies, who nevertheless read the magazine.

68. The *Cosmopolitan* was later renamed The *New Cosmopolitan* under the editorship of Marson and black Jamaican Aimee Webster.

69. The *Daily Gleaner*'s question of the week, in its December 23, 1899, issue was, "Should Girls Seek Employment Outside of the Home?" The general consensus was yes, but only if they have to.

70. W. Kirkpatrick, "Women's Activities—Some Thoughts and Suggestions," *Cosmopolitan,* July 28, 1928, 94.

71. See C.P.N., "Social Problems—Where Do We Stand?" *Cosmopolitan* 1, no. 3 (July 1928): 86; also see "The Age of Women" (editorial), *Cosmopolitan* 1, no. 11 (March 1929): 65–66.

72. K. D. Carnegie, "Sappho—The Lesbian Poetess," *Cosmopolitan* 1, no. 2 (June 1928): 44.

73. "Editorial Observations: The Coloured Follies," *Cosmopolitan* 1, no. 12 (April 1929): 99.

74. "The Colour-line" (editorial), and "Case of Seditious Libel Ended: Guess What's Happened?" both in *Cosmopolitan* 2, no. 8 (December 1929): 235 and 342, respectively.

75. In the inaugural issue the editors write, "'The Cosmopolitan' aims at being what the name itself would convey. . . . It can well be said of the people of our day as was said in connection with those of ages long past, 'Where there is no vision the people perish' and also that a country may be unmistakably judged by the standard of the literature she produces. Our chief aim is to develop literary and other artistic talents in our Island home. The Editor of our esteemed 'Daily' thinks that if Claude McKay had remained in Jamaica he never would have won such well deserved recognition, and we cannot but agree with him. It is a fact that local talent and ability in any field of art is not encouraged nor sufficiently appreciated in Jamaica by our people and our papers." Editorial, *Cosmopolitan* 1, no. 1 (May 1928): 1

76. See the excellent analysis of the *Cosmopolitan* in Leah Rosenberg, "Modern Romances: The Short Stories in Una Marson's *The Cosmopolitan* (1928–1931)," *Journal of West Indian Literature* 12, nos. 1–2 (November 2004): 171.

77. See Michelle Stephens, *Black Empire: The Masculine Global Imaginary of Caribbean Intellectuals in the United States, 1914–1962* (Durham: Duke University Press, 2005).

78. This is not to say that popular British literature was not also avidly consumed by the Caribbean reading classes in the early twentieth century. Turn-of-the-century romantic dramas such as *The Forsyte Saga* and the P. G. Wodehouse comic series were

also popular, but not necessarily associated with the modern, nor so accessible as American newspaper stories that were available for a few pennies.

79. Rosenberg, "Modern Romances," 172; Rosenberg counts fifteen of the twenty-five stories published in the magazine as romances.

80. "Kingston's Beauty Spots: The Goats," *Cosmopolitan* 1, no. 12 (April 1929): 99.

81. "Brighter Night Life," *Cosmopolitan* 1, no. 2 (June 1928): 64.

82. Una Marson, "Sojourn," *New Cosmopolitan,* February 1931, 8–27.

83. Rosenberg, "Modern Romances," 177.

84. See my detailed discussion of the "brown" characteristics of black romantic heroines in Caribbean romances in chapter 2 of this volume.

85. Marson, "Sojourn," 27.

86. See Rex Nettleford, *Mirror, Mirror: Identity, Race and Protest in Jamaica* (Kingston: LMH Publishing, 1970). See also Belinda Edmondson, "Trinidad Romance: The Invention of Jamaica Carnival," in Edmondson, *Caribbean Romances.*

87. See Orlando Patterson, "Context and Choice in Ethnic Allegiance: A Theoretical Framework and Caribbean Case Study," in *Ethnicity: Theory and Experience,* ed. Nathan Glazer and Daniel P. Moynihan, 305–409 (Cambridge: Harvard University Press, 1975), 318.

2. Brownness, Social Desire, and the Early Novel

1. William E. Cain, introduction to *Emmanuel Appadocca, or Blighted Life,* by Maxwell Philip, ed. S. Cudjoe (Amherst: University of Massachusetts Press, 1997), xvi, quoting L. B. Tronchin (principal of Port of Spain Model School), "The Great West Indian Orator," *Public Opinion,* December 18 and 21, 1888; and Gerard Besson and Bridget Brereton, eds., *The Book of Trinidad,* 2nd ed. (Port of Spain: Paria Publishing, 1992), 331.

2. Brereton et al., introduction to *Adolphus,* xxiv.

3. Anonymous, *Marly, or The Life of a Planter in Jamaica* (Glasgow: Richard Griffin, 1828), 24, as quoted in Burton, *Afro-Creole,* 35.

4. Gad Heuman, "White over Brown over Black: The Free Coloureds in Jamaican Society during Slavery and after Emancipation," *Journal of Caribbean History* 14 (1981):46–69, 60, as quoted in Burton, *Afro-Creole,* 35–36.

5. See Derek Walcott, "What the Twilight Says: An Overture," in *Dream on Monkey Mountain and Other Plays* (New York: Noonday Press, 1988), 4–40; as well as his famous poem "A Far Cry from Africa," in *Collected Poems, 1948–1984* (New York: Noonday Press, 1987), 17–18. In the Francophone context, see the elaboration of the *mestizaje* ideal in Edouard Glissant, *Caribbean Discourse: Selected Essays,* trans. J. Michael Dash (Charlottesville: University Press of Virginia, 1989).

6. "Decreolization" in this sense of the term comes from Richard Burton, who uses it to describe the cultural fragmentation of early creole society. See Burton, *Afro-Creole,* 36.

7. Ramchand, *West Indian Novel,* 40.

8. One of the more memorable scenes from the Manley campaign for the 1976 elections was his use of Rastafarian language and his brandishing of the "rod of correction," a gift he had received from Emperor Haile Selassie of Ethiopia and for

which he came to be known as Joshua. See Howard Campbell, "'Joshua' and the Rod of Correction," *Jamaica Gleaner* (online ed.), July 18, 2007.

9. For instance, see the excellent analysis of "dougla aesthetics," describing Afro-Indo-Trinidadian cultural moments, in Shalini Puri, *The Post-Colonial Caribbean* (New York: Palgrave Macmillan, 2004).

10. *Jane's Career* was published in Great Britain in 1914, but the novel was first serialized, then published, by the Gleaner Company in 1913, a year earlier, under the title *Jane: A Story of Jamaica*. De Lisser was the editor of the *Gleaner* around this time.

11. See Bridget Brereton, "Michel Maxwell Philip (1829–1888): Servant of the Centurion," *Antilia: Journal of the Faculty of Arts* (University of the West Indies) 1, no. 3 (1989), 6–7, as quoted in Selwyn Cudjoe, afterword to *Emmanuel Appadocca*, by Maxwell Philip, 270.

12. Selwyn Cudjoe, introduction to *Rupert Gray: A Study in Black and White*, by *Stephen Cobham* (Wellesley, MA: Calaloux Publications, 2004). Cudjoe states, in the afterword to *Emmanuel Appadocca*: "In its own way, *Emmanuel Appadocca* can be read as a nineteenth century response to the philosophies of slavery, racism, and European arrogance.... It also anticipates [Edward] Blyden's arguments on racial identity, the theories of Negritude and Pan-Africanism" (266).

13. The cover illustration for Calaloux Publications' edition of *Rupert Gray* is taken from a poster titled *African Women II* by Kathleen English-Pitts.

14. Kenneth Ramchand (*West Indian Novel*, 58) lauds the book but finally concludes that de Lisser becomes unsympathetic toward his black heroine as she becomes successful. Mervyn Alleyne refers to de Lisser as "the first competent Caribbean Novelist in English"; Alleyne, "H. G. DeLisser: The First Competent Novelist in English," *Carib* (Kingston) 1 (1979): 18–26. Feminist Jamaican critic Carolyn Cooper hails Claude McKay's novel *Banana Bottom* as the first black feminist novel, because of its black female protagonist Bita Plant, but she dismisses de Lisser's novel—the first Jamaican novel to use a Creole-speaking black woman as the protagonist, as Cooper herself notes—as being of apiece with early European travel writings, which saw Creole language and its speakers as no more than "a kind of curiosity—local color"; Carolyn Cooper, "'Only a Nigger Gal!': Race, Gender and the Politics of Education in Claude McKay's *Banana Bottom*," *Caribbean Quarterly* 38, no. 1 (March 1992): 40–54; and Cooper, *Sound Clash,* 285.

15. Author's interview with Lee, May 27, 2006. Lee is director of the Novelty Trading Company, Kingston, Jamaica, which distributes *The White Witch of Rose Hall*, as well as novels by American authors such as John Grisham

16. See Ramchand, *West Indian Novel,* 56.

17. "PM Urges Creative Use of National Themes in Creative Arts," *Daily Gleaner,* February, 27, 1971, as quoted in Laura Lomas, "Mystifying Mystery: Inscriptions of the Oral in the Legend of Rose Hall," *Journal of West Indian Literature* 6, no. 2 (1994): 70–86, quote at 71.

18. Lomas, "Mystifying Mystery," 71.

19. See Cobham, "Creative Writer and Jamaican Society," 61n24.

20. Ramchand, *West Indian Novel,* 54.

21. Thomas MacDermot [Tom Redcam, pseud.], *One Brown Girl And—* (Kingston: All Jamaica Library, Times Printery, 1909).

22. Brereton et al., introduction to *Rupert Gray*, xli, xxxv. The reference is to Norman Manley, founder of the People's National Party in Jamaica, who married Edna Manley, his English first cousin; and to Grantley Adams, the first prime minister of Barbados, who married white Barbadian Grace Thorpe in 1929. Of course, these alliances occurred much later than the period in which *Rupert Gray* was written. One might argue that the novel anticipated this new political class.

23. Review of *Rupert Gray*, *Mirror*, July 18, 1907, reprinted in Brereton et al., introduction to *Rupert Gray*, xxix. The authors of the introduction note that no other review or notice of *Rupert Gray* was published apart from this one in the radical *Mirror*.

24. Although I use "brown" as my preferred term for mixed-race people, I also use "colored" at times interchangeably to indicate the historical usage in the eighteenth and nineteenth centuries; the archival references are to "free coloreds," not to "browns." Quotation is from Brereton et al., introduction to *Adolphus*, xv.

25. B. Powrie, "The Changing Attitude of the Coloured Middle Class towards Carnival," *Caribbean Quarterly* 4, nos. 1 and 2, 224, as quoted in Daniel Segal, "'Race' and 'Colour' in Pre-Independence Trinidad," in *Trinidad Ethnicity*, ed. Kevin Yelvington (London: Macmillan Caribbean, 1993), 86.

26. Brereton et al., introduction to *Adolphus*, xvi.

27. "No person who is not above three Degrees removed in a lineal descent from the Negro Ancestor Exclusive shall be allowed to vote or poll in elections, and no one shall be deemed a Mulatto after the Third Generation." See Gregg, *Caribbean Women*, 19.

28. See Doris Garraway, *The Libertine Colony: Creolization in the Early French Caribbean* (Durham: Duke University Press, 2005), 29.

29. Throughout the eighteenth and nineteenth centuries, European travel writers penned several intriguing accounts, alternately contemptuous and admiring, of brown Caribbean women. I mention only two here. Well known are the observations of Lady Nugent, wife of the governor of Jamaica from 1801 to 1805, who notes in her diary that the white creole women are dismayed that she receives black and brown women in her home as guests: "the ladies told me strange stories of the influence of the black and yellow women, and Mrs. Bullock called them serpents." Elsewhere Lady Nugent remarks on a white captain who dies without seeing his white children but leaves all his property to his mulatto children. See Sylvia Wynter, "Lady Nugent's Journal," in Gregg, *Caribbean Women*, 312–13. Doris Garraway details French attitudes toward mulatto women in eighteenth-century Saint Domingue, noting that they were believed to be naturally more wanton than white women and shameless in their sexual exertions to retain their sway over white men. She describes free women of color as having more independence than white women of the period. Michel René d'Auberteuil's account of mulatto women is typical: "The mulâtresses are in general much less docile than mulatto men because they have arrogated to themselves an empire over most of the whites, founded on libertinage.... They are sober, avaricious, and proud" (Garraway, *Libertine Colony*, 230).

30. See Cudjoe, afterword to *Emmanuel Appadocca*, 254.

31. See Selwyn Cudjoe, introduction to *Free Mulatto*, by Jean-Baptiste Philippe, ed. S. Cudjoe (Wellesley, MA: Calaloux Publications, 1996), xiv.

32. The similarity of the plot of *Adolphus* to Philippe's scenario is noted in Brereton et al., introduction to *Adolphus*, xvii.

33. See Frantz Fanon, *Black Skin, White Masks* (1952; reprint, New York: Grove Weidenfeld, 1967), esp. chap. 2, "The Woman of Color and the White Man."

34. See n. 29 for primary sources in the Caribbean context. In addition, see Ramchand, *West Indian Novel,* 41; Fanon, *Black Skin, White Masks;* and more recently, chap. 4, "The Libertine Colony: Desire, Miscegenation, and the Law," in Garraway, *Libertine Colony.*

35. Another example of an early Caribbean antislavery novel is *The Slave Son,* also published in 1854, by Mrs. William Noy Wilkins, an Irish woman who lived for a time in Trinidad.

36. See Faith Smith, "Beautiful Indians, Troublesome Negroes, and Nice White Men: Caribbean Romances and the Invention of Trinidad," in Edmondson, *Caribbean Romances,* 170.

37. The Spanish islands seem to hold a particular fascination for the English as possessing a kind of model of brown, or creole, beauty. H. G. de Lisser, writing in *Planter's Punch,* asks rhetorically how the charms of Jamaica's "fair daughters" could compete with the charms of women in Costa Rica and Cuba: "That has been the unspoken question of Jamaicans" ("Fair Daughters of Jamaica," 4–5). One wonders, why the comparison with these Spanish-speaking Caribbean countries, exactly? I suggest it is their "brown" white population that may hold some allure for the Anglo society, a brown beauty that is acclaimed, and accepted, as "white."

38. Brereton et al., introduction to *Adolphus,* xvii.

39. In Louisiana, New Orleans in particular, the black population uses the term "griffon" to describe an ugly creole or light-skinned black from the traditional creole community—a reference to the mythical creature that is half lion and half eagle. In the Caribbean, terms like "bad red" are still heard to describe light-skinned blacks whose features are perceived to be awkwardly aligned ones of both races.

40. In racialist thought, brown or black skin in itself is not the characteristic of the inferior or degenerate moral character, but more so the shape of the nose, the angle of the forehead and jaw, and so forth. See the excellent reading of racialism and Enlightenment and Victorian views of the physical body in Sander Gilman, "Black Bodies, White Bodies," in *Race Writing and Difference,* ed. Henry Louis Gates Jr. (Chicago: University of Chicago Press, 1986); also, more recently, Sander Gilman, *Making the Body Beautiful: A Cultural History of Aesthetic Surgery* (Princeton: Princeton University Press, 1999).

41. Cudjoe, afterword to *Emmanuel Appadocca,* 268.

42. Lady Nugent famously remarked that the local whites in Jamaica spoke as badly as their servants and seemed to have more in common with them than with her: "The Creole language is not confined to the negroes. Many of the ladies, who have not been educated in England, speak a sort of broken English, with an indolent drawing of their words, that is very tiresome if not disgusting. I stood next to a lady one night, near a window, and, by way of saying something, remarked that the air was much cooler than usual; to which she answered,'Yes, ma'am, him rail-ly too fra-ish.'" Maria Nugent, *Lady Nugent's Journal,* ed. Frank Cundall (London: Adam and Charles Black, 1907), 32. As Burton notes in *Afro-Creole* (35n23), John Stewart, visiting Jamaica in the early 1800s, "thought that the local white women 'exhibit much of the Quashiba,' notably 'an awkward and ungraceful sort of affectation in their language and manner.'" Burton cites John Stewart, *An Account of Jamaica and Its Inhabitants* (London: Longman, Hurst, Rees and Orme, 1808), 160.

43. For detailed discussions on the representation of black Caribbean women in the nineteenth century, see Smith, *Creole Recitations;* and a primary source, Charles Kingsley, *At Last: A Christmas in the West Indies* (London: Macmillan 1889).

44. This characterization of Jimbo was different, apparently, from the way creole slaves saw Africans, in that they ridiculed what they thought to be African provincialism and backwardness. See Burton, *Afro-Creole,* chap. 1. Caribbean whites also subscribed to this view; in I. W. Orderson's *Creoleana,* the enslaved African who is a prince in his own country is given the option of returning there, but he prefers the "white man's ways" and willingly returns to Barbados as a slave. According to Doris Garraway, the benefits of creole birth were believed by Caribbean whites to accrue over generations, such that children of creole slaves were deemed smarter than their parents and were even thought to look "whiter." See Garraway, *Libertine Colony,* 252, quoting Moreau de Saint-Méry, *Description de la partie française de l'isle Saint-Domingue, 1784–1790.*

45. There have been several analyses of European views of white creole degeneracy in this period. Many of these look at Jean Rhys's tragic white creole in *Wide Sargasso Sea;* see Judith Raiskin, *Snow on the Cane Fields: Creole Writing and Women's Subjectivity* (Minneapolis: University of Minnesota Press, 1996). Local whites often blamed immoral behavior on the Irish and Scotch who came to the region as sailors and plantation or military personnel, and so the locals upheld a common English bias against these groups. For example, it is a duplicitous Irishman who seduces the mulatto half sister in *Creoleana* and a Scottish father who tries to rape his own mulatto child.

46. See Lewis, *Growth of the Modern West Indies;* Burton, *Afro-Creole;* and Ramchand, *West Indian Novel.*

47. All quotations from the text of *Rupert Gray* come from the 2006 University of the West Indies edition.

48. Deborah Thomas, "Modern Blackness: 'What We Are and What We Hope to Be,'" *Small Axe,* no. 12 (vol. 6, no. 2) (September 2002): 34; see also Tim Watson, *Caribbean Culture and British Fiction in the Atlantic World, 1780–1870* (Cambridge: Cambridge University Press, 2008), 187–88.

49. I am thinking here of the infamous image of a black man with large lips kissing a white woman that was used in a pamphlet intended to incite hatred of African Americans and repeal their gains under Reconstruction; it is reproduced in the documentary *Ethnic Notions* (1987).

50. This description parallels de Lisser's description of another black Jamaican heroine of African ancestry in his blood-and-sex romance *Psyche* (1952; reprint, Kingston: Macmillan Caribbean, 1980). The title character is a Mandingo slave whose beauty is ascribed to her Arab features "though her complexion is quite black. She has longish, soft hair; then look at her nose; it is positively hooked" (10).

51. H. G. de Lisser, *Jane's Career* (1913; reprint, Kingston: Heinemann, 1971).

52. See Kenneth Ramchand, introduction to *Jane's Career.*

3. Gentrifying Dialect, or the Taming of Miss Lou

1. Although linguists and other scholars have long since discarded the term "dialect" to describe Jamaican Creole speech (or any of the other Creole/Kreyol languages of the Caribbean), I use the anachronistic term because (1) during the period

when Louise Bennett made her mark as a poet entertainer, and indeed for most of the twentieth century, "dialect poetry" was the name used to describe the genre; and (2) despite the efforts of linguists and academics, the term "Creole" has never caught on in Jamaica. The popular term for Creole continues to be "patois" or "dialect." "Creole" is a term fraught with nationalist sentiment, implying acceptance for Caribbean languages that have been heretofore demonized. I also use "dialect" to suggest the preindependence lack of acceptance that to some extent still operates.

2. See Jahan Ramazani, *The Hybrid Muse: Postcolonial Poetry in English* (Chicago: University of Chicago Press, 2001), 106.

3. Bruce Golding, leader of the Jamaica Labour Party, as quoted in Howard Campbell, "Farewell Fit for a Queen," *Jamaica Gleaner*, August 10, 2006.

4. Naipaul, *Middle Passage*, 69, emphasis added. H. G. de Lisser's portrait of Mrs. Mason, the pretentious middle-class employer in *Jane's Career* (1913), echoes Naipaul's comment here.

5. Critics of Caribbean literature, like those of modern literature in general, tend to see value in literature associated with the kind of international "placelessness" of high modernism, or in avant-garde literary experimentation that is associated with the elite international marketplace. As a result, the literature that is discussed and analyzed tends to have these qualities, whether or not the works are popular in commercial terms (as with the poetry of Kamau Brathwaite or the fiction of Wilson Harris, for instance.) By contrast, literature that is locally or regionally popular tends not to have these qualities. One critic who made the argument that it is the critics alone who shape this distinction is Chris Bongie, in his essay "Exiles on Main Stream."

6. Although he argues that his dialect stories and poems arise from the Trinidadian carnival tradition of the "talk tent," Paul Keens-Douglas acknowledges the central influence of Jamaican pantomime, and Louise Bennett in particular, on his dialect poetry. Keens-Douglas studied at the University of the West Indies in Kingston, where he had the opportunity to listen to Louise Bennett perform her poetry and where he even performed in a Jamaican pantomime, *Hail Columbus*, with legendary Jamaican actors Ranny Williams and Oliver Samuels. See Victor D. Questel, introduction to *When Moon Shine*, by Paul Keens-Douglas (Port of Spain: College Press, 1979); and Paul Keens-Douglas, "'Where Talk Is Art'—How It All Began," http://paulkeensdouglas.com (accessed 2008).

7. See Louise Bennett, "Bennett on Bennett," interview with Dennis Scott, *Caribbean Quarterly* 14, nos. 1 and 2 (1968): 98: "You know, I wasn't ever asked to a Jamaican Poetry League meeting?... Most people thought that after all they couldn't discourse with me at all because I was going to talk to them in Jamaican dialect which they couldn't understand."

8. For this description of early Guyanese theater I am indebted to Errol Hill, Martin Banham, and George Woodyard, *The Cambridge Guide to Theatre* (Cambridge: Cambridge University Press, 2005), 463.

9. Julie Pearn, *Poetry in the Caribbean* (London: Hodder and Stoughton, 1985), 17, as quoted in Denise DeCaires Narain, *Contemporary Caribbean Women's Poetry* (London: Routledge, 2001), 69. Interestingly, Cupidon was specifically known for portraying dialect-speaking *women* onstage. More broadly speaking, the Jamaican theater scene was the oldest in the English-speaking Caribbean, spanning two centuries at

that time, and well regarded outside of the Caribbean in theater-going capitals such as New York City. For an account of early Jamaican theater, see Hill, *Jamaican Stage*.

10. See the review of *Susan Proudleigh* by "Our Dramatic Critic," *New Cosmopolitan*, February 8, 1931.

11. Denise DeCaires Narain, whose research and analysis of Miss Lou has influenced my discussion here, has a different interpretation of Caribbean laughter at dialect performance; she argues persuasively that the audience's laughter depends on its members—whether they are primarily middle or working class. If the former, the laughter comes from the recognition that "we can talk that talk too." If the latter, it has more indignation in it, along the lines of an early audience of Miss Lou's, whose members shouted at her, "is dat yuh mudder sen yuh a school fa?" (Is that what your mother sent you to school for?) See DeCaires Narain, *Contemporary Caribbean Women's Poetry*, 59.

12. See Gordon Rohlehr, "The Problem of the Problem of Form: The Idea of an Aesthetic Continuum and Aesthetic, Code-Switching in West Indian Literature," *Caribbean Quarterly* 31, no. 1 (1985): 1–52.

13. Author's telephone interview with anonymous writer, July 6, 2006.

14. See Colin Channer, "I Am Not in Exile," in *Catch Afire: New Jamaican Writing*, ed. Kwame Dawes, special issue of *Obsidian III: Literature in the African Diaspora* 2, no. 2 (Fall/Winter 2000–2001): 50–51, emphasis added.

15. See Marlon James's response, on "Iron Balloons Redux," Geoffrey Philp's Blog Spot, June 28, 2006, at 2:13 p.m., geoffreyphilp.blogspot.com/2006/06iron-balloons-redux.html. Marlon James has won accolades in the United States for his novel *John Crow's Devil* (2005).

16. Notable scholars write complimentary blurbs on the back of Hutchinson's poetry volumes, and one linguist reported, "I cannot help but see Joan Andrea's writing as another foundation stone in the construction of Jamaican as a formally written language." See Tanya Batson-Savage, "'Meck Mi Tell Yuh' Chats Good Jamaican," *Jamaica Gleaner* (online ed.), January 2, 2005.

17. See Mervyn Morris, "On Reading Louise Bennett, Seriously," winner of the 1963 Jamaica Festival essay competition, reprinted in *Jamaica Journal* 1 (1967): 69–74.

18. See Clyde McKenzie, "In Praise of Miss Lou," *Sunday Gleaner*, August 9, 2006, who recounts Mutabaruka's discussions with Miss Lou on his program *Musically Speaking*, on Kingston radio station IRIE-FM several years ago.

19. See Mel Cooke, "Serious Consideration for Miss Lou's Poetry," *Jamaica Gleaner* (online ed.), September 15, 2006.

20. Laurence Breiner, "The Half-Life of Performance Poems," *Journal of West Indian Literature* 8, no. 1 (1998): 27, drew my attention to the Bennett-McKay comparison; he states that McKay's early dialect poems are no longer performed outside of an academic setting.

21. As Louise Bennett relates it, her turn to dialect poetry came after an incident on a city tram car, which she tried to write about by reproducing the voices of the people on the car. See Mervyn Morris, introduction to *Selected Poems*, by Louise Bennett (1982; reprint, Kingston: Sangster's Publishing, 2003), v; also quoted in DeCaires Narain, *Contemporary Caribbean Women's Poetry*, 53.

22. See, for example, David Dabydeen and Nana Wilson-Tagoe, eds., *The Guide to West Indian and Black British Literature* (Rutherford, UK: Hansib Educational Publications, 1988).

23. See, for example, McKay's nostalgic evocation of peasant life in *Banana Bottom* (1933), or Jacques Romain's positioning of the peasantry as innately noble and Haitian, in contrast to the symbols of the philistine professional world exemplified by the shopkeeper and the policeman in *Masters of the Dew* (1944). Later novels like Michael Thelwell's *The Harder They Come* (1980) and Earl Lovelace's *The Dragon Can't Dance* (1978) elaborate on this motif when they identify the origins of modern urban alienation in earlier peasant traditions of resistance in the Caribbean.

24. "Them Belly Full (but We Hungry)" was produced as part of the *Natty Dread* album (Tuff Gong/Island Records, Kingston, 1974) by Bob Marley and the Wailers. The exact date for publication of Louise Bennett's poem "Dutty Tough" is not known, but it is certain that it was written in the 1940s or earlier; the poem appears in the 1966 edition of *Jamaica Labrish* under the section "Politics," which chronicles political upheavals in World War II–era Jamaica of the late 1930s and early 1940s.

25. See Bennett, "Bennett on Bennett," 98: "You know, I wasn't ever asked to a Jamaica Poetry League Meeting?...I did start to write before I started to perform!...People are not as accustomed to reading the dialect as they are to listening to it."

26. "On a Tramcar," Miss Lulu Sez, *Daily Gleaner,* 1949, as quoted in Morris, introduction to *Selected Poems,* v.

27. DeCaires Narain, *Contemporary Caribbean Women's Poetry,* 53, quoting Morris, introduction to *Selected Poems,* iv–v.

28. Carolyn Cooper, *Noises in the Blood: Orality, Gender and the "Vulgar" Body of Jamaican Popular Culture* (Durham: Duke University Press, 1995), 41.

29. DeCaires Narain, in *Contemporary Caribbean Women's Poetry,* argues that the women-of-words tradition that Louise Bennett records in her poetry is very different from the Man-of-Words persona of Roger Abrahams, *The Man-of-Words in the West Indies: Performance and the Emergence of Creole Culture* (Baltimore: Johns Hopkins University Press, 1983). From a different point of view, Jahan Ramazani sees Miss Lou as embodying precisely that persona (*Hybrid Muse,* 109). The main difference is that Abrahams asserted this tradition as a peculiarly masculine one, although verbal sparring—especially cursing—in the street has historically been identified with women in the Caribbean—albeit not with respectable women.

30. Bennett rejects Dennis Scott's assertion that she is a "professional entertainer of the middle-classes," saying, "I can't feel that I belong to any class or that I write for any class. The Jamaican peasant who speaks the dialect—not only the peasant, for we all speak the dialect to some extent" ("Bennett on Bennett," 101). Bennett's correction from "the peasant" to "we" underscores the multivalenced meaning of her poetry.

31. Ramazani, *Hybrid Muse,* 109.

32. See Lee Erwin, "Two Jamaican Women Writers and the Uses of Creole," in *Commonwealth and American Women's Discourse: Essays in Criticism,* ed. A. L. McLeod, 124–34 (New Delhi: Sterling Publishers Private, 1996), 126. Further, as Jeremy Poynting states, "It was not really until the work of Louise Bennett and Andrew Salkey...that the [Anancy] tradition was fully recuperated as an adult one"; Poynting, "From Ancestral to Creole: Humans and Animals in a West Indian Scale of Values," in *Monsters, Tricksters, and Sacred Cows: Animal Tales and American Identities,* ed. A. James Arnold (Charlotte: University of Virginia Press, 1996), 208.

33. See "Profile: Louise Simone Bennett," posted July 26, 2006, www.go-jamaica.com.

34. See Edmondson, *Making Men*, chap. 2.

35. Kamau Brathwaite, *History of the Voice: The Development of Nation Language in Anglophone Caribbean Poetry* (London: New Beacon Books, 1984), 27.

36. Walter Jekyll, *Jamaican Song and Story: Anancy Stories, Digging Sings, Ring Tunes, and Dancing Tunes*, with new introductory essays by Philip Sherlock, Louise Bennett, and Rex Nettleford (1906; reprint, New York: Dover Publications, 1966), x, as quoted in DeCaires Narain, *Contemporary Caribbean Women's Poetry*, 58.

37. I am indebted to Shalene Vasquez, who makes the connection between Derek Walcott's presence in Kingston, Louise Bennett's national Pantomime, and Walcott's subsequent play *Pantomime*, in "Laughing across Borders: Black Diasporic Literature and the Negotiation of Master Strategies" (Ph.D. diss., Rutgers University, 2006). It was Vasquez's connection that triggered my own here.

38. See Judy Raymond, "Beryl McBurnie, 1914–2000: Relentless Charm," *Trinidad Sunday Guardian*, April 2, 2000, 15, as quoted in Gregg, introduction to *Caribbean Women*, 84–85.

39. Derek Walcott, "Some Jamaican Poets," pts. 1 and 2, *Public Opinion* (Jamaica), August 3, 1957, 7, and August 10, 1957, 7, as quoted in Ramazani, *Hybrid Muse*, 110n41.

40. After developing his thesis that "nation language" distorts and transforms the European pentametric mode, Brathwaite writes, in reference to Bennett's poem "Dutty Tough," that "the tyranny of the pentametre can be seen/heard quite clearly here, although Miss Lou erodes and transforms this with the sound of her language. Its riddim sets up a counterpoint *against* the pentametre" (*History of the Voice*, 30n40).

41. See Barnes's discussion of the state's co-optation of popular culture in *Cultural Conundrums*.

42. Cooper, *Noises in the Blood*, 84, as quoted in Breiner, "Half-Life of Performance Poems," 27.

43. Ramazani, *Hybrid Muse*, 108.

44. See *The Star* (Kingston, Jamaica), December 16, 1971, and January 13, 1972; and Evon Blake, *Daily Gleaner*, January 27, 1979; as quoted in Morris, introduction to *Selected Poems*, xiii.

45. Rex Nettleford, introduction to *Jamaica Labrish*, by Louise Bennett (1966; reprint, Kingston: Sangster's Bookstores, 1972), 23.

46. Ramazani, *Hybrid Muse*, 113.

47. The details of the history of pantomime in Jamaica can be found in "LTM [Little Theatre Movement] Pantomime History—The Early Years," http://www.ltmpantomime.com (accessed 2006).

48. I am thinking here of Walcott's play, *Dream on Monkey Mountain* (1967), which uses the inversion theme to great effect. For a longer discussion of revisionings of European classics by Caribbean writers, see Edmondson, *Making Men*; also, Jonathan Goldberg's *Tempest in the Caribbean* (Minneapolis: University of Minnesota Press, 2004).

49. As quoted in Ruth Minott Egglestone, "A Philosophy of Survival: Anancyism in Jamaican Pantomime," in *The Society for Caribbean Studies Annual Conference Papers*, vol. 2, ed. Sandra Courtman (2001), 5; http://www.scsonline.freeserve.co.uk/olvol2.html.

50. Minott Egglestone's interview of Noel Vaz, December 18, 2000, ibid., 5n17.

51. For example, in 1963 the popular Trinidadian calypsonian the Mighty Sparrow wrote an acerbic hit, "Dan Is the Man in the Van," which ran through a list of old English rhymes to point out the vacuity of an English education.

52. See "LTM Pantomime History," 4. Jamaican theater critic Norman Rae notes with irony that the finale to *Soliday and the Wicked Bird* was a hymn containing the line, "England's green and pleasant land" (Norman Rae, e-mail to author, February 27, 2007). Nevertheless, Vera Bell's pantomime, like her poetry, appears to have been an extension of her role as an educator; she was the director of the Jamaica School of Arts and Crafts for a number of years.

53. Jahan Ramazani, in *Hybrid Muse,* calls this attitude of constant irony Louise Bennett's "Anancy poetics."

54. Louise Bennett, *Selected Poems,* ed. Mervyn Morris (1982; reprint, Kingston: Sangsters, 2003), 104.

55. The most well-known examples include Jean Rhys's *Wide Sargasso Sea* and V. S. Naipaul's *A Bend in the River,* revisions of *Jane Eyre* and *Heart of Darkness,* respectively.

56. DeCaires Narain, *Contemporary Caribbean Women's Poetry,* 55. Again, I am indebted to DeCaires Narain for noting the relationship between popular English poems and Bennett's verse. I have essentially replicated her argument here.

57. Bennett, *Selected Poems,* 116, as quoted in DeCaires Narain, *Contemporary Caribbean Women's Poetry,* 55.

58. Morris, "Reading Louise Bennett Seriously"; and Nettleford, introduction to *Jamaica Labrish.*

59. Naipaul himself was aware of the risk of criticizing the region when his work was underwritten by a government scholarship. He writes in the 1981 foreword to *The Middle Passage* that when Eric Williams asked him to write a nonfiction book about the Caribbean, "I hesitated. The novelist works towards conclusions of which he is often unaware; and it is better that he should. However, I decided to take the risk." The hostility to Naipaul in the Caribbean and other developing regions is well documented.

60. Jamaica Kincaid, *A Small Place* (New York: Virago Press, 1988), 49, as quoted in DeCaires Narain, *Contemporary Caribbean Women's Poetry,* 47.

61. DeCaires Narain, *Contemporary Caribbean Women's Poetry,* 57.

62. See Nate Chinen, "Jazz Is Alive and Well. In the Classroom, Anyway," *New York Times,* January 7, 2007.

63. Jean Binta Breeze, "Can a Dub Poet Be a Woman?" *Woman: A Cultural Review* 1 (1990): 47–49.

64. See Christian Habekost's interview of Jean Binta Breeze, in Habekost, *Verbal Riddim: The Politics and Aesthetics of African-Caribbean Dub Poetry* (Amsterdam: Rodopi, 1993), 45, as quoted in DeCaires Narain, *Contemporary Caribbean Women's Poetry,* 110.

65. Again, I am indebted to DeCaires Narain for her point: "[a] gendered reading of Caribbean poetry and its relationship to Creole-usage suggests that male protest poetry is associated with a declamatory public anger while the kind of Creole-use associated with Louise Bennett and women speakers generally is interpreted (and, indeed presents itself) as an intimate, humorous, private discourse, located in

relatively circumscribed domestic spaces" (*Contemporary Caribbean Women's Poetry,* 86). My interpretation differs slightly from DeCaires Narain's in that I see Miss Lou's positioning as public, not private, but disarmingly so, leavened with humor and an indirect use of social or political critique.

66. Bennett's work is now receiving more critical attention than it has in the past; in addition to entire chapters of literary criticism dedicated to her poetry by critics such as Jahan Ramazani, Denise DeCaires Narain, and Lloyd Brown, she has been anthologized in Dabydeen and Wilson-Tagoe, *Guide to West Indian and Black British Literature.*

67. See Bennett, "Bennett on Bennett," 101, 98 and 100.

68. For example, see Wikipedia's 2008 entry on the Mighty Sparrow, which alludes to his modest successes in England in the 1950s and to his controversial lyrics in such pieces as "Congo Man," a satirical song about cannibalism and interracial sex that was deemed so offensive it was banned from the local airwaves until 1989. Sparrow, like today's working-class rappers and dancehall artists, was also associated with urban, working-class violence: he was charged with shooting a man, an episode he chronicled in his local hit "Ten to One Is Murder." These differences aside, the parallels between the Mighty Sparrow and Miss Lou are numerous: both have enjoyed a long career spanning the pre- and postcolonial eras, and both are identified with an early nationalist government: the Mighty Sparrow was an early and ardent supporter of the government of Eric Williams, first prime minister of Trinidad and Tobago.

69. The Trinidadian writer Earl Lovelace does a hilarious send-up of academic appropriation of "oppositional" calypso lyrics in his novel *The Dragon Can't Dance,* underscoring his point that the people's language and experience lie beyond the agenda of one group.

4. Middlebrow Spectacle and the Politics of Beauty

1. The epigraph from Robert Love, editor of the *Jamaica Advocate,* is quoted in Patrick Bryan, *The Jamaican People, 1880–1902: Race, Class, and Social Control* (London: Macmillan, 1991), 233; the one from the *Port of Spain Gazette* is quoted in Gordon Rohlehr, *Calypso and Society in Pre-Independence Trinidad* (Port of Spain: G. Rohlehr, 1990), 22.

2. I owe the descriptive term "vulgar" in this context to Carolyn Cooper's groundbreaking work, *Noises in the Blood.*

3. Froude, *English in the West Indies,* 197–98.

4. In his travelogue, nineteenth-century English writer Charles Kingsley (of Barbadian descent) makes the following observations of the public behavior of black and Indian women at the races in Trinidad: "The Negresses, I am sorry to say, forgot themselves, kicked up their legs, shouted to bystanders, and were altogether incondite. The Hindoo women, though showing much more of their limbs than the Negresses, kept them so gracefully together, drew their veils around their heads, and sat coyly, half frightened, half amused, to the delight of their 'papas,' or husbands" (Kingsley, *At Last,* 2:262). I am grateful to Faith Smith, from whom I first discovered Kingsley's comments on black and Indian women, in her paper "Gentlemen and Jamettes: Gender and Creole Nationalism in Nineteenth-Century Trinidad," Caribbean Studies Association conference, Panama City, Panama, May 24–28, 1999.

5. Read, for example, the following description of the John Canoe—or Junkanoo—parade (an African-derived public masquerade, somewhat similar to carnival) in early nineteenth-century Jamaica: "But the beautiful part of the exhibition was the Set Girls. They danced along the streets, in bands from fifteen to thirteen. There were brown sets, and black sets, and sets of all intermediate gradations of colour.... I had never seen more beautiful creatures than there were among the brown sets—clear olive complexions, and fine faces, elegant carriages, splendid figures—full, plump, magnificent." See Michael Scott, *Tom Cringle's Log* (1821; reprint, http://www.scribd.com/doc/898606/Tom-Cringles-Log-by-Michael-Scott [accessed 2009], 207).

6. Vera Kutzinski, *Sugar's Secrets: Race and the Erotics of Cuban Nationalism* (Charlottesville: University Press of Virginia, 1994), chap. 2.

7. For example, after a public outcry in Spain, Iberia Airlines had to pull one of its television advertisements of Cuba, which showed voluptuous, brown-skinned women dancing and coddling a white baby to a driving reggaeton beat. See Reuters, "Spanish Airlines Cuts Cuban Aid after Sexism Complaint," May 22, 2007; also Coco Fusco, "Hustling for Dollars," *MS.*, September–October 1996, 60–70. There is some indication that the state of Bahia in Brazil is competing for European and American sex tourists with Cuba, using the same formula of black and brown women in their advertisements in those markets.

8. The Jamaican Dancehall Queen contest now has an international face: a recent winner was Junko, a Japanese national. Indeed the Dancehall Queen contest has been imported to several cities around the world. I suspect that Junko's reign as dancehall queen has more to do with the commercial imperatives of the dancehall industry than with Junko's skills as a dancer; in the same way that the expansion of the American beauty contest into international markets does not necessarily mean an acceptance of different types of ethnic beauty in the United States, so too the expansion of the dancehall franchise to include Japanese citizens and others may indicate an interest in building the franchise and nothing more. For a more detailed discussion of the racial politics of brown women, popular culture, and dancehall queens in Jamaica, see Edmondson, "Trinidad Romance."

9. Carlene Smith—"Queen Carlene"—appeared in the humorous video *How to Enjoy Jamaica: The Unofficial Guide,* produced by Kimberly Mais and Jeremy Francis (Kingston, Jamaica: Black Olive Entertainment, 1997). Ironically, when a dark-skinned Miss Jamaica, Sara Lawrence, resigned because she became pregnant, the former Dancehall Queen, who herself had a child out of wedlock, publicly castigated the disgraced beauty queen. See posting "More on Ms. Lawrence" by "yamfoot," March 17, 2007 (12:12 a.m.), on The next decade... what's in store? (blog), Yamfoot.net/archives/2007/03.html.

10. See the excellent analysis of this event in Natasha Barnes, "Face of the Nation: Race, Nationalisms and Identities in Jamaican Beauty Pageants," *Massachusetts Review* 35, nos. 3–4 (1994): 471–92; also published in chap. 2 of Barnes, *Cultural Conundrums.*

11. See "When the Reign Is Over: Miss Jamaica Festival Queens—Where Are They Now?" Roots and Culture: Independence 2003 sec., *Jamaica Gleaner* (online ed.), 2003.

12. The Miss Barbados controversy is not the first time tensions have arisen over the money showered on elite Caribbean women's contests at the perceived expense

of black calypsonians. Natasha Barnes describes the famous boycott of the calypso competition by black male calypsonians in Trinidad in 1957, after the winner of the Miss Carnival Queen pageant—essentially a debutante ball for Trinidad's white elite—received substantially more prize money than did all the winning carnival bands put together. See Barnes, "Face of the Nation," 475.

13. "Redwood, an Ideal Jamaican Mix."

14. Catherine Bremer, "Dreadlocked Miss Jamaica Puts Rastas in New Light," Youth Portal for Latin America and the Caribbean; http://www.youthlac.org/content/view/157/40/.

15. See Harris, "Dreadlocked Beauty a Bold Step."

16. See Krista Henry, "A Race to Beauty," *Jamaica Gleaner* (online ed.), August 27, 2006, emphasis added.

17. See Conrad McLeod, "Pregnant Pageant Winner Quitting," *Miami Herald*, March 15, 2007; Novia McDonald-White, "Pregnancy Dethrones Queen: Sara Lawrence Rules Out Abortion," *Jamaica Gleaner* (online ed.), March 15, 2007.

18. See McDonald-White, "Pregnancy Dethrones Queen"; Tony Deyal, "Wendy's Big Do," *Jamaica Gleaner* (online ed.), February 21, 2006; Attilah Springer, "There's Sex Out of Wedlock," *Trinidad Guardian* (online ed.), January 28, 2006.

19. One of the most popular winners of the Miss Jamaica contest, however, was 1973 winner Patsy Yuen, a Chinese Jamaican whose already skyrocketing popularity went even higher when she won the Miss World pageant, albeit by default—the real winner was dethroned—and thereby thrust Jamaica into the international spotlight. See Barnes, "Face of the Nation."

20. In Trinidad, the term "creole" usually refers to Afro-Trinidadians, although it also encompasses whites and mixed-race peoples. In short, creole refers to those who are descended from or who participate in the mixed cultural heritage of the society.

21. "No, Trinidad Isn't Guyana" (editorial), *Trinidad Express,* April 19, 1999.

22. "Dougla" is a term for someone of mixed Indian and African heritage and apparently derives from the Hindi word for "bastard."

23. Puri, "Canonized Hybridities, Resistant Hybridities," 25, 26. I am indebted to Puri's research and interpretation of the Drupatee Ramgoonai controversy, which I have essentially replicated here.

24. "Sabeeney: Look Out for Miss Japan," *Trinidad Express,* May 23, 1999.

25. Angela Martin-Hinds, "Nicole Takes off Braces," *Trinidad Express,* May 6, 1999.

26. Frank Phillip, "First Time Lucky for Miss Botswana," *Trinidad Express,* May 27, 1999.

27. Martin Henry, "Jamaica and Botswana," *Daily Gleaner,* June 3, 1999.

5. Organic Imports, or Authenticating Global Culture

1. Nestor García Canclini, *Hybrid Cultures: Strategies for Entering and Leaving Modernity* (Minneapolis: University of Minnesota Press, 1995), 147, as quoted in Puri, "Canonized Hybridities, Resistant Hybridities."

2. See Keith Nurse, "Bringing Culture into Tourism: Festival Tourism and Reggae Sunsplash in Jamaica," *Social and Economic Studies* 51, no. 1 (2002): 133.

3. Koningsbruggen, *Trinidad Carnival,* 240, as quoted in Aching, *Masking and Power,* 78.

4. Arjun Appadurai, "Disjuncture and Difference in the Global Economy," in *Colonial Discourse and Post-Colonial Theory: A Reader*, ed. Patrick Williams and Laura Chrisman (New York: Columbia University Press, 1994), 333–34.

5. Although the traditional treatment of carnival costumes is to discard them once the carnival is over—which is reminiscent of West African cultural practices of treating art as ephemeral—in recent years Trinidadian designer Peter Minshall has been circulating his pieces to the various carnivals staged in North America and Europe; he created pieces for the 1992 Barcelona Olympics.

6. Errol Hill, *The Trinidad Carnival: Mandate for a National Theatre* (Austin: University of Texas Press, 1972).

7. Editorial, *Port-of-Spain Gazette*, 1838, as quoted in Hill, *Trinidad Carnival*, 17.

8. See Gerard Aching's account of nineteenth-century carnival in Trinidad in *Masking and Power*, chap. 2.

9. Burton, *Afro-Creole*, 206.

10. Earl Lovelace both chronicled the politicization of carnival by the PNM and made the case for the increasing middle-classization of carnival in his classic novel *The Dragon Can't Dance* (1979). More recently, see Aching, *Masking and Power;* Koningsbruggen, *Trinidad Carnival*.

11. Burton, *Afro-Creole*, 208. See also Philip Scher's account of Trinidadian estrangement from carnival in "When 'Natives' Become Tourists of Themselves," in *Trinidad Carnival: The Cultural Politics of a Transnational Festival*, ed. Garth L. Green and Philip W. Scher (Bloomington: Indiana University Press, 2007).

12. In that Anglophone Afro-Caribbean immigrants are far more likely to live and go to school with African Americans than they are with white Americans (particularly in areas such as New York City), I posit that these interactions are far more likely to yield a certain cultural familiarity for African Americans with some forms of Caribbean culture. For research that supports this contention, see Ruben G. Rumbaut, "Immigrants from Latin America and the Caribbean: A Socioeconomic Profile," in *Immigrants and Immigrant Communities: A Focus on Latinos*, ed. Refugio I. Rochin (East Lansing, MI: Julian Samora Research Institute, 1996).

13. These statistics were compiled by the Central Statistics Office of Trinidad and Tobago, and sent to the author on April 12, 2007. I have added visitors from Venezuela to the total number of Caribbean and Caricom visitors, given that Venezuela is a close neighbor of the island. The number of visitors from North America has grown considerably in the last twenty years; Peter van Koningsbruggen reports that according to the Trinidad and Tobago Central Statistical Office data for 1985, 42 percent of the visitors came from North America and 39 percent came from the Commonwealth Caribbean (Koningsbruggen, *Trinidad Carnival*, 258).

14. Patricia Alleyne-Dettmers, "Black Kings: Aesthetic Representation in Carnival in Trinidad & Tobago and London," *Black Music Research Journal* 22, no. 2 (Autumn 2002): 241–58.

15. Anthropologist Patricia Moonsammy makes a case for carnival music—soca music—as a vehicle for forwarding women's empowerment in her essay "'Miss Good Reputation'? Divas, Warriors and Mothers Performing Power in Trinidad," presented at the Caribbean Studies Association annual conference, Trinidad and Tobago, May 30, 2006; in the essay Moonsammy dissects the lyrics and production of Hinds's music.

16. See Nicolette Bethel, "Peter Minshall on the Commercialization of Carnival," BlogWorld: Nicolette Bethel's Blog, December 22, 2006, http://nicobethel.net/blogworld. Peter van Koningsbruggen persuasively argues that the Americanization of carnival is not a recent event, as Minshall's comment implies. He traces the elaborate presentation of the Dimanche Gras show to the desire to appeal to the U.S. military presence on the island in the 1940s and the increased influence of Hollywood film spectacles of the 1950s postwar period. In other words, Trinidad carnival for the last sixty years has been steadily "Americanizing." See Koningsbruggen, *Trinidad Carnival,* 90, 258. Koningsbruggen also connects modern carnival to the U.S. presence during World War II when he suggests that the U.S. presence emancipated women to participate in the street parade; Americanness was associated with female freedom. For further discussion of the gender politics of "traditional mas'," see Pamela Franco, "The Invention of Traditional Mas and the Politics of Gender," in Green and Scher, *Trinidad Carnival.*

17. Koningsbruggen, *Trinidad Carnival,* 194; see also 218–19, in the section "Tourism without Tourists."

18. Ibid., 80.

19. See D. John, "Women in Mas'," in *Women in Mas',* ed. O. Baptiste (Port of Spain: Imprint Caribbean, 1988), 5–7, 90–92, 95–96, as quoted in Koningsbruggen, *Trinidad Carnival,* 80–81. For more on the revised role of Caribbean women in the public sphere, see my discussion in chapter 4.

20. See J. Stewart, "Patronage and Control in the Trinidad Carnival," in *The Anthropology of Experience,* ed. V. W. Turner and E. M. Bruner, 289–315 (Urbana: University of Illinois Press, 1986), as quoted in Koningsbruggen, *Trinidad Carnival,* 266.

21. Pan yards are the areas where the steel pans are made and where steel bands practice.

22. See Philip Scher, *Carnival and the Formation of a Caribbean Transnation* (Gainesville: University of Florida Press, 2003), 154–55; and Scher, "When 'Natives' Become Tourists of Themselves," 90–100.

23. Keith Nurse states that revenue for Trinidad's 2002 carnival was between US$50 million and US$67 million, although it's unclear whether that amount includes "on the road" revenue. See Nurse, "Bringing Culture into Tourism," 128.

24. Philip Scher, "Copyright and Heritage Tourism," *Anthropological Quarterly* 75 (Summer 2002): 453–84, quotation at 453.

25. See Milla C. Riggio, "Trinidad and Tobago Carnival," *Drama Review* 42, no. 3 (1998), as quoted in Scher, "Copyright and Heritage Tourism," 454.

26. John Cupid, "Trinidad Carnival Traditional Characters," *1st Carnival King and Queen of the World Magazine,* vol. 1 (1994): 16, as quoted in Scher, "Copyright and Heritage Tourism," 472.

27. Orlando Patterson, "Dollars in the Sand," *New York Times* (online ed.), January 2, 2007.

28. Scher, "Copyright and Heritage Tourism," 453; regarding Jamaica's legislation of copyright protection for Reggae Sunsplash from the World Intellectual Property Organization (WIPO), 471.

29. Koningsbruggen, *Trinidad Carnival,* 120.

30. I don't include a discussion of the British Virgin Islands or U.S. Virgin Islands carnivals here. For a more detailed account of Jamaica's carnival, see Edmondson, "Trinidad Romance"; my knowledge of Antigua's carnival comes primarily from the seminal essay on the convergence of tourism and carnival culture, Frank E. Manning, "Carnival in Antigua: An Indigenous Festival in a Tourist Economy," *Anthropos* 73, nos. 1–2 (1978): 191–204. My discussion of Barbados's Crop Over, the Virgin Islands' carnival, and Aruba's carnival is informed by Andre Hoyte, "The Story of Crop Over," public relations leaflet, National Cultural Foundation of Barbados (2007); Colleen Ballerino Cohen, "'This Is de Test': Festival and the Cultural Politics of Nation Building in the British Virgin Islands," *American Ethnologist* 25, no. 2 (May 1998): 189–214; and Robert W. Nicholls, "Old-Time Masquerading in the U.S. Virgin Islands" (St. Thomas: Virgin Islands Humanities Council, 1998); Victoria M. Razak, "Carnival in Aruba," 136–60, in Green and Scher, *Trinidad Carnival*.

31. Manning, "Carnival in Antigua," 196, 198–99.

32. Razak, "Carnival in Aruba," 143.

33. Junkanoo—also known as John Canoe—is not solely a Jamaican tradition. It may be found in the Bahamas as well as other nations.

34. Interview with Oneil Smith, in Claude Mills, "Revellers 'Bump and Wine' at Joker's Wild Beach J'Ouvert in Oracabessa, St. Mary," *Jamaica Gleaner* (online ed.), April 23, 2006.

35. "Jamaican Carnival," http://www.caribbeanchoice.com/jamaica/carnival/asp/April (accessed 2007).

36. Interview with Stamford Cockin, one of the directors of Bacchanal Jamaica, in Mills, "Revellers 'Bump and Wine.'"

37. Frederick Bayley, *Four Years' Residence in the West Indies* (London: William Kidd, 1832), 436, as quoted in Hilary Beckles, "Crop Over Fetes and Festivals in Caribbean Slavery," in *In the Shadow of the Plantation*, ed. Alvin O. Thompson, 246–63 (Kingston: Ian Randle, 2002).

38. Spouge, a combination of Jamaican ska and Trinidadian calypso, was a short-lived musical phenomenon in Barbados in the early to mid-1970s.

39. Like Trinidad's older carnival organizers, the original organizers of the revived Crop Over similarly lament the divergence of today's celebration from the earlier incarnation. In a post by "titilayo" on Caribbean Beat blog, August 23, 2006, 4:06 p.m., Caribbean-beat.blogspot.com/2006/08/after-crop-over/html, the blogger references a "sad" lecture about Emancipation Day (Crop Over's Jump Up falls on that day) given by former Yoruba Foundation director Elombe Mottley, who said that the current festival has diverged from what it was intended to be when it was revived in 1974.

40. "Crop Over: Carnival of Barbados," http://www.caribnet.com (accessed 2007); Barbados Crop Over Web site, www.barbados.org/cropover.htm (accessed 2007).

41. Hoyte, "Story of Crop Over," 5, 7.

42. There are endless combinations of these on various Web sites dedicated to Caribbean jokes: http://www.Caribwave.com, for example. They usually start with the line, "You know you are a Jamaican/Bajan/Trini/Guyanese when..."

43. For example, in acknowledgment of Barbados's nationalist-minded government, the first prime minister of Barbados, Grantley Adams, was initially tapped to head the short-lived West Indies Federation in the late 1950s.

44. Kirby Allain, public relations manager of the St. Lucia Tourist Board, in an e-mail message to the author, October 11, 2005.

45. See Neptune, *Caliban and the Yankees.*

46. See Warren Pinckney Jr., "Jazz in Barbados," *American Music* 12, no. 1 (Spring 1994): 62.

47. See Michelle Stephens's work on the influence of African American popular icons such as Paul Robeson and Harry Belafonte on Caribbean societies, in Stephens, "The First Negro Matinee Idol: Harry Belafonte and American Culture in the 1950s," in *Left of the Color Line: Race, Radicalism and Twentieth-Century Literature of the United States,* ed. Bill V. Mullen and James Smethurst (Chapel Hill: University of North Carolina Press, 2003).

48. Pinckney, "Jazz in Barbados," 67; Pinckney outlines the class-driven nature of the jazz venues in the early 1960s (81–82).

49. Ibid., 62–68; Elton Elombe Mattley, then director of the National Cultural Foundation of Barbados, was quoted in *Barbados/Caribbean Jazz Festival Magazine* (1985), as quoted in Pinckney, "Jazz in Barbados," 71.

50. All quotations and references are from Pinckney, "Jazz in Barbados," 74–75.

51. Ocho Rios Jazz Festival Web site, http://www.ochoriosjazz.com (accessed 2005).

52. "Evolution of the Fringe," http://www.stluciajazz.org (accessed 2006).

53. Beenie Man's presence notwithstanding, recent years have seen a rise in complaints that the jazz festivals are controlled by foreign commercial interests, foreign culture, and foreign artists. Some of the largest sponsors are, inevitably, American corporate interests like Black Entertainment Network. Some Caribbean musicians complain that the Americans deliberately marginalize Caribbean artists, who are overshadowed by the more famous Americans; or that it is the local organizers, not the foreign sponsors, who do not respect and advance local talent. When Elton John headlined Trinidad's Plymouth Jazz Festival, a group of Trinidadian pastors, somewhat predictably, decried that the singer was "advancing the homosexual agenda" in the country, although the singer was there only to perform. These signs of resentment suggest not so much the foreignness of jazz—after all, Elton John's music hardly qualifies—so much as a creeping sense of foreign control of what is supposed to be autonomous local culture, an inevitable consequence perhaps of the collision between international capital and local culture. For examples, see "BET: Caribbean Talent Not Shadowed [by American Artistes," *Daily Express* (Trinidad), June 1, 2006, 62; Keith Diaz, Steelbandsman, "Pan Getting Raw Deal at Jazz Show," Letters sec., *Trinidad Guardian* (online ed.), March 24, 2007; "Elton John Could Turn Us Gay, Says Archdeacon," *Daily Mail* (U.K.), March 16, 2007; Winston Lewis, "Dangerous to Allow John," Letters sec., *Trinidad Guardian* (online ed.), March 19, 2007.

54. "Jazz Festival of Class," Letters sec., *Daily Gleaner,* August 13, 2001.

55. Kamau Brathwaite, "Jazz and the West Indian Novel," in *Roots: Essays in Caribbean Literature* (1967; reprint, Ann Arbor: University of Michigan Press, 1993), 59, 56–58, 57, 108.

56. This information is from the official Web site of the Calabash Festival, http://www.calabashfestival.org (accessed 2006), emphasis added. Of the four largest sponsors of the 2006 Calabash Festival (contributing more than US$10,000, according to the program), however, only one was actually Jamaican: the Jamaica Tourist Board.

The other three were the Chase Fund, the U.S. State Department, and American Airlines. For clearly economic reasons, American corporate interests are never far from the vision of these local productions.

57. The "cultural" tourist is one who comes not for the beaches and general relaxation so much as to observe local culture; cultural tourists in Britain, for example, are estimated to stay 75 percent longer and spend 64 percent more per trip than "normal" tourists. Cultural tourists have been a target audience for Caribbean festival tourism since the inception of Jamaica's Reggae Sunsplash in 1978. See J. Myerscough, *The Economic Importance of the Arts in Britain* (London: Policy Studies Institute, 1988), 85–86, as quoted in Nurse, "Bringing Culture into Tourism," 129.

58. Channer, "Q & A with Author."

59. In 2006, *John Crow's Devil* was short-listed for both the Commonwealth Writer's Prize and the *Los Angeles Times* Book Prize, and was an Editor's Choice in the 2005 *New York Times Book Review*.

60. Colin Channer, "The Kingston 12 Overture," in *Iron Balloons: Hit Fiction from Jamaica's Calabash Writer's Workshop,* ed. Colin Channer (New York: Akashic Books 2006), 17. This volume, as well as all of the books on display at Calabash, have a local distributor, Novelty Trading Company based in Kingston, which distributes foreign as well as local literature.

61. Ibid., 12.

62. See Chandra Talpade Mohanty, "Women Workers and Capitalist Scripts," in *Feminist Genealogies, Colonial Legacies, Democratic Futures,* ed. M. Jacqui Alexander and Chandra Talpade Mohanty (London: Routledge 1997). Other scholars, however, such as Saskia Sassen, whose *Globalization and Its Discontents* is a better-known critique of globalization, have a more hopeful view of globalization than do postcolonial critics such as Alexander and Talpade Mohanty. I thank Sonali Perera for this distinction.

6. Transnational Communities and the New Pop Fiction

1. For a more detailed analysis of the impact of immigration on Caribbean literature, see the introduction to Edmondson, *Making Men;* also Carole Boyce-Davies, *Migrations of the Subject* (New York: Routledge, 1994).

2. Here I am thinking of characters such as the Rastafarian playwright Fire in Channer's *Waiting in Vain,* the rebel heroine Tan Tan who becomes the Midnight Robber in Hopkinson's eponymous novel, and the master-slave romance in Valerie Belgrave's *Ti Marie.*

3. I emphasize the U.S.-based community of Caribbean immigrants over the U.K.-based one because American influence extends to the English example as well. African American popular fiction has been instrumental in the creation of the British publisher of black popular fiction, X Press. The African American community provides a template for black metropolitan identity for newly American or British black immigrants to the United States or the United Kingdom.

4. In *No Telephone to Heaven,* the revolutionaries' final act is to attack a film set. The film is a foreign production of Jamaican history.

5. Saskia Sassen, *A Sociology of Globalization* (New York: W. W. Norton, 2007), 3, 169.

6. Neil Morley, "Opportunities in Paradise?" *Bookseller* (London, Publisher's Association), May 17, 2002, 31–32, quotation at 31.

7. There is a concrete reason that English Literature is no longer a compulsory subject in the English-speaking Caribbean. With the replacement of the England-based Cambridge "O" and "A" levels by the Caribbean-based CSEC (formerly CXC) and CAPE examinations has come a sea change in the relationship between regional examinations and the curriculum of individual schools.

8. Marlon James, "High Art, Low Art and Critical Thought," Marlon James among Other Things, March 13, 2007, http://www.marlon-james.blogspot.com.

9. Morley, "Opportunities in Paradise?" 32, quotation at 31.

10. See Norman Rae, "Isolation and Coronation: A Line from the Tower of Babble," *Sunday Gleaner,* August 28, 2005.

11. See Channer, "Kingston 12 Ouverture," 18.

12. The democratic innovations of Jamaica's recording industry are well chronicled in Norman Stolzoff, *Wake the Town and Tell the People* (Durham: Duke University Press, 2000). The popular depiction of Jamaica's recording industry in the iconic 1972 film *The Harder They Come* reveals a different view, however: a predatory industry, run by elites, who exploit working-class men and pay them almost nothing in return for their creative labor.

13. See Dinitia Smith's interview with Colin Channer in Dinitia Smith, "Emboldened by Reggae, Jamaican Writers Bust Out," *New York Times,* June 27, 2006; the stories in *Iron Balloons* are described as "hav[ing] none of the genteel Victorianism that has hung over Jamaican fiction in the past." A review of Channer's first novel, *Waiting in Vain* (1998), in the *Washington Post* hails it as "a clear re-definition of the Caribbean novel," implying that Channer's literary aesthetic is fundamentally different. See also Dawes, *Natural Mysticism,* chap. 3.

14. Colin Channer, "A Conversation with Colin Channer," http://www.aalbc.com/authors/colin.htm (accessed 2003), as quoted in Donette Francis, "Making Meaning of America, Audience and Authorship: Narrating the Limits of Diaspora in the Novels of Colin Channer," manuscript, April 2003, 1.

15. Calabash collaborator Kwame Dawes has described Channer as "Bob Marley with a pen," a quotation used frequently in the merchandising of Channer's novels.

16. Channer, "Q & A with Author," emphasis added

17. Colin Channer, *Passing Through* (New York: One World/Ballantine Books, 2004), 303–4.

18. See Colin Channer's biography in http://www.Answers.com, quoting the review of *Satisfy My Soul* by http://www.Africana.com. See also Felicia R. Lee, "Chick-Lit King Imagines His Way into Women's Heads," *New York Times,* July 29, 2004. Other critics have discussed Channer's images of black professionals in better detail than I provide here; for example, see Faith Smith, "You Know You're a West Indian If—Codes of Authenticity in Colin Channer's *Waiting in Vain*," Small Axe 10 (2001): 41–59.

19. Channer complains that he does not like the covers for his first two novels, both of which feature heavily charged erotic images of naked black men being watched by black women. He prefers the more dignified image on the cover of his third novel, *Passing Through*—a touristy image of a black woman in a tropical print swimsuit against a backdrop of colonial architecture. Still, he clearly has an

investment in erotica; speaking of *Passing Through*'s critical depth, he says, "Anyway, if my fans leave me 'cause they think I've gotten too sophisticated they'll come back for the sex!" See Channer, "Q & A with Author."

20. The ambivalence of black Caribbean populations toward African Americans has been fairly well documented. In the classic study by Mary Waters, *Black Identities: West Immigrant Dreams and American Realities* (Cambridge: Harvard University Press, 1999), Waters posits that, unlike other immigrant groups, black immigrants derive benefits from *not* assimilating in that they would become African Americans, and thus find themselves on the lower end of the American caste system. Their cultural difference, in other words, works in their economic favor.

21. See Channer's discussion of *Passing Through,* in Channer, "Q & A with Author."

22. When asked if he considered his recent Caribbean-focused novel, *The Girl with the Golden Shoes* (2007), a political novel, Channer responded that "it is a very political book, but it is political in the tradition of reggae, which has always seen politics as a complement to entertainment." Again, overt political content is relegated to an outdated anticolonial genre. See Colin Channer, "Social Consciousness in Literature," interview with Farai Chideya, National Public Radio, August 6, 2007.

23. In *Iron Balloons* Colin Channer describes the efforts of the organizers to reissue John Hearne's *Under the Window* and Roger Mais's *Brotherman,* which Channer calls "one of the most important novels in the Jamaican (and wider Caribbean) literary canon" See Channer, "Kingston 12 Ouverture," 22–23.

24. Author's interview with Suzzanne Lee, director, Novelty Trading Company, May 27, 2006. Lee explained that the success of *The White Witch of Rose Hall* probably resulted from tourist sales rather than local ones; 60 percent of the book's sales were in Montego Bay, home of Rose Hall, whereas most of Channer's sales were in Kingston.

25. Author's telephone interview with Nalo Hopkinson, July 7, 2006.

26. See Luan Gaines, "Curled up with a Good Book: An Interview with Nalo Hopkinson," http://www.curledup.com/naloint.htm (accessed 2006).

27. See Elizabeth Nunez, remarks at the Caribbean Women Writers Conference, Martinique, April 2002, as quoted in Francis, "Making Meaning of America."

28. See Terry McMillan's biography in http://www.Answers.com, which describes how the author organized her own book tours and contacted bookstores herself.

29. Author's telephone interview with Jaime Levine, senior editor, Warner Aspect Books, August 1, 2006.

30. Author's interview with Nalo Hopkinson, July 7, 2006.

31. Channer, "Q & A with Author."

32. Many early—and lurid—examples of Caribbean gothic literature can be found in the pages of Jamaica's *Daily Gleaner.* These usually involve supernatural phenomena such as obeah. H. G. de Lisser appeared to be catering to his readers' taste for the gothic in his terror tale *The White Witch of Rose Hall* (1928). Similarly, Edgar Mittelholzer utilized a Caribbean gothic tradition in his science fiction novel *My Bones and My Flute* (1955).

33. For example, the story line in *Midnight Robber* involves two planets, one a high-tech utopia named Toussaint, the other a primitive dystopia named New Half-Way Tree. Toussaint—as in the Haitian revolution's Toussaint L'Ouverture—as well

as Cockpit County—as in Jamaica's maroon homeland, Cockpit Country—remind Caribbean readers of the enslaved Africans of their ancestral past. New Half-Way Tree is an ironic allusion to one of Kingston's downtown areas, Half-Way Tree. The main character is Tan-Tan, a name well known to Trinidadians as a traditional character from carnival, and indeed carnival is a tradition that is central to the life of Toussaint.

34. Interview with Levine, July 7, 2006.

35. Author's telephone interview with Johnny Temple, August 9, 2006.

36. Akashic Books, http://www.akashicbooks.com (accessed 2006).

37. See David D. Kirkpatrick, "Winfrey Rescinds Offer to Author for Guest Appearance," *New York Times,* October 24, 2001.

38. Marlon James, in an interview with Nazma Muller, "The Mis-Education of Marlon James," *Jamaica Observer,* July 23, 2006.

39. African American book clubs have proliferated online. *Essence* magazine lists its favorite authors, highlights new ones, and features a local book club every month. African American book clubs have their roots in the literary societies formed in the early nineteenth century, when African Americans saw reading as a means to freedom and citizenship. For a history of African American reading clubs from the early nineteenth century to the present, see the informative analysis in Elizabeth McHenry, *Forgotten Readers.* The literature excavating the history of white American reading clubs is more extensive; particularly influential is Janice Radway, *A Feeling for Books: The Book-of-the-Month Club, Literary Taste, and Middle Class Desire* (Chapel Hill: University of North Carolina Press, 1997).

40. American best sellers are inevitably best sellers in the English-speaking Caribbean, according to Novelty Trading Company's Suzzanne Lee, who cites the prominence of American authors like John Grisham on Jamaica's best-seller lists.

41. African diaspora themes are to be found in the African American listings of all the major publishers, and certainly a cursory reading of Internet book clubs and amazon.com responses to Caribbean-authored, U.S.-published books suggests that African American readers are well represented among their readers. Further, venues like *Essence* magazine promote diaspora connections in their advocacy of books by authors from Africa to the Caribbean.

42. James interview, in Muller, "Mis-Education of Marlon James."

43. Critics have noted the rise of the black pop lit phenomenon. My source here is the excellent article by Curdella Forbes, "X Press Publications: Pop Culture, 'Pop Lit' and Caribbean Literary Criticism: An Essay of Provocation," *Anthurium: A Caribbean Studies Journal* 4, no. 1 (Spring 2006): 3. For an analysis of "yardie" fiction, see Loretta Collins, "Raggamuffin Cultural Studies: X-Press Novels' Yardies and Cop Killers Put Britain on Trial," *Small Axe* 9 (March 2001): 70–96; and Grant Farred, "The Postcolonial Chickens Come Home to Roost: How *Yardie* Has Created a New Postcolonial Subaltern," *South Atlantic Quarterly* 100, no. 1 (Winter 2001): 288–305.

44. Forbes, "X Press Publications," 5. Forbes notes that a quote from a character in one of X Press's yardie novels, Patrick Augustus's *Baby Father* (2003) appears, almost verbatim in a 2001 *New Nation* article quoting X Press publisher Dotun Adebayo: "I remember this Ku Klux Klan guy on TV, saying 'If you wanna hide anything from

a nigga, put it in a book.' From that moment I started reading the books in the store voraciously. African history books especially, to learn bout those old ancient... civilizations and how we lived before we were brought out here to Babylon."

45. See Krista Thompson, *An Eye for the Tropics,* 4, 167.

46. There are interesting variants on the racist stereotypes of black Caribbean servants who cater to white tourists' desires. Iberia Airlines recently had to pull ads for Cuba as a vacation destination for Spaniards: "Spanish airline Iberia has cut an advertisement showing black Cuban women in bikinis bottle feeding a baby tourist as he sings 'feed me mulattas... come on little mamas, take me to my cot' after complaints it was sexist.... The animated cartoon shows young Cuban women driving the baby to the beach, dancing for him and massaging him after he is transported to the Caribbean island via the Iberia Web site." Reuters, "Spanish Airlines Cuts Cuba Ad After Sexism Complaint," May 22 2007.

47. Channer, "Q & A with Author."

48. Ian Strachan, *Paradise and Plantation: Tourism and Culture in the Anglophone Caribbean* (Charlotte: University of Virginia Press, 2002).

49. This image is a familiar one of a tourist in the Caribbean; the cover of *Passing Through* is similar to that of Brian Antoni's novel, *Paradise Overdose* (1994), which features a white, not black, woman, back to the viewer, in a wide-brimmed hat and a swimsuit, facing the Caribbean sea.

50. There have been many critical appraisals of this novel, most of them ambivalent or critical. As Curdella Forbes astutely notes, most critics who do not investigate popular literature were eager to discuss *Ti Marie* because of the author's status as a serious artist as well as the book's historical setting in the slavery era. See Forbes, "X Press Publications"; also Smith, "Beautiful Indians, Troublesome Negroes, and Nice White Men"; Carolyn Cooper, "Perverse Romance," *Third World Quarterly* 11, no. 4 (1989): 289–93; Steve Harney, "Men Goh Respect All o' We: Valerie Belgrave's *Ti Marie* and the Invention of Trinidad," *World Literature Written in English* 30, no. 2 (1990): 110–19.

51. William Tanifeani, "Interview with Valerie Belgrave; Novelist, Visual Artist," *Wasafiri,* no. 11 (Spring 1990): 24.

52. Maisha Tulivu Fisher, "Choosing Literacy: African Diaspora Participatory Literacy Communities," research report, Center for Latin American Studies, University of California Berkeley, summer 2002; http://socrates/berkeley.edu:7001/ Research/graduate/summer2002/fisher/index.html.

53. Description on the front cover of the 1988 ed. of *Ti Marie* (Kingston: Heinemann).

54. Boyd Tonkin, "Anthony C. Winkler: A Playful Pirate of the Caribbean," *Independent* (online ed.), January 5, 2007.

55. Anthony Winkler, *The Lunatic* (Kingston: Kingston Publishers Ltd., 1987), 56.

56. Tonkin, "Anthony C. Winkler."

57. Much criticism has been devoted to the dilemma of the Caribbean's white authors, who, for a time, were considered inauthentic. See Kamau Brathwaite's infamous remarks on Jean Rhys, in *Contradictory Omens: Cultural Diversity and Integration in the Caribbean* (Kingston: Savacou Publications, 1974), for example. See also Kim Robinson-Walcott, "Claiming an Identity They Thought We Despised: Contemporary

White West Indian Writers and Their Negotiation of Race," *Small Axe* no. 14 (vol. 7, no. 2) (September 2003): 93–110.

58. There are a number of Web sites dedicated to Caribbean humor. For a more detailed analysis of the importance of the Internet in maintaining and constructing Caribbean identities, see Daniel Miller and Don Slater, *The Internet: An Ethnographic Approach* (Oxford: Berg Publishers, 2001).

Bibliography

Abrahams, Roger. *The Man-of-Words in the West Indies: Performance and the Emergence of Creole Culture.* Baltimore: Johns Hopkins University Press, 1983.

Aching, Gerard. *Masking and Power: Carnival and Popular Culture in the Caribbean.* Minneapolis: University of Minnesota Press, 2002.

"Adolphus, A Tale" (Anonymous) and "The Slave Son" (Mrs. William Noy Wilkins). With an introduction by Bridget Brereton, Rhonda Cobham, Mary Rimmer, Karen Sanchez-Eppler, and Lise Winer. Ed. Lise Winer. Kingston: University of the West Indies Press, 2003.

Akashic Books. http://www.akashicbooks.com (accessed 2006).

Alleyne, Mervyn. "H. G. DeLisser: The First Competent Novelist in English." *Carib* (Kingston) 1 (1979): 18–26.

Alleyne, Mike. "Positive Vibration? Textual Hegemony and Bob Marley." In *Caribbean Romances: The Politics of Regional Representation,* ed. Belinda Edmondson. Charlottesville: University Press of Virginia, 1999.

Alleyne-Dettmers, Patricia. "Black Kings: Aesthetic Representation in Carnival in Trinidad & Tobago and London." *Black Music Research Journal* 22, no. 2 (Autumn 2002): 241–58.

Anonymous. *Marly, or The Life of a Planter in Jamaica.* Glasgow: Richard Griffin, 1828.

Appadurai, Arjun. "Disjuncture and Difference in the Global Economy." In *Colonial Discourse and Post-Colonial Theory: A Reader,* ed. Patrick Williams and Laura Chrisman. New York: Columbia University Press, 1994.

Ashcroft, Bill, Gareth Griffiths, and Helen Tiffin. *The Empire Writes Back: Theory and Practice in Post-Colonial Literatures.* New York: Routledge, 1989.

Ballerino Cohen, Colleen. "'This Is de Test': Festival and the Cultural Politics of Nation Building in the British Virgin Islands." *American Ethnologist* 25, no. 2 (May 1998): 189–214.

Barbados Advocate. "Mr. Bernard Grant Addresses Literary Society." January 4, 1930, 4.

Barbados Crop Over. http://www.barbados.org/cropover.htm (accessed 2007).

Barnes, Natasha. *Cultural Conundrums: Gender, Race, Nation, and the Making of Caribbean Cultural Politics.* Ann Arbor: University of Michigan Press, 2006.

———. "Face of the Nation: Race, Nationalisms and Identities in Jamaican Beauty Pageants." *Massachusetts Review* 35, nos. 3–4 (1994): 471–92.

Batson-Savage, Tanya. "'Meck Mi Tell Yuh' Chats Good Jamaican." *Jamaica Gleaner* (online ed.), January 2, 2005.

Bayley, Frederick. *Four Years' Residence in the West Indies.* London: William Kidd, 1832.

Beacon. "Local Fiction." Editorial. Vol. 1, no. 10 (January–February 1932).

Becca, Tony. "The Missing Cricket Fans." *Jamaica Gleaner* (online ed.), April 1, 2007.

Beckles, Hilary. "Crop Over Fetes and Festivals in Caribbean Slavery." In *In the Shadow of the Plantation,* ed. Alvin O. Thompson, 246–63. Kingston: Ian Randle, 2002.

———. *A History of Barbados.* New York: Cambridge University Press, 1990.

Belgrave, Valerie. *Ti Marie.* London: Heinemann, 1988.

Bennett, Louise. "Bennett on Bennett." Interview with Dennis Scott. *Caribbean Quarterly* 14, nos. 1 and 2 (1968): 97–101.

———. *Jamaica Labrish.* With an introduction by Rex Nettleford. 1966. Reprint. Kingston: Sangster's Bookstores, 1972.

———. *Selected Poems.* Ed. Mervyn Morris. 1982. Reprint. Kingston: Sangster's Publishing, 2003.

Besson, Gerard, and Bridget Brereton, eds. *The Book of Trinidad.* 2nd ed. Port of Spain: Paria Publishing, 1992.

Bethel, Nicolette."Peter Minshall on the Commercialization of Carnival." BlogWorld: Nicolette Bethel's Blog. December 22, 2006. http://nicobethel.net/blogworld.

Bongie, Chris. "Exiles on Main Stream: Valuing the Popularity of Postcolonial Culture." *Postmodern Culture* 14, no. 1 (2003): 3.

Boyce-Davies, Carole. *Migrations of the Subject.* New York: Routledge, 1994.

Brathwaite, Kamau. *Contradictory Omens: Cultural Diversity and Integration in the Caribbean.* Kingston: Savacou Publications, 1974.

———. *History of the Voice: The Development of Nation Language in Anglophone Caribbean Poetry.* London: New Beacon Books, 1984.

———. "Jazz and the West Indian Novel." In *Roots: Essays in Caribbean Literature.* 1967. Reprint. Ann Arbor: University of Michigan Press, 1993.

Breeze, Jean Binta. "Can a Dub Poet Be a Woman?" *Woman: A Cultural Review* 1 (1990): 47–49.

Breiner, Laurence. "The Half-Life of Performance Poems." *Journal of West Indian Literature* 8, no. 1 (1998): 27.

Bremer, Catherine. "Dreadlocked Miss Jamaica Puts Rastas in New Light." Youth Portal for Latin America and the Caribbean. http://www.youthlac.org/content/view/157/40 (accessed 2007).

Brereton, Bridget. "Michel Maxwell Philip (1829–1888): Servant of the Centurion." *Antilia: Journal of the Faculty of Arts* (University of the West Indies) 1, no. 3 (1989): 6–7.

———. *Race Relations in Colonial Trinidad, 1870–1900.* Cambridge: Cambridge University Press, 1979.

Brereton, Bridget, Rhonda Cobham, Mary Rimmer, Karen Sanchez-Eppler, and Lise Winer. Introduction to *"Adolphus, A Tale" (Anonymous) and "The Slave Son" (Mrs. William Noy Wilkins).* Ed. Lise Winer. Kingston: University of the West Indies Press, 2003.

Brereton, Bridget, Rhonda Cobham, Mary Rimmer, and Lise Winer. Introduction to *Rupert Gray: A Study in Black and White,* by Stephen Cobham. Ed. Lise Winer. Kingston: University of the West Indies Press, 2006.

Bryan, Patrick. *The Jamaican People, 1880–1902: Race, Class, and Social Control.* London: Macmillan, 1991.
Burton, Richard D. E. *Afro-Creole: Power, Opposition and Play in the Caribbean.* Ithaca: Cornell University Press, 1997.
C.P.N. "Social Problems—Where Do We Stand?" *Cosmopolitan* 1, no. 3 (July 1928): 86.
Cain, William E. Introduction to *Emmanuel Appadocca, or Blighted Life,* by Maxwell Philip. Ed. S. Cudjoe. Amherst: University of Massachusetts Press, 1997.
Calabash Literary Festival. http://www.calabashfestival.org (accessed 2006).
Campbell, Howard. "Farewell Fit for a Queen." *Jamaica Gleaner* (online ed.), August 10, 2006.
———. "'Joshua' and the Rod of Correction." *Jamaica Gleaner* (online ed.), July 18, 2007.
Carnegie, K. D. "Sappho—The Lesbian Poetess." *Cosmopolitan* 1, no. 2 (June 1928): 44.
Carpenter, McDonald. "Calypsos Not Art." *TG,* February 8, 1944.
———. "Europe's Culture Cast Our Own." *TG,* February 25, 1944.
Channer, Colin. "A Conversation with Colin Channer." http://www.aalbc.com/authors/colin.htm (accessed 2003).
———. "I Am Not in Exile." In *Catch Afire: New Jamaican Writing,* ed. Kwame Dawes. Special issue of *Obsidian III: Literature in the African Diaspora* 2, no. 2 (Fall–Winter 2000–2001): 43–56.
———. "The Kingston 12 Overture." In *Iron Balloons: Hit Fiction from Jamaica's Calabash Writer's Workshop,* ed. Colin Channer. New York: Akashic Books, 2006.
———. *Passing Through.* New York: One World/Ballantine Books, 2004.
———. "Q & A with Author." http://www.colinchanner.com (accessed 2006).
———. "Social Consciousness in Literature." Interview with Farai Chideya. National Public Radio, August 6, 2007.
———. *Waiting in Vain.* New York: One World/Ballantine Books, 1998.
Chinen, Nate. "Jazz Is Alive and Well. In the Classroom, Anyway." *New York Times,* January 7, 2007.
Cobham, Rhonda. "The Creative Writer and Jamaican Society, 1900–1950." Ph.D. diss., University of St. Andrews, 1981. Ann Arbor: University Microfilms International, 1983.
Cobham, Stephen. *Rupert Gray: A Study in Black and White.* With an introduction by Bridget Brereton, Rhonda Cobham, Mary Rimmer, and Lise Winer. Ed. Lise Winer. 1907. Reprint. Kingston: University of the West Indies Press, 2006.
———. *Rupert Gray: A Study in Black and White.* Ed. and with an introduction by Selwyn Cudjoe. 1907. Reprint. Wellesley, MA: Calaloux Publications, 2004.
"Colin Channer." http://www.Answers.com (accessed 2007).
Collins, Loretta. "Raggamuffin Cultural Studies: X-Press Novels' Yardies and Cop Killers Put Britain on Trial." *Small Axe* no. 9 (vol. 5, issue 1) (March 2001): 70–96.
Cooke, Mel. "Serious Consideration for Miss Lou's Poetry." *Jamaica Gleaner* (online), September 15, 2006.
Cooper, Carolyn. *Noises in the Blood: Orality, Gender and the "Vulgar" Body of Jamaican Popular Culture.* Durham: Duke University Press, 1995.
———. "'Only a Nigger Gal!': Race, Gender and the Politics of Education in Claude McKay's *Banana Bottom.*" *Caribbean Quarterly* 38, no. 1 (March 1992): 40–54.

———. "Perverse Romance." *Third World Quarterly* 11, no. 4 (1989): 289–93.
———. *Sound Clash: Jamaican Dancehall Culture at Large.* New York: Palgrave Macmillan, 2004.
Cordle, Edward A. *Overheard: A Series of Poems Written by the Late Edward A. Cordle.* Barbados: C. F. Cole, Printer and Publisher, 1903.
Cosmopolitan. "The Age of Women." Editorial. Vol. 1, no. 11 (March 1929): 65–66.
———. "Brighter Night Life." Vol. 1, no. 2 (June 1928): 64.
———. "Case of Seditious Libel Ended: Guess What's Happened?" Editorial. Vol. 2, no. 8 (December 1929): 342.
———. "The Colour-line." Editorial. Vol. 2, no. 8 (December 1929): 235.
———. Editorial. Vol. 1, no. 1 (May 1928).
———. "Editorial Observations: The Coloured Follies." Vol. 1, no. 12 (April 1929): 99.
———. "Kingston's Beauty Spots: The Goats." Vol. 1, no. 1 (April 1929): 99.
"Crop Over: Carnival of Barbados." http://www.caribnet.com (accessed 2007).
Cudjoe, Selwyn. Afterword to *Emmanuel Appadocca, or Blighted Life,* by Maxwell Philip. Ed. S. Cudjoe. 1854. Reprint. Amherst: University of Massachusetts Press, 1997.
———. Introduction to *Free Mulatto,* by Jean-Baptiste Philippe. Ed. S. Cudjoe. Wellesley, MA: Calaloux Publications, 1996.
———. Introduction to *Rupert Gray: A Study in Black and White,* by Stephen Cobham. Ed. S. Cudjoe. Wellesley, MA: Calaloux Publications, 2004.
Cundall, Frank. *A History of Printing in Jamaica.* Kingston: Institute of Jamaica, 1935.
Cupid, John. "Trinidad Carnival Traditional Characters." *1st Carnival King and Queen of the World Magazine* 1 (1994): 16–17.
Dabydeen, David, and Nana Wilson-Tagoe, eds. *The Guide to West Indian and Black British Literature.* Rutherford, UK: Hansib Educational Publications, 1988.
Daily Express (Trinidad). "BET: Caribbean Talent Not Shadowed by American Artistes." June 1, 2006, 62.
Daily Gleaner. "Jazz Festival of Class." Letters to the Editor. August 13, 2001.
———. "Nancy Story Competition." December 23, 1899, 11.
———. "PM Urges Creative Use of National Themes in Creative Arts." February 27, 1971.
———. "Question of the Week: 'Should Girls Seek Employment Outside of the Home?'" December 23, 1899, 1.
Daily Mail (U.K.). "Elton John Could Turn Us Gay, Says Archdeacon." March 16, 2007.
Daily Telegraph. Letter from Charlotte. Daily News Letter sec. November 29, 1898.
———. "Welcoming *The Jamaica Times.*" Editorial. November 29, 1898.
Davies, Carole Boyce. *Migrations of the Subject.* New York: Routledge, 1994.
Dawes, Kwame. *Natural Mysticism: Towards a New Reggae Aesthetic.* London: Peepal Tree Press, 1999.
DeCaires Narain, Denise. *Contemporary Caribbean Women's Poetry.* London: Routledge, 2001.
de Lisser, H. G. "The Fair Daughters of Jamaica: Characteristics." *Planter's Punch* 1, no. 6 (1925–26): 4–5.

———. "The Jamaica Nobility; Or, The Story of Sir Mortimer and Lady Mortimer." *Planter's Punch* 2, no. 1 (1926–27).
———. *Jane's Career*. 1913. Reprint. Kingston: Heinemann, 1971.
———. *Psyche*. 1952. Reprint. Kingston: Macmillan Caribbean, 1980.
Deyal, Tony. "Wendy's Big Do." *Jamaica Gleaner* (online ed.), February 21, 2006.
Diaz, Keith. "Pan Getting Raw Deal at Jazz Show." Letters. *Trinidad Guardian* (online ed.), March 24, 2007.
Downing, Marlon. "Libertas C, or Died for Cuba." *Jamaica Times*, May 27, 1899, 7.
Edmondson, Belinda. "African-American Manhood in the Making of Caribbean (Inter)Nationalism." *Small Axe* no. 20 (vol. 10, issue 2) (June 2006): 261–68.
———. *Making Men*. Durham: Duke University Press, 1999.
———. "Race, Privilege, and the Politics of (Re)Writing History." *Callaloo* 16, no. 1 (1993): 180–91.
———. "Trinidad Romance: The Invention of Jamaica Carnival." In *Caribbean Romances: The Politics of Regional Representation*, ed. B. Edmondson. Charlottesville: University Press of Virginia, 1999.
Ehrenreich, Barbara, and Annette Fuentes. *Women in the Global Factory*. Boston: South End Press, 1985.
Erwin, Lee. "Two Jamaican Women Writers and the Uses of Creole." In *Commonwealth and American Women's Discourse: Essays in Criticism*, ed. A. L. McLeod, 124–34. New Delhi: Sterling Publishers Private, 1996.
"Evolution of the Fringe." St. Lucia Jazz Festival Web site. http:www.stluciajazz.org (accessed 2006).
Fanon, Frantz. *Black Skin, White Masks*. 1952. Reprint. New York: Grove Weidenfeld, 1967.
———. *The Wretched of the Earth*. New York: Grove Press, 1965.
Farred, Grant. "The Postcolonial Chickens Come Home to Roost: How *Yardie* Has Created a New Postcolonial Subaltern." *South Atlantic Quarterly* 100, no. 1 (Winter 2001): 288–305.
Fonseca, Carlisle. "Carvalho." *Jamaica Times*, May 6, 1899, 13.
Forbes, Curdella. "X Press Publications: Pop Culture, 'Pop Lit' and Caribbean Literary Criticism: An Essay of Provocation." *Anthurium: A Caribbean Studies Journal* 4, no. 1 (Spring 2006): 3.
Fowler, Henry. "A History of Theatre in Jamaica." *Jamaica Journal* 2, no. 1 (1968): 54.
Francis, Donette. "Making Meaning of America, Audience and Authorship: Narrating the Limits of Diaspora in the Novels of Colin Channer." Manuscript. April 2003.
Franco, Pamela. "The Invention of Traditional Mas and the Politics of Gender." In *Trinidad Carnival: The Cultural Politics of a Transnational Festival*, ed. Garth L. Green and Philip W. Scher. Bloomington: Indiana University Press, 2007.
Frazier, Franklin. *Black Bourgeoisie*. New York: Collier, 1957.
Freeman, Carla. *High Tech and High Heels in the Global Economy*. Durham: Duke University Press, 2000.
Froude, James Anthony. *The English in the West Indies*. London: Longman's Green, 1888.
Fusco, Coco. *English Is Broken Here*. New York: New Press, 1995.

———. "Hustling for Dollars." *MS,* September–October 1996, 60–70.

Gaines, Luan. "Curled Up with a Good Book: An Interview with Nalo Hopkinson." http://www.curledup.com/naloint.htm (accessed 2006).

García Canclini, Nestor. *Hybrid Cultures: Strategies for Entering and Leaving Modernity.* Minneapolis: University of Minnesota Press, 1995.

Garraway, Doris. *The Libertine Colony: Creolization in the Early French Caribbean.* Durham: Duke University Press, 2005.

Gikandi, Simon. *Writing in Limbo: Modernism and Caribbean Literature.* Ithaca: Cornell University Press, 1992.

Gilman, Sander. "Black Bodies, White Bodies." In *Race Writing and Difference,* ed. Henry Louis Gates Jr. Chicago: University of Chicago Press, 1986.

———. *Making the Body Beautiful: A Cultural History of Aesthetic Surgery.* Princeton: Princeton University Press, 1999.

Glissant, Edouard. *Caribbean Discourse: Selected Essays.* Trans. J. Michael Dash. Charlottesville: University Press of Virginia, 1989.

Goldberg, Jonathan. *Tempest in the Caribbean.* Minneapolis: University of Minnesota Press, 2004.

Gonzalez, Anson. "Race and Colour in Pre-Independence Trinidad and Tobago Novel." Ph.D. diss., University of the West Indies, St. Augustine, Trinidad, 1982.

Goudie, Sean X. *Creole America: The West Indies and the Formation of Literature and Culture in the New Republic.* Philadelphia: University of Pennsylvania Press, 2006.

Green, Garth L., and Philip Scher, eds. *Trinidad Carnival: The Cultural Politics of a Transnational Festival.* Bloomington: Indiana University Press, 2007.

Gregg, Veronica, ed. *Caribbean Women: An Anthology of Non-Fiction Writing, 1890–1980.* South Bend, IN: University of Notre Dame Press, 2005.

H. G. D. "A Peculiar Love Scene." Amusements of the People sec. *Jamaica Times,* July 1, 1899, 5.

Habekost, Christian. *Verbal Riddim: The Politics and Aesthetics of African-Caribbean Dub Poetry.* Amsterdam: Rodopi, 1993.

Harney, Steve. "Men Goh Respect All o' We: Valerie Belgrave's *Ti Marie* and the Invention of Trinidad." *World Literature Written in English* 30, no. 2 (1990): 110–19.

Harris, S. "Dreadlocked Beauty a Bold Step." Letters to the Editor. *Jamaica Gleaner,* March 28, 2007.

Hart, Ansell. "Colour Prejudice in Jamaica." *Jamaica Journal* 4, no. 4 (December 1970).

Hebdige, Dick. *Subculture: The Meaning of Style.* London: Methuen, 1979.

Henry, Krista. "A Race to Beauty." *Jamaica Gleaner* (online ed.), August 27, 2006.

Henry, Martin. "Jamaica and Botswana." *Daily Gleaner,* June 3, 1999.

Heuman, Gad. "White over Brown over Black: The Free Coloureds in Jamaican Society during Slavery and after Emancipation." *Journal of Caribbean History* 14 (1981): 46–69.

Hill, Errol. *The Jamaican Stage, 1655–1900: Profile of a Colonial Theatre.* Amherst: University of Massachusetts Press, 1992.

———. *The Trinidad Carnival: Mandate for a National Theatre.* Austin: University of Texas Press, 1972.

Hill, Errol, Martin Banham, and George Woodyard. *The Cambridge Guide to Theatre.* Cambridge: Cambridge University Press, 2005.

Hopkinson, Nalo. *Midnight Robber.* New York: Aspect, 2000.

How to Enjoy Jamaica: The Unofficial Guide. Video produced by Kimberly Mais and Jeremy Francis. Black Olive Entertainment, Kingston, Jamaica, 1997.
Hoyte, Andre. "The Story of Crop Over." Public relations leaflet. National Cultural Foundation of Barbados, 2007.
Husband, Joseph. "The Citadel or The Ring of Dessalines." *Planter's Punch* 1, no. 6 (1925–26).
Jamaica Gleaner. "Redwood, an Ideal Jamaican Mix." Online ed. March 25, 2007.
———. "When the Reign Is Over: Miss Jamaica Festival Queens—Where Are They Now?" Roots and Culture: Independence 2003 sec. Online ed. 2003.
Jamaica Telegraph. Editorial. November 29, 1898.
Jamaica Times. Amusements of the People sec. July 22, 1899, 13.
———. Editorial. December 24, 1898.
———. "Is Novel-Reading Injurious?" Editorial. December 10, 1898, 9.
———. "The Revival Balm Station of Mother Ackinson." Amusements of the People sec. December 10, 1898, 5.
———. "Weekly Prize Story." July 22, 1899, 13.
———. "Winkler's Choir Leader." December 17, 1898, 5.
"Jamaican Carnival." http://www.caribbeanchoice.com/jamaica/carnival/asp/April (accessed 2007).
James, C. L. R. "The Artist in the Caribbean." *Radical America,* May 4, 1970, 62–63. Originally given as a lecture at the University of the West Indies, Mona Jamaica, 1959.
James, Marlon. Comment on "Iron Balloons Redux." Geoffrey Philp's Blog Spot, June 28, 2006, at 2:13 p.m. http://geoffreyphilp.blogspot.com/2006/06iron-balloons-redux.html.
———. "High Art, Low Art and Critical Thought." Marlon James among Other Things, March 13, 2007. http://www.marlon-james.blogspot.com.
James, Winston. "Becoming the People's Poet: Claude McKay's Jamaican Years, 1889–1912." *Small Axe* no. 13 (vol. 7, no. 1 (March 2003): 17–45.
Jarrett-Macaulay, Delia. *The Life of Una Marson.* Manchester, UK: Manchester University Press, 1998.
Jekyll, Walter. *Jamaican Song and Story: Annancy Stories, Digging Sings, Ring Tunes, and Dancing Tunes.* With new introductory essays by Philip Sherlock, Louise Bennett, and Rex Nettleford. 1906. Reprint. New York: Dover Publications, 1966.
John, D. "Women in Mas'." In *Women in Mas',* ed. O. Baptiste. Port of Spain: Imprint Caribbean, 1988.
Judah, G. F. (George Fortunatus). *The Newspaper History of Jamaica.* 1899. Reprint. University of the West Indies Department of Library Studies. Working Papers on West Indian Printing (Mona, Jamaica), ser. 1, no. 9a (1975): 1–7.
Keens-Douglas, Paul. *When Moon Shine.* With an introduction by Victor D. Questel. Port of Spain: College Press, 1979.
———. "'Where Talk Is Art'—How It All Began." Entertainment sec. http://www.paulkeensdouglas.com/articles (accessed 2008).
Kincaid, Jamaica. *A Small Place.* New York: Virago Press, 1988.
Kingsley, Charles. *At Last: A Christmas in the West Indies.* 2 vols. London: Macmillan, 1889.

Kirkpatrick, David D. "Winfrey Rescinds Offer to Author for Guest Appearance." *New York Times,* October 24, 2001.

Kirkpatrick, W. "Women's Activities—Some Thoughts and Suggestions." *Cosmopolitan* 1, no. 3 (July 1928): 94.

Koningsbruggen, Peter van. *Trinidad Carnival: A Quest for a National Identity.* London: Macmillan, 1997.

Kutzinski, Vera. *Sugar's Secrets: Race and the Erotics of Cuban Nationalism.* Charlottesville: University Press of Virginia, 1994.

Lacey, Marc. "In Jamaican Politics, Just about Everything Is Cricket." *New York Times* (online ed.), April 2, 2007.

Lamming, George. *The Pleasures of Exile.* London: Allison and Busby, 1960.

Lee, Felicia R. "Chick-Lit King Imagines His Way into Women's Heads." *New York Times,* July 29, 2004.

Levine, George. *Highbrow, Lowbrow: The Emergence of Cultural Hierarchy in America.* Cambridge: Harvard University Press, 1988.

Lewis, Gordon K. "The Contemporary Caribbean." In *Caribbean Contours,* ed. Sidney W. Mintz and Sally Price. Baltimore: Johns Hopkins University Press, 1985.

———. *The Growth of the Modern West Indies.* New York: Monthly Review Press, 1968.

———. *Main Currents in Caribbean Thought.* Baltimore: Johns Hopkins University Press, 1983.

Lewis, Winston. "Dangerous to Allow John." Letters. *Trinidad Guardian* (online ed.), March 19, 2007.

Lien, Dennis. Review of Edgar Mittelholzer's *My Bones and My Flute. Fantasy and Science Fiction* (Hoboken) 109, no. 6 (December 2005): 162.

Livingston, W. P. *Black Jamaica: A Study in Evolution.* London: Sampson, Low Marston, 1899.

Lomas, Laura. "Mystifying Mystery: Inscriptions of the Oral in the Legend of Rose Hall." *Journal of West Indian Literature* 6, no. 2 (1994): 70–86.

Love, Robert. Editorial. *Jamaica Advocate.* December 15, 1894.

———. "Study Your Business." Editorial. *Jamaica Advocate,* December 15, 1894, 3.

Lovelace, Earl. *The Dragon Can't Dance.* Port of Spain: Longman, 1979.

"LTM [Little Theatre Movement] Pantomime History—The Early Years." History of the Pantomime/Perspective of the Early Years. http://www.ltmpantomime.com (accessed 2006).

MacDermot, Thomas [Tom Redcam, pseud.]. *One Brown Girl And—.* Kingston: All Jamaica Library, Times Printery, 1909.

———. "The Present Conditions of Jamaica and Jamaicans." *Canadian Magazine,* October 1899, 503–4.

MacDonald, Scott B. *Trinidad and Tobago: Democracy and Development in the Caribbean.* New York: Praeger, 1986.

MacGregor James, Alexander. *Four Stories and a Drama of Old Jamaica.* Kingston: Gleaner Co. Ltd. Printers, 1921.

———. "The Mysterious Murder." *Jamaica Times,* December 17, 1898, 13.

Manning, Frank E. "Carnival in Antigua: An Indigenous Festival in a Tourist Economy." *Anthropos* 73, nos. 1–2 (1978): 191–204.

Marley, Bob, and the Wailers. "Them Belly Full (but We Hungry)." *Natty Dread.* Tuff Gong/Island Records, Kingston, 1974.

Marly, or The Life of a Planter in Jamaica. Glasgow: Richard Griffin, 1828.

Marson, Una. "Sojourn." *New Cosmopolitan,* February 1931, 8–27.

Martin, Tony. *Literary Garveyism: Garvey, Black Arts, and the Harlem Renaissance.* Dover: Majority Press, 1983.

Martin-Hinds, Angela. "Nicole Takes off Braces." *Trinidad Express,* May 6, 1999.

Marx, Karl. *Grundrisse: Foundations of the Critique of Political Economy.* London: Penguin Books, 1973.

Matthews, Augustus. *The Lying Hero, or an Answer to J. B. Moreton's Manners and Customs of the West Indies.* St. Kitts (St. Eustatius): Edward Luther Low Printery, 1793.

McDonald-White, Novia. "Pregnancy Dethrones Queen: Sara Lawrence Rules Out Abortion." *Jamaica Gleaner* (online ed.), March 15, 2007.

McHenry, Elizabeth. *Forgotten Readers: Recovering the Lost History of African American Literary Societies.* Durham: Duke University Press, 2002.

McKay, Claude. *Banana Bottom.* New York: Harcourt Brace Jovanovich, 1932.

McKenzie, Clyde. "In Praise of Miss Lou." *Jamaica Gleaner* (online ed.), August 9, 2006.

McLeod, Conrad. "Pregnant Pageant Winner Quitting." *Miami Herald,* March 15, 2007.

Miller, Daniel, and Don Slater. *The Internet: An Ethnographic Approach.* Oxford: Berg Publishers, 2001.

Mills, Claude. "Revellers 'Bump and Wine' at Joker's Wild Beach J'Ouvert in Oracabessa, St. Mary." *Jamaica Gleaner* (online ed.), April 23, 2006.

Minott Egglestone, Ruth. "A Philosophy of Survival: Anancyism in Jamaican Pantomime." In *The Society for Caribbean Studies Annual Conference Papers,* vol. 2, ed. Sandra Courtman. 2001. http://www.scsonline.freeserve.co.uk/olvol2.html.

Mirror. Review of *Rupert Gray.* July 18, 1907

Moonsammy, Patricia. "'Miss Good Reputation'? Divas, Warriors and Mothers Performing Power in Trinidad." Paper presented at the Caribbean Studies Association annual conference, Trinidad and Tobago, May 30, 2006.

Morley, Neil. "Opportunities in Paradise?" *Bookseller* (London, Publisher's Association), May 17, 2002, 31–32.

Morris, Mervyn. Introduction to *Selected Poems,* by Louise Bennett. 1982. Reprint. Kingston: Sangster's Publishing, 2003.

———. "On Reading Louise Bennett, Seriously." *Jamaica Journal* 1 (December 1967): 69–74. First published in 1963.

Muller, Nazma. "The Mis-Education of Marlon James." Interview with James Marlon. *Jamaica Observer,* July 23, 2006.

Myerscough, J. *The Economic Importance of the Arts in Britain.* London: Policy Studies Institute, 1988.

Naipaul, V. S. *The Middle Passage.* 1962. Reprint. New York: Vintage, 1981.

———. *A Turn in the South.* New York: Vintage, 1989.

Neptune, Harvey. *Caliban and the Yankees: Trinidad and the United States' Occupation.* Chapel Hill: University of North Carolina Press, 2007.

Nettleford, Rex. Introduction to *Jamaica Labrish,* by Louise Bennett. Reprint. Kingston: Sangster's Bookstores, 1972.

———. *Mirror, Mirror: Identity, Race and Protest in Jamaica.* Kingston: LMH Publishing, 1970.

BIBLIOGRAPHY

New Cosmopolitan. Review of H. G. de Lisser's *Susan Proudleigh,* by "Our Dramatic Critic." February 8, 1931.

New York Times. "What Jamaica Will Show." May 1, 1893.

Nicholls, Robert W. "Old-Time Masquerading in the U.S. Virgin Islands." St. Thomas: Virgin Islands Humanities Council, 1998.

North, Michael. *The Dialect of Modernism: Race, Language and Twentieth Century Literature.* Oxford: Oxford University Press, 1994.

Nugent, Maria. *Lady Nugent's Journal.* Ed. Frank Cundall. London: Adam and Charles Black, 1907.

Nurse, Keith. "Bringing Culture into Tourism: Festival Tourism and Reggae Sunsplash in Jamaica." *Social and Economic Studies* 51, no. 1 (2002): 127–43.

Ocho Rios Jazz Festival Web site. http://www.ochoriosjazz.com (accessed 2005).

Olivier, Sydney. *Jamaica the Blessed Island.* London: Faber and Faber, 1936.

Page, Malcolm. "Review Essay: West Indian Writers." *Novel: A Forum for Fiction* 3, no. 2 (Winter 1970): 167–72.

Patterson, Orlando. "Context and Choice in Ethnic Allegiance: A Theoretical Framework and Caribbean Case Study." In *Ethnicity: Theory and Experience,* ed. Nathan Glazer and Daniel P. Moynihan, 305–409. Cambridge: Harvard University Press, 1975.

———. "Dollars in the Sand." *New York Times* (online ed.), January 2, 2007.

Pearn, Julie. *Poetry in the Caribbean.* London: Hodder and Stoughton, 1985.

Philip, Maxwell. *Emmanuel Appadocca, or Blighted Life.* With an introduction by William E. Cain and an afterword by Selwyn Cudjoe. Ed. S. Cudjoe. 1853. Reprint. Amherst: University of Massachusetts Press, 1997.

Philippe, Jean-Baptiste. *Free Mulatto.* Ed. Selwyn Cudjoe. 1824. Reprint. Wellesley, MA: Calaloux Publications, 1996.

Phillip, Frank. "First Time Lucky for Miss Botswana." *Trinidad Express,* May 27, 1999.

Philp, Geoffrey. "Iron Balloons Redux." Geoffrey Philp's Blog Spot, June 28, 2006. geoffreyphilp.blogspot.com/2006/06iron-balloons-redux.html.

Pinckney, Jr., Warren. "Jazz in Barbados." *American Music* 12, no. 1 (Spring 1994): 58–88.

Pope-Hennessy, James. *Verandah: Some Episodes in the Crown Colonies, 1867–1889.* New York: Knopf, 1964.

Poynting, Jeremy. "From Ancestral to Creole: Humans and Animals in a West Indian Scale of Values." In *Monsters, Tricksters, and Sacred Cows: Animal Tales and American Identities,* ed. A. James Arnold. Charlottesville: University of Virginia Press, 1996.

"Profile: Louise Simone Bennett." Posted July 27, 2006. www.go-jamaica.com.

Puri, Shalini. "Beyond Resistance: Notes toward a New Caribbean Cultural Studies." *Small Axe* no. 14 (vol. 7, no. 2) (September 2003): 23–38.

———. "Canonized Hybridities, Resistant Hybridities: Chutney Soca, Carnival, and the Politics of Nationalism." In *Caribbean Romances: The Politics of Regional Representation,* ed. Belinda Edmondson. Charlottesville: University of Virginia Press, 1999.

———. *The Post-Colonial Caribbean.* New York: Palgrave Macmillan, 2004.

Radway, Janice. *A Feeling for Books: The Book-of-the-Month Club, Literary Taste, and Middle Class Desire.* Chapel Hill: University of North Carolina Press, 1997.

Rae, Norman. "Isolation and Coronation: A Line from the Tower of Babble." *Sunday Gleaner,* August 28, 2005.
Raiskin, Judith. *Snow on the Cane Fields: Creole Writing and Women's Subjectivity.* Minneapolis: University of Minnesota Press, 1996.
Ramazani, Jahan. *The Hybrid Muse: Postcolonial Poetry in English.* Chicago: University of Chicago Press, 2001.
Ramchand, Kenneth. Introduction to *Jane's Career.* Kingston: Heinemann, 1971.
———. *The West Indian Novel and Its Background.* London: Faber and Faber, 1970.
Raymond, Judy. "Beryl McBurnie, 1914–2000: Relentless Charm." *Trinidad Sunday Guardian,* April 2, 2000.
Razak, Victoria M. "Carnival in Aruba." In *Trinidad Carnival: The Cultural Politics of a Transnational Festival,* ed. Garth Green and Philip W. Scher, 136–60. Bloomington: Indiana University Press, 2007.
Reuters. "Spanish Airlines Cuts Cuba Ad after Sexism Complaint." May 22, 2007.
Riggio, Milla C. "Trinidad and Tobago Carnival." *Drama Review* 42, no. 3 (1998).
Robinson-Walcott, Kim. "Claiming an Identity They Thought We Despised: Contemporary White West Indian Writers and Their Negotiation of Race." *Small Axe* no. 14 (vol. 7, no. 2) (September 2003): 93–110.
Rohlehr, Gordon. *Calypso and Society in Pre-Independence Trinidad.* Port of Spain: G. Rohlehr, 1990.
———. "The Problem of the Problem of Form: The Idea of an Aesthetic Continuum and Aesthetic, Code-Switching in West Indian Literature." *Caribbean Quarterly* 31, no. 1 (1985): 1–52.
Rosenberg, Leah. "Modern Romances: The Short Stories in Una Marson's *The Cosmopolitan* (1928–1931)." *Journal of West Indian Literature* 12, nos. 1–2 (November 2004): 170–83.
———. *Nationalism and the Formation of Caribbean Literature.* New York: Palgrave Macmillan, 2008.
Rumbaut, Ruben G. "Immigrants from Latin America and the Caribbean: A Socioeconomic Profile." In *Immigrants and Immigrant Communities: A Focus on Latinos,* ed. Refugio I. Rochin. East Lansing, MI: Julian Samora Research Institute, 1996.
"Sabeeney: Look Out for Miss Japan." *Trinidad Express.* May 23, 1999.
Sander, Reinhard, ed. *From Trinidad: An Anthology of Early West Indian Writing.* London: Hodder and Stoughton, 1978.
———. *The Trinidad Awakening: West Indian Literature of the 1930s.* New York: Greenwood Press, 1988.
Sassen, Saskia. *Globalization and Its Discontents.* New York: New Press, 1998.
———. *A Sociology of Globalization.* New York: W. W. Norton, 2007.
Scher, Philip. *Carnival and the Formation of a Caribbean Transnation.* Gainesville: University of Florida Press, 2003.
———. "Copyright and Heritage Tourism." *Anthropological Quarterly* 75 (Summer 2002): 453–84.
———. "When 'Natives' Become Tourists of Themselves." In *Trinidad Carnival: The Cultural Politics of a Transnational Festival,* ed. Garth L. Green and Philip W. Scher. Bloomington: Indiana University Press, 2007.
Scott, David. *Refashioning Futures: Criticism after Postcoloniality.* Princeton: Princeton University Press, 1999.

Scott, Michael. *Tom Cringle's Log.* 1821. Reprint. http://www.scribd.com/doc/898606/Tom-Cringles-Log-by-Michael-Scott (accessed 2009).
Segal, Daniel. "'Race' and 'Colour' in Pre-Independence Trinidad." In *Trinidad Ethnicity,* ed. Kevin Yelvington. London: Macmillan Caribbean, 1993.
Smith, Dinitia. "Emboldened by Reggae, Jamaican Writers Bust Out." *New York Times,* June 27, 2006.
Smith, Faith. "Beautiful Indians, Troublesome Negroes, and Nice White Men: Caribbean Romances and the Invention of Trinidad." In *Caribbean Romances: The Politics of Regional Representation,* ed. Belinda Edmondson. Charlottesville: University of Virginia Press, 1999.
———. *Creole Recitations: John Jacob Thomas and Colonial Formations in the Late Nineteenth-Century Caribbean.* Charlottesville: University of Virginia Press, 2002.
———. "Gentlemen and Jamettes: Gender and Creole Nationalism in Nineteenth-Century Trinidad." Caribbean Studies Association conference, Panama City, Panama, May 24–28, 1999.
———. "You Know You're a West Indian If...": Codes of Authenticity in Colin Channer's *Waiting in Vain.*" *Small Axe* no. 10 (vol. 5, no. 2) (September 2001): 41–59.
Spotlight. Editorial. December 1951, 12.
Springer, Attilah. "There's Sex Out of Wedlock." *Trinidad Guardian* (online ed.), January 28, 2006.
Stallybrass, Peter, and Allon White. *The Politics and Poetics of Transgression.* Ithaca: Cornell University Press, 1986.
Stephens, Michelle. *Black Empire: The Masculine Global Imaginary of Caribbean Intellectuals in the United States, 1914–1962.* Durham: Duke University Press, 2005.
———. "The First Negro Matinee Idol: Harry Belafonte and American Culture in the 1950s." In *Left of the Color Line: Race, Radicalism and Twentieth-Century Literature of the United States,* ed. Bill V. Mullen and James Smethurst. Chapel Hill: University of North Carolina Press, 2003.
Stewart, J. "Patronage and Control in the Trinidad Carnival." In *The Anthropology of Experience,* ed. V. W. Turner and E. M. Bruner, 289–315. Urbana: University of Illinois Press, 1986.
Stewart, John. *An Account of Jamaica and Its Inhabitants.* London: Longman, Hurst, Rees and Orme, 1808.
Stolzoff, Norman. *Wake the Town and Tell the People.* Durham: Duke University Press, 2000.
Strachan, Ian. *Paradise and Plantation: Tourism and Culture in the Anglophone Caribbean.* Charlotte: University of Virginia Press, 2002.
Swan, Bradford Fuller. *The Spread of Printing (Western Hemisphere): The Caribbean Area.* Amsterdam: Vangendt, 1970.
Talpade Mohanty, Chandra. "Women Workers and Capitalist Scripts." In *Feminist Genealogies, Colonial Legacies, Democratic Futures,* ed. M. Jacqui Alexander and Chandra Talpade Mohanty. London: Routledge, 1997.
Tanifeani, William. "Interview with Valerie Belgrave; Novelist, Visual Artist." *Wasafiri* no. 11 (Spring 1990): 24.
"Terry McMillan." http://www.Answers.com (accessed 2007).
Thomas, Deborah. *Modern Blackness: Nationalism, Globalization, and the Politics of Culture in Jamaica.* Durham: Duke University Press, 2004.

Thomas, Deborah. "Modern Blackness:'What We Are and What We Hope to Be.'" *Small Axe,* no. 12 (vol. 6, no. 2) (September 2002): 25–48.
Thompson, Krista. *An Eye for the Tropics: Tourism, Photography and Framing the Caribbean Picturesque.* Durham: Duke University Press, 2006.
Tiffin, Helen. "The Institution of Literature." In *A History of Literature in the Caribbean,* vol. 2: *English and Dutch-Speaking Regions,* ed. A. James Arnold. Philadelphia: John Benjamins Publishing, 2001.
Tinling, E. D. "Anancy Wishes to Learn to Read, and the Result." *Daily Gleaner,* December 23, 1899.
Titilayo. Comment on "After Crop-Over." Caribbean Beat Blog, August 23, 2006, at 4:06 p.m. Caribbean-beat.blogspot.com/2006/08/after-crop-over/html.
Tonkin, Boyd. "Anthony C. Winkler: A Playful Pirate of the Caribbean." *Independent* (online ed.), January 5, 2007.
Trinidad. "A Commentary." Editorial. Vol. 1, no. 2 (Easter 1930).
Trinidad Express. "No, Trinidad Isn't Guyana." Editorial. April 19, 1999.
———. "Sabeeney: Look Out for Miss Japan." May 23, 1999.
Tronchin, L. B. "The Great West Indian Orator." *Public Opinion,* December 18 and 21, 1888.
Tulivu Fisher, Maisha. "Choosing Literacy: African Diaspora Participatory Literacy Communities." Research report. Center for Latin American Studies, University of California, Berkeley, summer 2002. http://socrates/berkeley.edu:7001/Research/graduate/summer2002/fisher/index.html.
Uddenberg, Tian, and Karen Vaucrosson. "Lists from the San Fernando Gazette Trinidad West Indies, 1865–1896." National Archives, Port of Spain, 2002 (self-published).
Vargas-Cetina, Gabriela. "Music, Silence, Noise and the Uncomfortable Scribe: Studying Trova Music in Yucatan, Mexico." Paper presented at the Society for the Humanities, Cornell University, Fall, 2006.
Vasquez, Shalene. "Laughing across Borders: Black Diasporic Literature and the Negotiation of Master Strategies." Ph.D. diss., Rutgers University, 2006.
wa Thiong'o, Ngũgĩ. *Decolonising the Mind: The Politics of Language in African Literature.* London: Heinemann Educational Books, 1982.
Walcott, Derek. *Collected Poems, 1948–1984.* New York: Noonday Press, 1987.
———. "Some Jamaican Poets." *Public Opinion* (Jamaica), August 3 and 10, 1957.
———. "What the Twilight Says: An Overture." In *Dream on Monkey Mountain and Other Plays,* 4–40. New York: Noonday Press, 1988.
Waters, Mary. *Black Identities: West Immigrant Dreams and American Realities.* Cambridge: Harvard University Press, 1999.
Watson, Tim. *Caribbean Culture and British Fiction in the Atlantic World 1780–1870.* Cambridge: Cambridge University Press, 2008.
Wilson, Peter J. *Crab Antics: The Social Anthropology of English-Speaking Negro Societies in the Caribbean.* New Haven: Yale University Press, 1973.
Winkler, Anthony. *The Lunatic.* Kingston: Kingston Publishers Ltd., 1987.
Wong Chin Foo. "The Mandarin's Daughter: A Romance of Chinese Life, ch. 1." *Jamaica Times,* July 8, 1899, 13.
Wright, Richardson. *Revels in Jamaica.* 1937. Reprint. Kingston: Bolivar Press, 1986.

Wynter, B. P. "A Negro's Christmas Message to His Race in Jamaica." *Daily Gleaner*, December 23, 1899, 12.

Wynter, Sylvia. "Lady Nugent's Journal." In *Caribbean Women: An Anthology of Non-Fiction Writing, 1890–1980,* ed. Veronica Gregg. South Bend, IN: University of Notre Dame Press, 2005.

Yamfoot. Posting on "More on Ms. Lawrence." The next decade...what's in store? (blog). March 17, 2007 (12:12 a.m.). Yamfoot.net/archives/2007.03.html.

Index

abolitionist movement, 53, 62
Abrahams, Roger, 98, 187
Aching, Gerard, 172n26
Adams, Grantley, 182n23, 195n43
Adolphus, 50, 58–60, 68, 71, 76, 78, 84
Africa, Africaneity: 9, 11, 67; in carnival, 131; diaspora of, 155; heritage in Caribbean, 72, 79, 84, 137; stereotypes of, 67, 79
African American literature, 94, 158, 178n53; "ghetto," 162; modernism, 170n16
African Americans: 45, 46, 48, 197n3; authors, 63, 153; book clubs, 156, 160, 200n39; and Caribbean immigrants, 149, 193n12; Caribbean views of, 37, 46, 199n20; and carnival, 135; critics, 93; culture, 7; debating societies, 36; immigration to Jamaica, 37; in jazz, 46, 140; marketing to, 200n41; Marxism and, 177n40; middle class, 36, 177n40; performers in the Caribbean, 44, 196n47; readers, 148, 155–56, 157, 160, 163; and Reconstruction, 184n47; self-determination of, 73; slave testimonials of, 62; stereotypes of, 92, 93; and tourism, 163; compared with West Indians, 36
African diaspora, 156
Africans: in the Caribbean, 184n44; in Caribbean literature, 70, 184n44; slavery and, 184n44; women, 53
Afro-Caribbean population: aesthetics of, 51; and education, 174n4; images of men, 67–68; images of women, 110, 113; and respectability, 110, 111, 124
Afrocentrism, 67, 100, 135; and beauty pageants, 129
Alleyne, Mervyn, 181n14
Alleyne-Dettmers, Patricia, 131
All Jamaica Library, 55, 173n12
America, American, 16; actors in Jamaica, 177n49; creoles in, 183n39; cultural studies, 10; culture, 7; influence in the Caribbean, 15, 128, 148, 151; and modernity, 47; popular culture, 19, 39, 63;

and race, 44; readers, 148, 156, 157, 159; religions in the Caribbean, 173n39; Revolutionary War, 35; views of, 93. *See also* United States
American Company of Comedians, 35, 177n49
American fiction, 8, 18 159; anti-slavery novel, 61–63; in the Caribbean, 200n40; popular fiction, 47, 51; white readers of, 156, 157, 159. *See also* African American literature
Amerindians, 10
Anancy stories, 21, 22, 96, 98, 101
Antigua, 107
Appadurai, Arjun, 127
Appiah, Anthony, 9
Aruba: carnival in, 135–36
Ashcroft, Bill, 50
Asia: female leaders of, 112; globalization in, 173n36; images of women in, 125
Asian Caribbean population, 48; women, 111, 121. *See also* Chinese (Caribbean); Indo-Caribbean population; Indo-Trinidadians

"Back to Africa," 100, 106
Back to Africa Movement, 100, 104
Banana Bottom, 23, 82
"Bans o' Killing," 102
Barbados Advocate, 177n39, 178n51
Barbados Gazette, 24
Barbados, 12, 173n3; Adams, Grantley, 182n23, 195n43; African identity in, 137; beauty pageants in, 118; Caribbean nationalism and, 195n43; cricket in, 173n3; Crop Over in, 134, 137–39, 195n39; jazz in, 140; middle class in, 173n3; Miss Barbados controversy, 191–92n12; planter class in, 173n3; Pringle, Rachel, 58; Sobers, Sir Garfield, 118; spouge, 136, 195n38; sugar industry in, 137; tourism, 137; working class in, 173n3; Yoruba Foundation, 136, 195n39

217

INDEX

Barbados Jazz Festival, 140. *See also* jazz: festivals in the Caribbean
"barracks yard" literature. *See* "yard" literature
"barrel" culture, 15, 19
Beacon (Trinidad), 3, 43
Beacon group (Trinidad), 94, 169n6
beauty pageants (Caribbean), 1, 2, 4, 7, 16, 112, 118, 192n19; and Afrocentrism, 129; black women and, 119, 120; brownness and, 116, 121; Indo-Trinidadian women and, 121–22; Miss Barbados controversy, 191–92n12; Miss Jamaica controversy, 116; race in, 116–23; Rastafarians in, 119, 120; socialism and, 117
Beenie Man, 141, 142, 196n53
Belgrave, Valerie, 149; *Ti Marie,* 197n2n, 163, 167
Bell, Vera, 104
Bennett, Louise, 6, 86–109, 185n1, 185n6, 186n11, 190n65; and Afrocentrism, 95; "Colonization in Reverse," 106; critiques of, 92–93; "Dutty Tough," 96; "On a Tram Car," 97; and pantomime, 102–4; "Pinnicle," 100; and politics, 102
Bim (Barbados), 40, 87
black British fiction, 161–62, 197n3
Black Entertainment Television (BET), 130, 139, 196n53
black nationalism, 73, 110, 112. *See also* nationalism
Black Power Revolts (Trinidad), 129
Blacks: images of, 60, 68, 70, 80; racial stereotypes of, 110, 114. *See also* Afro-Caribbean population
Blackwell, Chris, 20
Blyden, Edward, 52, 181n12
Bob Marley and the Wailers, 20. *See also* Marley, Bob
Bolívar, Simón, 72
Bongie, Chris, 9
Bongo Jerry, 88
Bradshaw, Sonny, 142
Brathwaite, Kamau, 94, 99, 142, 185n5; on Louise Bennett, 188n40; and "nation-Language," 91, 188n40. *See also* "nation-language"
Breakspeare, Cindy, 117
Breiner, Laurence, 101
Brereton, Bridget, 52, 56
British empire, 162, 127. *See also* England: Caribbean colonies of
British literature, 52; black British, 197n3; in Caribbean, 179n78

brown population, 13, 53, 57, 66, 83, 173n2; aesthetics, 6, 7, 51–52, 80, 116; "brownness," 56–57; as a racial category, 182n24; society, 69; women, 58, 59, 70; women, early descriptions of, 182n29. *See also* mulattos
Burnie, Beryl, 100
Burns, Robert, 25, 34
Burton, Richard, 13, 129
Butler, Octavia, 8, 157, 173n33

Calabash Literary Festival, 143–45, 154; sponsors of, 196–97n56; Writer's Workshop, 145–46
calypso, 13, 16, 112, 113, 122, 169n6; competitions, 123, 192n12
Canclini, Nestor García, 126
cannes brûlées, 129, 134. *See also* carnival
Caribbeana, 24
Caribbean fiction, 3–4, 148, 163, 174n6, 185n5; American influence on, 197n2; authors of, 145; Caribbean immigrants and, 148–49, 199n20; early, 31–36, 38–40, 48–49; "gothic," 199n32; local versus global, 149–55; modernism in, 170n16; plantation imagery in, 162–68; white authors of, 201n57
Caribbean Review of Books, 151
Caribbean studies, 147
Caribbean Voices, 40
Caricom, 130
carnival, 7, 13, 14, 16, 114, 126, 128–39; African Americans and, 135; African retentions of, 131; Americanization of, 194n16; in Antigua, 135; in Aruba, 135; bands, 192n12; and commerce, 133; competitions, 125; costumes of, 193n5; de-Africanizing of, 131; European attitudes toward, 131; feminization of, 132–33; history of, 128–30; immigrants and, 135; j'ouvert, 131; in Jamaica, 136–37; in "jamettes" in, 173n34; middle class attitudes toward, 131; multiculturalism and, 131; music of, 193n15; National Carnival Commission and, 133; in North America, 133; Pan-Caribbean identity and, 132; pretty mas', 131; revenue from, 194n23; "talk tent," 185n6; tourism, 130, 133, 135; traditional, 133, 200n33; Trinidad-style, 134; ugly mas', 131; in the Virgin Islands, 134, 195n30
Carpenter, McDonald, 169n6
Cezair Thompson, Margaret, 163

INDEX 219

Channer, Colin, 9, 15, 17, 92, 143, 144, 149, 152; and Calabash Literary Festival, 143; *The Girl with the Golden Shoes,* 199n22; *Iron Balloons,* 145, 160, 199n23; marketing of novels, 198n19; novels of, 168; *Passing Through,* 153, 163, 168, 199n19; reggae aesthetic, 171n20; *Satisfy My Soul,* 153; "urban relationship" novels of, 156, 158, 168; *Waiting in Vain,* 15, 16, 153, 154, 197n2. *See also* Calabash Literary Festival

Charles, Eugenia, 112

Chase, Sam, 88

Chavarría, Daniel, 159

Chicago Defender, 44

Chinese (Caribbean), 42. *See also* Asian Caribbean population

Cliff, Michelle; *No Telephone to Heaven,* 150

Cobham, Rhonda, 42, 52, 56, 74, 75, 173n2

Cobham, Stephen, 56; *Rupert Gray,* 6, 52, 53, 56–57, 66, 72, 73, 75

Code Noir, 57

Collymore, Frank, 40

colonies (Caribbean), 127. *See also* British empire

Cooper, Carolyn, 97, 101, 144, 171n25; critique of *Jane's Career,* 181n14; and reggae studies, 144

Cordle, Alexander, 6; *Overheard,* 6, 88

Corsbie, Ken, 87

Cosmopolitan (Jamaica), 43–45

Craft, William and Ellen, 62

Creole (language), 27, 40, 45, 81, 86, 88, 90, 97–98, 185n1; in literature, 94, 181n1, 184n14; of Pan-Caribbean, 157

Creoleana, 58

Creole Day (St. Lucia), 139

creoles, 11; culture, 143; as slaves, 184n44; spaces of, 122; in Trinidad, 192n20. *See also* white creoles

creolization, 11; and modernity, 125; segmentary, 49; synthetic, 49. *See also* decreolization

cricket, 16–17, 135, 173n3

Crop Over (Barbados), 134, 137–39, 195n39; and tourism, 137

Cuba: literature, 39; nationalism, 115; revolutionary war, 35; sex in advertising of, 191n7, 201n45

Cudjoe, Selwyn, 52, 56, 62, 66, 181n12

Cupidon, Ernest, 90, 185n9

Daily Chronicle (Guyana), 176n31

dancehall, 171n25; dancehall queens (Jamaica), 115–16; Japanese in, 191n8

Dawes, Kwame, 144, 152

DeCaires Narain, Denise, 97, 98, 99, 105, 107, 186n11, 186n29, 189–90n65

decreolization, 51. *See also* creolization

de Lisser, H. G., 12, 42, 54, 78, 81, 171n21, 176n31; *Jane's Career,* 6, 52, 53, 54–55, 66, 77, 80–85; and Marcus Garvey, 179n66; *Morgan's Daughter,* 80; race of, 173n2, 177n44; and *Planter's Punch,* 40, 43; *Psyche,* 171n19, 184n48; *Susan Proudleigh,* 80, 90; *Under the Jamaican Sun,* 80; *White Witch of Rose Hall,* 54, 154, 199n24

Dessources, George Numa, 50, 55; *Adolphus,* 50, 58–60, 68, 71, 76, 78, 84

dialect, 86; performances, 90; poetry, 34, 88, 106, 170n10, 185n1; speakers of, 70; stories, 45; in theater, 81, 90, 100; in Trinidad and Guyana, 88; and working class, 169n10. *See also* Creole (language); dub poets

dialectical tradition, 9, 170n18, 174n9

dimanche gras, 129. *See also* carnival

douglas (Trinidad), 13, 172n25, 192n22

Douglass, Frederick, 62, 63

Dragon Can't Dance, 150, 172n30, 187n23, 190n69, 193n10

DuBois, W. E. B., 46; and double consciousness, 46

dub poets, 6, 108, 169n10. *See also* dialect: poetry

East Indians. *See* Indo-Caribbean

education, 30, 151, 171n22, 174n4, 198n7

elections. *See* suffrage

Emmanuel Appadocca, 6, 58, 60, 52, 53, 64, 76

England: Caribbean colonies of, 127; Caribbean literary history, 152; Englishness of, 66, 72, 73; traditions of, 12, 23, 113; writers of, 113, 114. *See also* British empire; British literature

Eyre, Edward, 178n55

Fanon, Frantz, 20, 59; *Wretched of the Earth,* 20

Fitzwilliam, Wendy, 121

Focus (Jamaica), 40, 87

Forbes, Curdella, 161, 201n50

Franzen, Jonathan: *The Corrections,* 159

Frazier, Franklin E., 177n40

free coloreds, 62. *See also* mulattos; brown population

Free Mulatto, 58, 59

Freeman, Carla, 19, 173n36

Froude, James Anthony, 113

INDEX

Garvey, Marcus, 1, 25, 83, 120; and Back to Africa Movement, 104; criticism of, 42, 45; as national hero, 117; and *Negro World,* 25; and U.N.I.A., 25
"ghetto" literature, 162
Gilroy, Paul, 10, 125; *The Black Atlantic,* 10
Gleaner (Jamaica), 25, 45, 94, 176n31
globalization, 8, 9, 19, 20 127, 128, 146; critics of, 173n36; and fiction, 149–50; and middle-class, 146
Goudie, Sean, 7
Great Britain. *See* England
Griffiths, Gareth, 50
Guyana, 10, 14; theater, 88; literature of, 172n33, 176n31

Haiti, 42; in literature, 157, 199n33. *See also* Saint-Domingue
Hanna, Lisa, 116
Harder They Come, The (film), 198n12
Harlem Renaissance, 93, 95
Hearne, John: *Under the Window,* 199n23
Hill, Errol, 129, 171n21
Hinds, Alison, 131
Hindus, Hinduism (Trinidad), 122
Hispanic Caribbean, 115, 151, 183n37
Hispanics: race relations among, 70
homophobia (Caribbean), 196n53
Hopkinson, Nalo, 149, 173n33; *Brown Girl in the Ring,* 155; *Midnight Robber,* 155, 197n2
Hosein (Trinidad), 134
Hurston, Zora Neale, 93
Hutchinson, Joan Andrea, 93
hybridity, 7, 13; aesthetics of, 51–52

immigrants (Caribbean), 15, 168, 199n20; and African Americans, 193n12; American influence on, 197n2; as readers, 148–49
indentured laborers, 121
India: 13, film industry of, 9, 11
Indians (Caribbean). *See* Indo-Caribbean population; Indo-Trinidadians
Indo-Caribbean population, 14; aesthetics of, 51; politics of, 122; women, 113. *See also* Indo-Trinidadians
Indo-Trinidadians: and carnival, 129; festivals of, 134; nationalism of, 122. *See also* Indo-Caribbean population
informatics, 19
intermarriage, 37, 56
Island Records, 101

Jamaica, 13, 18, 23, 115; Anancy stories of, 21, 22, 96, 98, 101; beauty pageants in, 116–17, 119–21; book sales in, 160; carnival in, 136–37; dialect poetry in, 170n10; dub poets in, 170n10; education in, 174n4; elite of, 27, 40; in fiction, 163; in film, 164; history of printing in, 174n10; jazz festivals, 141; Jews in, 178n60; middle class reading in, 178–79n65; minstrelsy in, 35; music, 145, 152; newspaper culture of, 24–34; printer's strike, 83; recording industry, 198n12; socialism in, 167; television shows, 163; theater, 177n49, 185n6, 185n9, 188n47; tourism in, 170n12; working class culture in, 172n25; writers, 154
Jamaica Advocate, 25, 110
Jamaica Carnival, 136–37
Jamaica Labour Party (JLP), 116
Jamaica Poetry League, 96, 185n7
Jamaica Telegraph, 24
Jamaica Times, 28, 36, 42, 45
James, Alexander MacGregor, 39
James, C. L. R., 3, 9, 10, 13, 94, 107; *Beyond A Boundary,* 17; and cricket, 16; *Minty Alley,* 4, 55
James, Marlon, 92, 151, 161; *John Crow's Devil,* 145, 159–60
"jamettes," 113, 173n34
Jane's Career, 6, 52, 53, 54–55, 66, 77, 80–85
jazz, 7, 8, 18, 106, 127; and Caribbean culture, 142; in Caribbean literature, 142; compared with calypso, 143; festivals in the Caribbean, 139–43, 196n53; in Jamaica, 141–42; jazz aesthetic, 143; musicians, 46; resentment of, 196n53; and tourism, 141
Jekyll, Walter, 99; *Jamaica Song and Story,* 99
Jews (Jamaica), 38, 40
Jim Crow (U.S.), 36, 44. *See also* America; United States
John Canoe. *See* Junkanoo
John, Elton, 196n53
Jounee Kweyol. *See* Creole Day
j'ouvert, jouvay. *See* carnival
Junkanoo, 136, 191n5

Keens-Douglas, Paul, 87, 97, 185n6
Kincaid, Jamaica, 5, 9, 107; *A Small Place,* 107
Kingsley, Charles, 190n4
Koningsbruggen, Peter van, 14, 127, 130, 172n26, 194n16
Kutzinski, Vera, 115
Kyk-Over-Al (Guyana), 40, 87

Lady Nugent, 182n29, 183n42
Lamming, George, 3, 10

INDEX

Lara, Brian, 17
Latin America, 16; nationalism, 72; publishing in, 151
Levine, Jaime, 157
Lewis, Gordon, 23, 50
literary festivals, 127. *See also* Calabash Literary Festival
Little Carib Dance Theater (Trinidad), 100
Livingston, W. P., 174n4
Lomas, Laura, 54
Love, Robert, 26, 112; and *Jamaica Advocate,* 25, 110
Lovelace, Earl: *The Dragon Can't Dance,* 150, 172n30, 187n23, 190n69, 193n10

MacDermot, Thomas, 52, 55, 77–79; and All Jamaica Library, 173n12; *Becka's Buckra Baby,* 55; *One Brown Girl And—,* 52, 55, 66, 72, 77–79, 85; and race, 177n47
Mais, Roger, 92; *Brotherman,* 199n23
Manley, Edna, 182n22
Manley, Michael, 51, 180–81n8
Manley, Norman, 103, 182n22
Manning, Frank, 135
Marly, 51
Marley, Bob, 2, 6, 95, 117, 119, 126, 145; comparisons to, 198n18; lyrics of, 152; marketing of, 155; music of, 154; "Them Bellyful (But We Hungry)," 96; and the Wailers, 20
Marson, Una, 16, 29; and *Cosmopolitan,* 29
Martin, Sidney, 88
Marx, Karl, 170n4, 170n12
Marxism, 19
masquerade, mas'. *See* carnival
McAndrew, Wordsworth, 87
McKay, Claude, 12, 23, 34, 54, 82, 94, 95, 98, 161, 171n21, 179n75, 181n14, 187n23; *Banana Bottom,* 23, 82; *Constab Ballads,* 34; *Songs of Jamaica,* 34
McMillan, Terry, 8, 18, 153, 155; *How Stella Got Her Groove Back,* 163–64
mestizaje, 115, 180n5
mestizo identity, in Aruba, 135
middle class: 12, 25, 42, 81, 84; in Aruba, 135; audience, 9; in Barbados, 27; beauty pageants, 124; black women of, 125; brown and black, 2, 22–23, 25, 30–31, 36–37, 40–41, 114; and carnival, 130, 131; culture of, 4, 8–9, 11–20, 49; and dialect, 87, 90; early black, 30, 174n6; globalization, 146; in Guyana, 22; identity, 7, 79; institutions of, 14; in Jamaica, 22, 26, 38, 41, 44; and jazz, 140; Marxist views of, 170n14; "middleclassization," 14, 15; in the nineteenth century, 26; origins of, 91; peasant traditions, 101; status and, 5; theater, 93; in Trinidad, 22, 30, 166. *See also* professional class
Mighty Gabby, 118, 119
Mighty Sparrow, 109, 189n51, 190n68
Minshall, Peter, 193n5
minstrelsy, 92, 93; in Jamaica, 35
Minty Alley, 4, 55
Mirror (Trinidad), 56
Miss Barbados controversy, 118–19, 123
missionaries, 23
Miss Lou. *See* Bennett, Louise, 86
Mittelholzer, Edgar: *Corentyne Thunder,* 10; *Children of Kaywana,* 171n19; *My Bones and Flute,* 172n33
Moonsammy, Patricia, 193–94n15
Morant Bay Rebellion, 55
Morris, Mervyn, 53, 93, 107
Mosley, Walter, 8
Muharram. *See* Hosein
mulattos, 57; images of, 60; rights of, 57, 58; rape and, 69; in U.S., 63; women, 182n18. *See also* brown population
Mutabaruka, 93, 107

Naipaul, V. S., 3, 36, 40, 82, 86, 94, 98, 107; *A House for Mr. Biswas,* 35; *The Middle Passage,* 107, 177n43, 189n59; *The Mimic Men,* 82; *Overcrowded Barracoon,* 176n35
nationalism. and black women, 121; in Caribbean, 45; of Indo-Trinidadians, 122; Jamaican, 48, 176n38; Latin America, 72; in romance novels, 49, 56–57, 72, 74–77; and theater, 103. *See also* black nationalism; Pan-Africanism
"nation-language," 91, 100
Negritude, 181n12
Neptune, Harvey, 7, 169n6
Nettleford, Rex, 49, 102, 107
New Era (Trinidad), 30
New York Evening Post, 36
New York Times, 144, 159, 160, 170n10

Olivier, Sydney, 171n21, 176n38; and Jamaican middle class, 176n38
One Brown Girl And—, 52, 55, 66, 72, 77–79, 85
Onoura, Oku, 88
Orderson, J. W.: *Creoleana,* 58

Pan-Africanism, 52, 53, 54, 56, 57, 83, 140, 181n12
Pan-Caribbean: culture, 128, 130; language of, 157; and nationalism, 173n3

Panday, Basdeo, 122
pantomime (Jamaica), 100, 103, 105, 185n6, 188n47
pardos, 65. See also brown population
Patterson, Orlando, 49; *Children of Sisyphus,* 143
peasantry, 23, 45, 113, 175n21; resistance traditions of, 187n23
People's National Movement (PNM), 129
Philip, Maxwell Michel, 58, 62–63, 74, 78; *Adolphus,* 50, 58–60, 68, 71, 76, 78, 84
Phillipe, Jean-Baptiste, 58, 60; *Free Mulatto,* 58, 59
Pinckney, Warren, Jr., 140
planters, plantocracy, 39, 41, 45, 54, 73, 88; images of, 149
Planter's Punch (Jamaica), 40, 43
Plummer, Denyse, 123
popular fiction (Caribbean), 148–68; early, 34–39, 47–85. See also "ghetto" literature; romance novels; science fiction; "urban relationship" novels; "yardie" fiction; "yard" literature
Port of Spain Gazette, 110, 113, 129
postmodernism, 9
Pringle, Rachel, 58
printer's strike (Jamaica), 83
professional class, 17, 131. See also middle class
professionalism, 15, 16
Puri, Shalini, 13, 122, 172n25; *The Caribbean Postcolonial,* 13

quadroons, 65. See also brown population

racial ideology, 183n40; in marketing, 155–57
racial stereotypes, 102, 114
Rae, Norman, 151
Ramazani, Jahan, 98, 103
Ramchand, Kenneth, 23, 51, 53, 54, 55, 82, 171n22, 174n6, 181n14
Ramgoonai, Drupatee, 122
Ramleela, 134
rapso, 107
Rastafarianism, Rastafarians, 1, 20, 51, 149; in popular fiction, 194n2; and politics, 181n8
Razak, Victoria, 135
Redcam, Tom. See MacDermot, Thomas
Redwood, Zahra, 1, 119
reggae aesthetic, 171n20
reggae, 2, 13, 109: reggae aesthetic, 171n20; Reggae Sunsplash, 126; studies, 144

respectability, 15, 124; women and, 110, 111, 131
Rohlehr, Gordon, 91
romance novels, 15, 16, 48–50, 149, 159; nationalism in, 49, 56–57, 72, 74–77; and planter class, 167; representations of slavery in, 164
Rosenberg, Leah, 46, 48
Roumain, Jacques: *Masters of the Dew,* 187n23

Saint-Domingue, 58. See also Haiti
salsa, 13
Sander, Reinhard, 176n36, 177n43
San Fernando Gazette (Trinidad), 30
Sassen, Saskia, 150
science fiction, 17, 155, 156, 159, 168; black writers of, 172–73n33; Caribbean, 172n33
Scott, David, 14
Scott, Dennis, 108
Selvon, Samuel, 177n43
Set Girls (Jamaica), 191n5
sexuality, 79; and aesthetics, 171n20; black, 79; of brown women, 84; marketing of, 171n19; and sexual harassment, 80; in tourism, 191n7. See also women
Shearer, Hugh, 54, 55
Simpson, Portia, 112
slavery, 39 53, 60, 63, 111, 114; and Africans, 184n44; images of, 162; in literature, 166, 184n48, 201n50
Smith, Faith, 63–64, 198n18
Sobers, Sir Garfield, 118
soca, 16, 131. See also calypso
Spotlight (Jamaica), 45
spouge, 136, 195n38
stickfighting, 113, 125
St. Lucia Jazz Festival, 139, 141–42. See also jazz: festivals in the Caribbean
suffrage (Jamaica), 54, 102
Swanzy, Henry, 40

Temple, Johnny, 158, 160
theater: Derek Walcott and, 100; in Jamaica, 103; and nationalism, 103, 104
Thomas, Deborah, 14
Thomas, John Jacob, 56, 174n9
Thompson, Krista, 162
Tiffin, Helen, 50
Ti Marie, 163, 164–66, 197n2n
tourism (Caribbean), 47, 109, 114, 128: African Americans and, 163; and carnival, 130–33; "cultural," 144, 197n57; culture

of, 131; ethnic stereotypes and, 132; "festival," 126; "heritage," 133; history of, 162; intra-Caribbean, 141; and jazz, 141; and literature, 143; in nineteenth century, 170n12; and race, 146; Reggae Sunsplash and, 126; sexual advertising for, 191n7; and Trinidad carnival, 193n13; U.S. influence on, 127
Toussaint L'Ouverture, 74, 199n33
trade unions, 83
Trinidad and Tobago, 6, 14, 18; anti-Asian nationalism in, 175n29; Asians in, 176n36; "barracks yard" literature of, 166; beauty pageants in, 123–25; black and Indian women, views of, 190n4; Black Power revolts in, 129; carnival figures, 155; and carnival tourism, 193n13, 194n16; creoles in, 192n20; "douglarization" in, 172n25; early literature of, 30–33, 50; folk characters of, 149; history of, 74; homophobia in, 196n53; Hosein in, 134; immigrants to Aruba, 135; jazz in, 196n53; newspaper culture of, 30–32; society, 13; theater in, 100; Trinidad Awakening, 50, 176n37; U.S. occupation of, 7, 139; Williams, Eric, 107, 129; Williams, Sylvester, 53
Trinidadian, 50
trova music, 8
Trump, Donald, 123

Uncle Tom's Cabin, 53, 62, 63
United Negro Improvement Association (U.N.I.A.), 173n3
United States: consumer culture of, 128; globalization in, 173n36; influence of, 151–62; newspapers in Caribbean, 180n78; occupation of Trinidad, 139, 7; publishers in, 155; Revolutionary War, 35. See also America, American
University of the West Indies, 99, 100, 103, 144
Up From Slavery, 36
"urban relationship" novels, 156

Vaz, Noel, 103, 104
Venezuela: beauty pageants in, 124; influence of, 64; *pardos,* 65; in Trinidadian literature, 64–65

Vera, Yvonne, 171n20
Victoria Quarterly (Jamaica), 24

Walcott, Derek: 6, 40, 51, 94, 99, 103, 162–63; *Dream on Monkey Mountain,* 188n48; and pantomime, 100; "Ruins of A Great House," 162; *Ti-Jean and His Brothers,* 100
Ward Theater (Jamaica), 90, 170n12, 178n60
Washington, Booker T., 25, 73; *Up From Slavery,* 36
wa Thiong'o, Ngũgĩ, 94; *Decolonising the Mind,* 103
Webber, A. R. F., 176n31
Webster, Aimee, 179n68
Wells Brown, William: *Clotel,* 63
West Indies Federation, 136, 195n43
white creoles, 38, 67, 79, 182n29, 183n42; degeneracy of, 184n45; in Jamaican theater, 171n21; as readers, 168, 169. See also creoles
Williams, Eric, 107; and PNM, 129
Williams, Sylvester, 53
Wilson, Peter, 18; *Crab Antics,* 18
Winer, Lise, 56
Winfrey, Oprah, 120; *Oprah's Book Club,* 9
Winkler, Anthony: *Going Home to Teach,* 167; *The Lunatic,* 163, 167; *The Painted Canoe,* 167
Wolfe, Charles, 105, 106
women, women's culture, 8, 16, 18; Afro-Caribbean, 110, 113, 115, 124; Asian, 115; Asian-Caribbean, 121; birth control and, 44; brown, 114, 115; employment and, 44; Indo-Trinidadian, 121; and politics, 111, 112; as readers, 56; working class, 111, 113, 116. See also beauty pageants
working class, 2, 12, 14, 15; black, 114, 122, 161; calypsos and, 123; culture of, 4, 10, 97, 144; icons of, 117; in Jamaica, 25, 98, 172; nonwhite, 129; poetry of, 107; women, 111, 113, 116. See also peasantry

"yardie" fiction, 161–62. See also black British fiction
"yard" literature, 166. See also *Jane's Career; Minty Alley*
Yoruba Foundation (Barbados), 136, 195n39

PR9205.05 .E357 2009

Edmondson, Belinda

Caribbean middlebrow :
leisure culture and the
middle class   NOV 2 2 2010